Agricultural Change and Rural Poverty

Variations on a Theme by Dharm Narain

Edited by JOHN W. MELLOR and GUNVANT M. DESAI

Published for the International Food Policy Research Institute

THE JOHNS HOPKINS UNIVERSITY PRESS

Baltimore and London

The Johns Hopkins University Press,
701 West 40th Street,
Baltimore, Maryland 21211
The Johns Hopkins Press Ltd, London

The paper in this book is acid-free and meets the guidelines for
permanence and durability of the Committee on Production Guidelines
for Book Longevity of the Council on Library Resources.

Library of Congress Cataloging in Publication Data

Main entry under title:

Agricultural change and rural poverty.
  Bibliography: p.
  Includes index.
  1. Agriculture—Economic aspects—Developing countries—Congresses. 2. Agricultural innovations—Economic aspects—Developing countries—Congresses. 3. Rural poor—Developing countries—Congresses. 4. Farm income—Developing countries—Congresses. I. Narain, Dharm. II. Mellor, John Williams, 1928–   . III. Desai, Gunvant M. IV. International Food Policy Research Institute.

HD1417.A4475 1985   338.1'09172'4   85-50
ISBN 0-8018-3275-6 (alk. paper)

Contents

List of Tables

List of Figures

Preface

During the past two decades there has been increasing concern that the development strategies of the 1950s and 1960s would neither eliminate nor even greatly reduce rural poverty—even as the pervasive nature of that poverty became more widely recognized. This increase in concern coincided with the drama of the major biological breakthroughs in food production associated with the "green revolution." A debate began on whether there was a causal relation between the technology of the green revolution and the incidence of rural poverty. The conclusion of this debate is of importance not only because food is vital but because population growth is placing greater pressure on existing food supplies and because limited land area is shifting the means of expanding food production towards yield-increasing technology. If the means of increasing food production are associated with immiserizing processes, the prospects for the poor are bleak, and policies must be sought to break such a connection.

Beyond this contemporary debate about the green revolution, mitigation of poverty requires knowledge of what are now recognized as enormously complex causes. Empirical identification of these causes is a formidable task because of the conceptual issues involved in defining the many dimensions of poverty, the data constraints in measuring its incidence, and the econometric problems in estimating the relationships between the causal factors and the poverty levels. The papers in this volume analyze these questions from several points of view. A notable finding pointed up in these papers is the enormous short-term fluctuation in the number of rural people in absolute poverty. Why this fluctuation occurs and what can and should be done about it is an important issue. The papers also note substantial differences in the levels of poverty from one place to another despite similarities in average income and stage of development. Such differences provide the basis for understanding more about the causes of poverty and hence the means of treating it.

India offers an immense data base on poverty superimposed on a highly variegated background. Time series measuring poverty can be generated for India that are impossible to construct for other developing countries, and comparable data are available for widely divergent conditions. Thus the papers in this volume draw heavily on Indian data. Several questions are then raised: How does African poverty, for example, differ from Indian poverty, and how must remedial measures be accordingly modified? How can the longer development experience of Japan be appropriately viewed in this context? What other lessons can be learned from Southeast Asia?

This volume originates from Dharm Narain's unfinished research on the forces behind temporal changes in rural poverty. At the heart of his efforts was the idea that rural poverty is a function of the growth performance of agriculture, of prices of commodities consumed by the rural poor, and of a set of trend factors. Unfortunately, he passed away just when results of his efforts were beginning to emerge.

To discuss and extend Dharm Narain's work, persons familiar with his research who are scholars in their own right were invited to write papers covering different aspects of rural poverty. These papers and comments on them were discussed in a workshop in New Delhi on 11–14 April 1982. The present volume is a collection of the papers that developed from that conference.

As work in planning and developing the volume proceeded, it quickly became evident that Dharm Narain's focus on the growth performance of agriculture and on prices was on the surface controversial, in depth prescient, and in practice multifaceted. In other words, it was well suited to efforts originating from different perspectives. Thus this volume presents a diverse set of papers that approach the central themes set out by Dharm Narain from a multitude of angles and perceptions.

The volume includes a prelude by Raj tracing Dharm Narain's thinking on the role of agricultural prices in the growth performance of Indian agriculture, which is so vital for poverty alleviation. The first chapter is a précis by Desai of Dharm Narain's unfinished research on trends in rural poverty in India. The contributions by Sen, Bliss, Mellor, and Srinivasan discuss the theoretical underpinnings of Dharm Narain's conceptualization and explore various relations behind it. The paper by Kumar deals with the complexities of causal links between poverty defined in terms of minimum income and minimum nutritional requirements for the poor.

The next set of papers examines the problem of rural poverty in India in temporal, cross-sectional, and policy contexts. Ahluwalia extends his well-known time series of poverty estimates to the 1970s and reexamines the relationships between rural poverty, agricultural production, and prices in the light of Dharm Narain's ideas as well as those of the others. Bardhan tests the "trickle-down" hypothesis using cross-sectional data at three levels of aggregation. Rao, Gupta, and Sharma discuss cross-sectional variations in rural poverty by focusing on institutional, infrastructural, and technological variables. Dantwala reviews the performance of Indian agriculture after the introduction of high-yield varieties from the viewpoint of the rural poverty problem. Ahmed's comments on Dantwala's paper also offer a brief discussion of the roots of rural poverty in Bangladesh and the policies required to tackle it.

The next papers focus on experiences in three different parts of the world from different angles. Hayami and Kikuchi examine the Marxian hypothesis of how polarization of peasant communities contributes to the misery of the poor by drawing on Japan's historical experience and more recent evidence from the Philippines. Mangahas discusses various aspects of poverty in the Philippines and comments on the data constraints to understanding poverty. Hirashima demonstrates how advances in irrigation and technical education in agriculture paved the way for poverty alleviation in Japan. Lele highlights the central role that poor agricultural performance plays in the poverty of sub-Saharan Africa. Finally, Parthasarathy and Vyas comment on papers discussing rural poverty in India, the Philippines, Japan, and Africa.

Collectively, the contributions cover a wide range of conceptual, empirical, and policy issues related to the problem of rural poverty. Although the papers use Dharm Narain's formulation as a starting point, there are many variations on the theme. They demonstrate the complexities of the problem and the disagreements that exist in dealing with it. They also, however, indicate that it is possible to draw certain conclusions, to settle some of the controversies, and to develop a meaningful perspective for tackling one of the most severe problems of our day. The final chapter is an attempt in this direction.

In preparing this volume, we received invaluable help and encouragement from all of the contributors. We are aware how much of this is due to their deep affection and great esteem for Dharm Narain.

J. W. M.
G. M. D.

Prelude

K.N. RAJ

A distinctive feature of Dharm Narain's scholarly output is that almost all of it was devoted to the study of responses of Indian agriculture to various kinds of stimuli, given the constraints within which it operates. Dharm Narain's major published works were not numerous, and most of them took the form of short and concise papers. Yet his intellectual contribution to the understanding of various dimensions of agricultural development has been immense and beyond dispute outstanding. This is not only because whatever he wrote was characterized by careful and meticulous examination of all available data within a well-considered theoretical frame but also because of his deep insights and the refreshing way in which he skillfully wove these insights into his interpretations of the most complex phenomena. The soundness of his contributions ensures that they will stand the test of time; however, the exacting standards he set for himself and the quiet but stubborn professional integrity he preserved throughout dissuaded him from attempting anything grandiose.

Throughout the 1950s Dharm Narain focused his attention almost wholly on the response of Indian agriculture during the colonial period to changes in the relative prices of important crops through shifts in the allocation of land under cultivation. He chose to study a question on which several unsubstantiated doctrines commanded wide acceptance: the perverse responses of farmers in traditional agrarian communities to economic stimuli. Owing to the confidence with which some of the doctrines were generally presented and the common distrust of available agricultural statistics, few had even contemplated undertaking such a study. Dharm Narain's leisurely temperament and persistence were required to break this spell.

The task was deemed formidable. Not only did Dharm Narain lack time-series data on areas under crops and relative prices for the period 1900–1939 but he had selected for close study no less than six crops in as many parts of the country as he could find continuous data for. The collection and compilation of all the data, as well as the graphic method he adopted for identifying and examining systematically such relations as could be inferred from them (sometimes most ingeniously by drawing the price and the area series on separate sheets of tracing paper and comparing the two by moving one sheet over the other), were much more time-consuming than would appear reasonable now with various mechanical aids for data processing. But perhaps the most time-consuming of all was Dharm Narain's own fastidiousness about everything. Not only did the inferences drawn in every instance have to be just right, no more and no less than could be sustained on the basis of the available evidence, but they had to be the only ones that could be legitimately drawn; and they had to be demonstrated and expressed with the greatest possible precision and economy of words.

One unfortunate result was that the pioneering nature of his work and the novelty of his findings perhaps were not fully appreciated initially by many who saw the final product only after it came out as a book (Narain 1965). By then, some econometric studies testing similar hypotheses for particular crops had already been published in professional journals abroad, and more than common perception was required to note that despite the seemingly unsophisticated methods that he used, and partly because of them, the fare that Dharm Narain provided was in some ways richer and subtler. The richness was owing to his identification of different kinds of area response to price changes (for instance, sugarcane compared with cotton); the subtlety was owing to his identification of the various constraints operative on several crops (particularly foodgrains) and thereby discouragement of untenable generalizations about the nature and extent of the responsiveness to such price changes.

Well before the work on area response was completed, Dharm Narain turned his attention to the response of marketed surpluses in agriculture to changes in relative prices and to the related possibility of using the terms of trade between agricultural and nonagricultural products as a device for transferring resources from the agricultural to the non-agricultural sector. The first evidence that his work had taken this direction was in the form of a theoretical paper (Narain 1957). This was followed a few years later, characteristically, by a careful empirical investigation into the distribution of the marketed surplus of agricultural produce by size-level of holding (Narain 1961).

Highlighted in these contributions was, essentially, the importance of distinguishing clearly between the component of the marketed surplus that could be traced to the farmers' demand for money for meeting obligations fixed in terms of money (such as land tax and possibly rent) and the component exchanged for other nonagricultural goods. After analyzing the nature of the factors that would affect the latter (as well as the direction in which each of them would operate), Dharm Narain concluded that the effect of worsening the terms of trade for agriculture on this truly commercial component of the surplus was likely to be adverse. Dharm Narain drove home the need for caution on this account further by demonstrating that in India in the early 1950s as much as half of the marketed surplus appeared to comprise distress sales from small-sized holdings (most of them evidently due to the heavy burden of fixed money obligations). Less than half of the marketed surplus was a commercial surplus with potentiality for further growth.

This note of caution and the lessons that Dharm Narain drew about the difficulties inherent in the formulation of an appropriate price policy for agricultural produce (particularly for foodgrains) in India not only were very timely but reflected the personality of one who shunned facile generalizations of the kind that have been abundant in the literature. They also stood him in good stead when he became the chairman of the Agricultural Prices Commission. It was a one-man commission for some time, but his firm understanding of the issues involved and his modest, unabrasive manner made it possible for Dharm Narain to resist pressures that others in that position might have found difficult to resist.

During this period and after, Dharm Narain's intellectual concerns focused increasingly on the response of Indian agriculture to advances in seed-cum-fertilizer technology. He was deeply impressed by the advances in this sphere and by the need to depend on them still more, but he was also disturbed by the lack of any evidence of acceleration in the rate of growth of agricultural output and by the emerging imbalances among crops and regions in the country. He discussed some of these issues in a sharp and stimulating address (Narain 1972) and devoted the following years to examining their implications in further depth.

The first issue that he addressed was why the rate of productivity increase in Indian agriculture was only slightly higher in the 1960s, when there was substantial extension in the use of high-yield varieties and fertilizers, than in the 1950s, when there was no basis for any significant technological change. He also explored the effect of price and nonprice factors on the sources of productivity increase. He presented his findings in a very important paper on productivity growth in Indian agriculture (Narain 1976).

Dharm Narain stressed two significant points in this paper. First, most of the increase in productivity in the 1950s came from shifts in the cropping pattern in the country as a whole—from foodgrain to non-foodgrain crops (which generally yielded higher value of output per hectare); from lower-value foodgrain crops (such as jowar and bajra) to higher-value ones (such as wheat); and shifts of some important crops (such as rice) from low-yield regions to high-yield regions. Second, in the

1960s, in contrast, as much as two-thirds of the overall productivity increase was from increase in "pure" yield, whose rate of growth was in fact two and one-half times as high as in the 1950s. Though it was widely known that yield increases were more important in the latter decade, the nature of the changes in cropping pattern and in location that took place in these decades raises very interesting questions about their future role.

Above all, the detailed examination of the role of price and nonprice factors in productivity growth enabled Dharm Narain to reiterate an earlier conclusion, namely, that while the play of market forces could be an effective determinant of the share of nonfoodgrain crops in total cropped area and even in bringing about locational shifts, there were severe limits to what could be achieved through changes in relative prices. This he demonstrated also with reference to the important question of how far the use intensity of vital inputs such as fertilizers could be raised by changes in the crop-fertilizer price ratio, showing that while the ratio had to be maintained within a favorable range, the magnitude of the increases in input required was such that the price instrument could not possibly be relied upon to bring them about. "It underscores the fact," he observed in what was perhaps the strongest statement he permitted himself to make, "that an oversimplistic and therefore excessive preoccupation with price can do more harm than good by distracting attention from the harder but more important tasks which belong in the nonprice world of achieving technological breakthroughs and releasing such real constraints as stand in the way of their becoming a reality on the farmers' fields."

There was one other possible alternative—belonging to the "nonprice world"—for relaxing the real constraints on growth in agriculture: increasing cropping intensity and expanding gross cropped area. This became the next aspect to which he turned his attention, and it was the subject of the last brochure that he completed on the impact of irrigation and labor availability on multiple cropping in India (Narain and Roy 1980).

The analysis was based on the hypothesis that multiple cropping must depend not only on the extent of irrigated area but also on the quality of irrigation, as well as the availability of adequate family labor in cultivator households. This hypothesis was tested with reference to both interstate variations in cropping intensity and variations in cropping intensity among different farm-size groups and was found to be consistent with the available data. The results clearly implied that "land reforms designed to rectify the existing imbalance between the availability of land and labor can exert a significantly favorable effect on cropping intensity because smaller farms tend to use irrigation and labor more intensively."

The results were also used to project the rate of increase in gross cropped area that could be achieved by the proposed program of irrigation development in the Sixth Plan period. This exercise led to the very interesting and encouraging conclusion that even if there were no improvement in the growth rate of productivity compared with that of the 1960s, agricultural output could grow at about 3.5 percent per annum if this program were executed and its potential for raising cropping intensity were realized adequately. If the execution of the program helped also to raise crop yields, a rate of growth of output of even 4 percent per annum was within the reach of Indian agriculture.

This was a result to which Dharm Narain obviously attached much importance. Although he did not deal at length with questions of equity in any of his writings, he was very deeply concerned about them and had stressed that if any dent was to be made in rural poverty, the rate of growth of agricultural output would have to be over 3.5 percent per annum (Narain 1972). If the constraints on agricultural growth proved to be more serious, there was also the danger of land's being diverted from nonfoodgrain to foodgrain crops on account of demographic pressure. This could retard the whole process of development in other ways.

It is within this carefully built framework of ideas relating to agricultural development in India that one has to consider the meaning and purpose of the venture on which Dharm Narain embarked just before he passed away. It was clearly an effort to understand whether the trends in rural poverty in different states within India (on which much work had meanwhile been done by others) could be explained with reference to not only the rates of growth recorded in agriculture but also the pressure on foodgrain availability as reflected in the direction and extent of foodgrain prices. This was obviously a very fruitful line of inquiry and would have in his hands led to conclusions illuminated by his many deep insights. Some of the questions he raised form the subject matter of this volume. It might be risky, of course, to extrapolate any of the inferences he drew from the limited exercises he initiated, since he had his own way of examining them further and often chose to emphasize what inferences should *not* be drawn. It is only natural that friends, saddened by the loss of such a man, should wish to draw attention to what he was trying to do when he passed away, but we must be careful not to indulge in speculations that would violate the high standards he observed in intellectual matters.

AGRICULTURAL CHANGE AND RURAL POVERTY

NOTE: In this book, numerical subscripts are set on the base line: C_1 C_2, whereas lettered subscripts are positioned partly below the base line: C_i C_x.

1 Trends in Rural Poverty in India: An Interpretation of Dharm Narain

GUNVANT M. DESAI

> A great deal of effort has been invested in recent years in quantifying the dimensions of absolute poverty in terms of the absolute numbers or the proportion of the population lying below some arbitrarily defined poverty line. The interest of this paper, however, centers not so much on the level of absolute poverty as on the temporal variations therein. For want of time-series of reasonable length on poverty estimates, it is understandable that work on the forces that accentuate or alleviate poverty should be lacking. However, for India, at any rate, this lacuna has been filled by Montek Ahluwalia who prepared annual estimates of the proportion of the rural population in absolute poverty for almost a decade and a half and subjected the series to statistical analysis. In preparing this paper we are doubly indebted to him: We make use of his poverty estimates and our analysis seeks to build from where he left.

With these words, Dharm Narain began drafting his study on rural poverty in India just before his death. Unfortunately, the only other material on this subject found in his papers comprises several computer printouts of his attempts to build on Ahluwalia's (1978b) analysis.

This chapter presents my understanding, based on discussions with Dharm Narain over several months, of the significance he attributed to his statistical results. It is no substitute for what Dharm Narain had to say. He had endless patience to reflect on statistical results and an inimitable way of expressing what he saw in them.

Ahluwalia's (1978b) three major findings based on all-India evidence serve as a backdrop to Dharm Narain's results: First, there was no discernible trend between the mid-1950s and the early 1970s in the incidence of poverty in rural India, measured as the percentage of the

1

rural population in poverty (POV). A linear trend fitted to Ahluwalia's estimates yields the following results:*

$$POV = 45.59 + 0.393 \text{ TIME} \qquad (1.1)$$
$$(13.73) \quad (1.04) \qquad R^2 = 0.09$$

Second, improved agricultural performance, measured as an increase in the net domestic product in agriculture per head of rural population at 1960/61 prices (NDPARP), was definitely associated with reduced incidence of rural poverty. In equation (1.2), POV in year t is a function of NDPARP in year t or a function of the average value of NDPARP in t and t-1 years (ANDPARP).

$$POV = 106.524 - 0.337 \text{ NDPARP}** \qquad (1.2)$$
$$(5.30) \quad (2.89) \qquad R^2 = 0.43$$
$$POV = 132.953 - 0.492 \text{ ANDPARP}**$$
$$(5.53) \quad (3.52) \qquad\qquad R^2 = 0.53$$

Third, as shown in equation (1.3), there was no underlying time trend in the incidence of rural poverty, even after allowing for changes associated with agricultural performance.

$$POV = 132.808 - 0.491 \text{ ANDPARP}** - 0.003 \text{ TIME} \qquad (1.3)$$
$$(3.05) \qquad\qquad\qquad (0.01) \qquad R^2 = 0.53$$

Dharm Narain thought that agricultural performance and time (representing the influence of other forces) were relevant in explaining temporal changes in poverty through regression analysis. But he also saw the need to expand Ahluwalia's specification by including nominal prices of commodities consumed by rural poor as an explanatory variable.

To be sure, Dharm Narain was well aware of the relations between changes in nominal prices of some commodities consumed by the poor and their real incomes. However, because of the rural poor's small share in the marketed agricultural surplus; rigidities in rural wages, which were increasingly monetized; and the widespread dependence of the poor on market purchases for consumption needs, he thought that changes in the nominal price of the consumption basket of the poor had a far greater and more immediate impact on their ability to cross the poverty line than on their incomes, whether they were producers of these commodities or farm laborers.

Dharm Narain estimated two equations in which he added price as an explanatory variable to NDPARP and TIME. In equation (1.4), the price

*Figures in parentheses below regression coefficients in equations 1.1 to 1.6 are t ratios. Two asterisks (**) indicate that the regression coefficient is significantly different from zero at the 5 percent level; a single asterisk (*) indicates that it is significantly different from zero at the 1 percent level.

variable is the consumer price index for agricultural laborers (CPIAL). In equation (1.5) it is the index number of wholesale price of foodgrains (IFGP). He estimated these equations after logarithmic transformation of the variables.

$$\text{LPOV} = 4.592 - 0.631 \text{ LNDPARP*} \tag{1.4}$$
$$(-3.595)$$
$$+ 0.582 \text{ LCPIAL*} - 0.174 \text{ LTIME*}$$
$$(8.537) \qquad\qquad (-7.353) \qquad R^2 = 0.93$$

$$\text{LPOV} = 6.072 - 0.841 \text{ LNDPARP*} \tag{1.5}$$
$$(-4.837)$$
$$+ 0.499 \text{ LIFGP*} \quad - 0.025 \text{ LTIME}$$
$$(8.022) \qquad\qquad (-7.029) \qquad R^2 = 0.91$$

Inclusion of price as an independent variable increased the explanation of the variation in rural poverty substantially, as shown by the R^2s of equations (1.4) and (1.5). It also made the regression coefficient of TIME highly significant, with a *negative* sign. The upshot of Dharm Narain's results, then, is that it is not enough to take into account agricultural performance and time to explain temporal variations in rural poverty; it is equally necessary to consider changes in the nominal prices of goods consumed by the poor. After allowance is made for the changes in the incidence of poverty associated with agricultural performance and the nominal price of the rural poor's consumption basket, there was a definite *downward* trend in the incidence of rural poverty between 1956/57 and 1970/71. This was owing to the influence of other factors operating over time. Among the factors that Dharm Narain had in mind were the employment generated through building of socioeconomic overheads in rural areas, support to traditional cottage and village industries, growth of the tertiary sector in rural areas resulting from agricultural development at an unprecedented pace, land reforms, development of cooperative institutions, and growth in health, education, and other services. He attached maximum importance to the land reforms of the 1950s. Perhaps because of this, he used TIME as an explanatory variable after logarithmic transformation.

Dharm Narain's findings critically depend on the inclusion of the nominal price of the rural poor's consumption basket as an explanatory variable. After Ahluwalia expressed reservations, we had extensive discussions on this issue. Ahluwalia thought that use of CPIAL to estimate poverty percentages would produce a spurious positive correlation between the price variable and POV (equation 1.4). Dharm Narain did not agree. According to him, the estimates of poverty percentages in different years were based on (1) the National Sample Survey Organisation's findings on the distribution of household expenditure and (2) poverty lines in

Figure 1.1. Percentage of rural population in poverty (POV) and consumer price index for agricultural laborers (CPIAL), 1956/57–1970/71

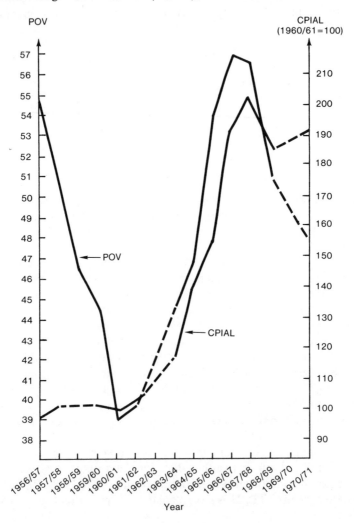

current-value terms. Although measurement of the poverty lines was statistically influenced by CPIAL, its influence on the distribution of household expenditure was causal rather than statistical. Only if it is assumed that the distribution of household expenditure remained unchanged over time can one say that the use of CPIAL in estimating poverty percentages will produce a spurious positive correlation between

Figure 1.2. Percentage of rural population in poverty (POV) and net domestic product in agriculture per head of rural population (NDPARP) at 1960/61 prices, 1956/57–1970/71

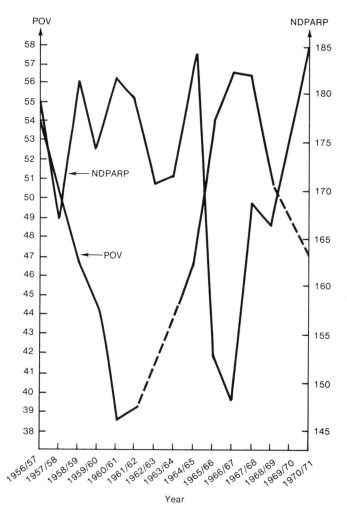

POV and CPIAL. Clearly, such an assumption is not justified on a priori grounds. Sen's paper in this volume elegantly supports this reasoning.

The data used by Dharm Narain to estimate the equations also support the insights provided by his specification (figs. 1.1 and 1.2). There was no trend in the incidence of rural poverty between 1956/57 and 1970/71, as Ahluwalia observed. But there were no yearly fluctuations either. The figures show that the percentage of the rural population in poverty declined continuously from 54.1 in 1956/57 to 38.9 in 1960/61, rose to 56.6 in 1966/67, and then fell to 47.5 in 1970/71. If the missing observations for 1962/63 and 1969/70 are ignored, the changes in each subperiod were in only one direction. During the entire fifteen-year period, the percentage of the rural population in poverty moved between an upper bound of 57 percent and a lower bound of 39 percent.

A decline of 15 percentage points in the incidence of rural poverty during 1956/57–1960/61 was associated with neither a decline in the price variable nor an improvement in agricultural performance. Thus, TIME as a proxy for the other factors, notably land reforms, becomes relevant in explaining the reductions in the incidence of rural poverty. On the other hand, the sharp rise in the level of rural poverty during 1960/61–1966/67 was closely associated with a steep rise in CPIAL and a fall in NDPARP. The use of TIME in logarithmic form explains why this variable alone could not offset the poverty-aggravating effects of rising nominal prices in the face of deteriorated agricultural performance. In the last subperiod, downward changes in the poverty levels clearly were associated with impressive gains in agricultural performance and much less upward pressure on prices.

The above scrutiny of the data suggests that the statistical significance of Dharm Narain's results was not due to spurious correlation between POV and CPIAL. In fact, in the first and third subperiods, when rural poverty declined continuously, prices were quite stable. This cannot be overemphasized. Not only does it dispel doubts about spurious correlation between the price variable and poverty percentages in Dharm Narain's results but it highlights the importance of a stable price environment in mitigating the incidence of rural poverty.

Among the forces that accentuate or alleviate rural poverty, the impact of changes in the price of the poor's consumption basket has received, at best, only passing attention. Dharm Narain's genius lay in developing a simple but insightful equation to drive home this point. His unfinished research assumes added significance because he was second to none in understanding the complexities of eradicating massive poverty and in using agricultural prices as instruments of public policy to promote growth with equity.

2   Dharm Narain on Poverty: Concepts and Broader Issues

AMARTYA SEN

One day in 1973 when Dharm Narain was passing through London en route to America, I attempted a guided tour of London. As we passed through Drury Lane, I said: "This is a very famous street, Dharm. It is called Drury Lane, of which you have no doubt heard." "Why," he asked, "is it famous?" Recognizing—sadly—that I did not know the answer, I told the tourist in no uncertain terms: "Don't fuss. It is just famous, that is all." Dharm Narain looked around, paused, and pointed to the Theatre Royal: "It must be because of that theater, I think. Looks quite grand, possibly old." There was Dharm Narain quietly confident on his home ground, that is, able to produce a coherent and plausible explanation from a tiny bit of information in a completely new territory.

In empirical economics, no one else could get so much out of so little and with such ease. This is worth bearing in mind in interpreting Dharm Narain's involvement in poverty research in general and the equations in this book in particular. In pursuing these equations, it may be a mistake to look for a grand design aimed at unearthing the whole truth behind poverty, and indeed, Dharm Narain would have been most skeptical of such a design. He was not, I think, searching for a "unified field theory," but pointing to the insight that we can get about nature and causes of poverty from a rudimentary—and incomplete—characterization involving these simple variables. He was, as usual, capturing some important aspects of a complex reality in a simple and elegant way.

The variables in Dharm Narain's equations are:

1. an index of rural poverty x (he chose the simple index of the head-count ratio, giving the percentage of rural population below the poverty line);
2. a price index p (he considered two, viz., the consumer price index for agricultural laborers and the index of wholesale foodgrain prices);
3. an index of average real income of the rural population y (he took

the net domestic agricultural product per head of the rural population); and

4. an indicator of other influences that change over time t (he chose time itself).

And he proposed that poverty may be seen as being determined by the other three variables:

$$x = f(y,p,t) \tag{2.1}$$

In his data fits, he tried out a particular form of this general equation, namely, linear in logarithms, but I do not think that that was a central feature of what he was after.

Is there anything unusual about this characterization? Using time in this way is rare, but it is a very sensible method when (1) the changes in question (e.g., land reform) are difficult to quantify and (2) they have a monotonic impact (e.g., land reform over time always reducing rather than raising poverty). However, the really interesting feature of Dharm Narain's formulation relates, not to time, but to the use of the price index. There would have been nothing special about it at all had it been used along with an index of *money* income, since price correction would then have been essential. But y is *real* income—already discounted for price changes—and the price index is being brought *once again* into the story, and that is the significant issue. The charge of double counting is the dog that did not bark.

Why not? The short answer is that Dharm Narain is concerned here, not with mean prosperity, but specifically with poverty. However, with a given relative distribution, the mean income would also be a good guide to the level of poverty. So a longer answer is that Dharm Narain is rejecting the usefulness of the assumption of constant distribution. But should not that take him towards supplementing y by some index of distribution rather than by a general price index? If Dharm Narain were looking just for consistency relations rather than for causation, the answer would be yes. But he *is* looking for causation. And thus it is the causal role of price changes that Dharm Narain is choosing to emphasize in his analysis of poverty. That is the main novelty of his analysis, and it is on that focus that this chapter concentrates.

Price Index: Recovery versus Command

We can distinguish between two different exercises in which the price index plays a role in the "determination" of the consumption by people, including the poor. From the point of view of the *observer*, for example, the economist studying poverty, the price index is useful to recover the real consumption picture from the nominal consumption data given in money terms. This is a problem, not for the *observed* persons, for example, the poor who are being studied, but for the person "determining" real consumption from nominal consumption data. I shall call this the recovery problem. In contrast, the consumption opportunities that people, including the poor, have can in fact depend on the prices that they actually have to pay. The simplest case is that of a person with a given money income, or a given amount of some particular good to sell. What he can buy depends on the prices of the various goods; the prices thus "determine" his consumption in the causal sense. This is a problem primarily for the *observed* person himself, since his actual command over goods and services depends on these prices. This I shall call the command problem. The command problem is also of interest to the observer, for example, the economist, only because he is interested in knowing the situation that the observed person actually faced. While the economist is thus concerned with both the recovery problem and the command problem, they are totally different types of exercises. This contrast is relevant to the inter- esting methodological issue that Montek Ahluwalia put to Dharm Narain regarding the latter's approach and the good statistical fit he had got.

> The statistical problem arises because we have no independent measure of poverty which does not use the price index to derive the poverty measure. If we had such a measure (e.g., if the NSS [National Sample Survey Organisation] had directly measured calory consumption) and then used prices as explanatory variable, and your results were obtained, they would certainly demonstrate the conclusion you wish to assert. As it stands the price index is being used to estimate the poverty percentage itself and therefore figures on both sides of the equation. I fear this may produce a spurious positive correlation between poverty and prices. To illustrate the point I suspect if you took the NSS nominal consump- tion data, and used the wholesale price index for Brazil to first estimate poverty, and then tried to explain poverty thus estimated in terms of the price index, you are very likely to get a good fit simply because this variable figures on both sides of the equation. Clearly this would be unacceptable.[1]

Ahluwalia's point is well worth considering, particularly since it raises an important general issue regarding Dharm Narain's approach and its empirical verification.

The distinction between the recovery problem and the command problem is important in this context. Dharm Narain was concerned with the command problem and not the recovery problem, whereas Ahluwalia's point can be seen as involving both. But as far as the recovery problem is concerned, the objection to using Brazilian prices for Indian consumption is straightforward, and it obviously does not turn on the remoter issue of spurious correlation in any fit like Dharm Narain's. Using Brazilian prices in this way would not recover Indian consumption figures, and thus the measure of poverty that would be obtained in this way would not be appropriate at all. Thus the variable with which a spurious correlation would be obtained would not be a measure of poverty.

Suppose that the recovery problem were correctly performed. Would this problem of spurious fit still apply because the price index "figures on both sides of the equation"? Clearly not. How the real consumption picture is recovered is not directly relevant as long as it is recovered. Suppose that the money values of consumption from which the recovery was to be done had been obtained—for whatever reason—by evaluating Indian consumption bundles at Brazilian prices. To recover the Indian consumption data, we would have to use Brazilian prices. But once this had been done, Brazilian prices would have no further role to play. If we tried out a fit with the poverty measure (thus obtained from recovered consumption data using Brazilian prices) against Brazilian prices, we would not prima facie expect any relation at all. Thus, the mere fact that the same price index "figures on both sides of the equation" need not precipitate a spurious good fit. The real issue is whether the price index used for the recovery problem does make us recover the consumption data. If it does, then there is no prima facie reason to expect any fit with the price index used in the recovery problem.

That the same price index can be used both in the recovery problem and in the command problem does not imply that a relation of the kind that Dharm Narain finds must of necessity be observed. Let us take another hypothetical example. Let it be the case that physical consumption remains invariant with respect to price changes, for example, because wages adjust correspondingly and immediately (and the system is homogeneous of degree zero) or because the government supplements income until the physical consumption is restored. In this case, we would have the same price index on both sides of the equation, once for the recovery problem to get the poverty estimate and again for Dharm Narain's model centered on the command problem. But we would not prima facie expect to find any relation between the price index and variations of poverty and consumption, since these variations must be due to influences *other than* price changes (since prices have no influence on actual consumption in this case). So if we did use the right price index to recover actual consumption, there would be no reason why its use as an explanatory variable must lead to a good fit, unless there were some real reason for that fit, such as wages falling behind prices, affecting the command problem. And that was precisely what Dharm Narain was after.

So the real issue is whether the recovery problem is being correctly performed, not whether some price index is figuring on both sides of the equation. The price paid by the potentially poor for food and other goods is a real influence on their actual poverty (in the absence of compensation through wage adjustment or public policy). Dharm Narain was emphasizing that real causal link, to be distinguished from the computational issue underlying the recovery problem. Ahluwalia's worry would become real and important if the recovery problem were wrongly performed and if the price index used in that wrong calculation happened to be the same as—or closely related to—the price index for testing the fit of Dharm Narain's economic relations.[2] That is, of course, primarily an empirical issue. It can be dealt with by examining whether the prices used in the recovery exercise are the right ones to use for that exercise. If they are not, then the possibility of spurious relation is indeed present. But in that case—more immediately—the poverty estimate itself is wrong, and we need not care whether the fit is good or not. Dharm Narain took the poverty estimates to be correct, under which condition his approach certainly stands. If the poverty estimates were wrong, and the prices used in the recovery exercise with NSS data were not the actual prices faced by the respondents, then we should correct our poverty estimates before considering the question of causation. What is ruled out is the possibility that the poverty estimation is correct while Dharm Narain's causal model is producing a spurious fit because of the use of the price index on both sides of the equation. The fact that the same index appears on both sides of the equation is in itself neither here nor there.

Fuller Specification

The variables used by Dharm Narain can be incorporated in a fuller model, giving a more complete account. But a fuller picture is not necessarily a better one. A partial picture is typically consistent with several different fuller models, and there may be substantial loss of generality in choosing any particular fuller specification. Further, a partial picture of the kind that Dharm Narain presents does not overstate our understanding of how the economy operates, whereas a fuller model might do just that. Nevertheless, it is interesting to consider examples of how the Dharm Narain relations may be embedded in a fuller model.

For this purpose, I shall use a model that I have presented elsewhere to interpret the causation of the Bengal famine of 1943 (Sen 1981b, app. B). There are five occupation groups:

1. agricultural capitalists and landlords;
2. peasants;
3. urban and semiurban workers;
4. rural workers (agricultural laborers); and

5. rural household producers (craftsmen, barbers, etc.).

It might be noted that in the context of rural poverty, the relevant occupation groups are groups 2, 4, and 5. The number of persons in occupation group i is n_i for $i = 1, \ldots, 5$. The output of peasant farms—taken to be units of foodgrains—is q_2 per peasant, and the output is q per person of w_3 landed class in nonpeasant farms. The wage rates per person are w_3 and w_4, respectively, for urban and rural workers. The output per rural household worker is taken to be unity (with the units appropriately defined), and the money income per rural household worker is v, which obviously also reflects the price of one unit of household product. The proportions of the nonpeasant and the peasant foodgrain outputs marketed are m_1 and m_2, respectively (cf. Narain 1961). Finally, c_i and h_i represent the proportion of money income that members of occupation group i spend on foodgrains and rural household goods, respectively; furthermore, $c_1 = c_2 = h_3 = 0$, and $c_4 + h_4 = c_5 + h_5 = 1$.

The model was used to calculate the foodgrain entitlement of each occupation group, defined as the maximum amount of foodgrains that can be commanded by a member of that group. Denoting the food entitlement per head of occupation group i as e_i, we obtain the following:

$$e_1 = q_1 - (n_4 w_4 / n_1 p) \qquad (2.2)$$
$$e_2 = q_2$$
$$e_3 = w_3 / p$$
$$e_4 = w_4 / p$$
$$e_5 = [n_1 q_1 m_1 h_1 + n_2 q_2 m_2 h_2 + n_4 h_4 (w_4 / p)] / n_5 (1 - h_5)$$

It is obvious that, other things given, a rise in foodgrain prices worsens the foodgrain entitlements of occupation groups 3 (urban workers), 4 (rural workers), and 5 (rural household producers); keeps the foodgrain entitlement of group 2 (peasants) unchanged; and increases the foodgrain entitlement of group 1 (agricultural capitalists). This is clearly in line with Dharm Narain's analysis of the impact of foodgrain prices on poverty.

However, one cannot simply assume that foodgrain prices rise with everything else given. In my explanation of the Bengal famine of 1943, in the context of which this model was employed, it was assumed that urban workers were protected from the effect of rising foodgrain prices as a result of rationing and control by a public subsidy. A sharp increase in urban real income was taken as the prime mover in getting foodgrain prices p, to rise, hitting at the rural workers and household producers, who provided the bulk of the famine victims. Such a model is not appropriate in other contexts, especially since the urban sector is often sluggish and the urban workers are often not protected against rising foodgrain prices. (In 1942–43, protecting urban workers against rising foodgrain prices was seen as a wartime necessity by the British government, then in power, in its anxiety to avoid any political trouble in Calcutta [Sen 1981b, 56–57].)

A more appropriate prime mover in the present context is a restriction of foodgrain sales by the larger producers, leading to an increase in foodgrain prices. Such a restriction—in the stylized picture of this model—is best represented by a decline in m_1. Its impact on foodgrain prices, p, can be worked out from the following equation:

$$p = (n_3 w_3 c_3 + n_4 w_4 c_4) / [n_1 q_1 m_1 (1 - h_1) + n_2 q_2 m_2 (1 - h_2)] \qquad (2.3)$$

A reduction in m_1 will (1) *increase* foodgrain prices, p; (2) *reduce* the food entitlement of rural and urban workers; (3) *reduce* the food entitlement of rural household producers; (4) *keep unchanged* the peasants' food entitlement; and (5) *increase* the food entitlement of agricultural capitalists (Sen 1981b, app. B, 179–84). And these qualitative effects will all remain unchanged, even if wages rise in proportion to rises in prices, but not by as much.

While Dharm Narain's analysis is in line with all this as far as the price index, p, is concerned, he is, of course, also concerned with other forces operating on rural poverty. The average agricultural income per unit of rural population is taken by Dharm Narain as a separate influence. This can be captured in the present context by q_1 and q_2. Whereas a reduction of q_1 will reduce the food entitlement of groups 3, 4, and 5 through an increase in prices, a reduction of q_2 will *in addition* directly reduce the food entitlement of group 2 (peasants).

This is no more than a simple illustration of how Dharm Narain's relations might be embedded in a fuller model. Many other ways of characterizing these relations can be explored. Dharm Narain was outlining a common denominator of a *class* of such models.

Policy Issues

The policy issues related to Dharm Narain's analysis are of some importance. It is useful to divide the policy picture into the short and the long run. Unlike Dharm Narain's third explanatory variable, time, the other two, agricultural income and price index, can both shift very quickly over time, depending on economic circumstances. Dharm Narain's analysis points to these two short-run variables for monitoring change and anticipating rapid accentuation of poverty.

It might be interesting to consider how Dharm Narain's analysis might have changed the governmental anticipation of two famines in South Asia that I have studied—the Bengal famine of 1943 and the Bangladesh famine of 1974. In December 1942 the Indian government was deeply complacent about the food situation in India, including that in Bengal.

The food availability in Bengal during 1942 had been 32 percent higher than in 1941, and although the December 1942 harvest was smaller than that in December 1941, it was still quite a bit higher than that in December 1940. Statistically the shortage seemed small. In January 1943 the viceroy wrote the secretary of state for India in London that he was trying to "screw a little (rice) out of" Bengal (Mansergh 1971, doc. no. 362). As it happens, destitution had already begun in remoter rural areas in Bengal, and within a few months Bengal was experiencing the worst famine in centuries.

How would Dharm Narain's focus have affected the reading of the situation? Dharm Narain concentrates not on the food problem as such but on poverty, which clearly is the right perspective for anticipating famines. In terms of Dharm Narain's variable of agricultural income per head, nothing disastrous would have been seen. Agricultural income in 1942 had been high, and the lower harvest of December 1942 would not have reduced income drastically. It is the price variable that gives the clue to the impending crisis. Although in 1942 food availability in Bengal was 32 percent higher than in 1941 and the output of rice—the staple food in the region—was 41 percent higher, the price of rice shot *up* by 90 percent during 1942 (Sen 1981b, chap. 6). This price rise—fed by a war boom— would gather momentum in the following months and ultimately kill millions of rural workers, household producers, and others. Already by December 1942 the Dharm Narain warning bells were tolling ferociously. Those running the government chose to concentrate on other indicators and had to take the consequence of sacrificed lives.

Similarly, in Bangladesh the indicator of food supply and even Dharm Narain's variable of average agricultural income did not indicate any catastrophe in the offing in the middle of 1974. But the price index of foodgrains—Dharm Narain's indicator—rose very sharply indeed, paving the way for the famine (ibid., chap. 9).

In combating oncoming famines, early diagnosis is more than half the battle, and from that point of view Dharm Narain's indicators have strategic importance. The long-run need, however, is different: to make sure that distress situations do not occur rather than to concentrate on immediate relief based on early diagnosis of distress. Here, too, Dharm Narain's relations have great importance. The focus on average real income (corrected for price changes) is not particularly unusual. But the use of the price index on its own as a further variable is less common, and it has the effect of capturing the commercial nature of modern destitution in developing countries such as India. A major weapon in combating poverty over the long run as well as the short run is to keep food prices low. This approach conflicts rather sharply with the view that the way out of Indian poverty is to enhance incentives to grow more food through higher food prices—a view that has gained some considerable ground in India. Dharm Narain's focus on the negative effects of higher food prices is important, not because the incentive effects are clearly negligible, for they may not be, and as far as the relative allocation of resources between different crops is concerned, Dharm Narain's own work (1965) has pointed towards strong price effects. The real issue is that irrespective of whether the indirect effects of high food prices in raising rural incomes through incentives are strong, the direct effects of high food prices on poverty are substantial. Even if the indirect positive effects were powerful, which is far from obvious, the direct effects would remain immediate and important.

Insofar as higher agricultural prices increase output and agricultural income, these effects will be represented by Dharm Narain's second explanatory variable, agricultural income per head, y. Thus, there might be a deep conflict between the two variables p and y pushing in different directions in response to a policy of high agricultural prices. What is crucially important in this context is the fact that the two types of effects do not necessarily—indeed, do not even typically—work on the same group of people. The increase in agricultural income as a consequence of higher agricultural prices clearly does benefit the larger farmers and possibly even the peasants. On the other hand, depending on the nature of the technological change and the extent of slack in the rural labor market, the wage laborers may or may not gain from this incentive effect.

The concentration on the average situation can be terribly misleading. The role of food prices as a divisive influence is important here. Poverty in a commercial economy is not simply a matter of output and availability but also one of purchase and command. Dharm Narain has helped us to focus on this crucially important question.

Extensions

In what directions might this approach be extended? First, we can use less crude measures of poverty than the head-count ratio. Measures that are distribution-sensitive have been proposed recently by me (1973) and others.[3] The number of people below the poverty line can be very deceptive as a measure of poverty. For example, in Bangladesh, while the proportion of the rural population below the poverty line (with a calorie intake equal to 90 percent of the recommended intake) *fell* by about 19 percent between 1968/69 and 1975, the proportion in "extreme poverty" (80 percent or less of the recommended calorie intake) *rose* by 64 percent (Khan 1977, table 48; Sen 1981b, 150–53). A measure of poverty that puts all the weight on just one dividing line can hide a great deal. There is no reason why Dharm Narain's approach must be used only with the head-count measure of poverty; extensions are clearly possible.

Second, while either the index of food prices or the laborer's cost of living is a good supplement to average real income in analyzing poverty, some index of money wages and some measure of rural unemployment could be used to supplement the picture further. The price variable adds to the explanation of poverty even on its own insofar as its impact is not eliminated by corresponding wage adjustment. However, the response of wages may vary a great deal from one situation to another. The important lead given by Dharm Narain takes explicit note of the commercial basis of modern poverty, but that lead has to be supplemented by other parameters of commerce and exchange.

Finally, it is worth noting that the price index used by Dharm Narain is a part of the picture of *opportunities* that the potentially poor have of acquiring different bundles of goods. It is not directly a measure of the *actual bundle* of goods. The motivation behind looking at opportunities can vary. Even if our interest is ultimately only in the actual bundle of goods, examining the opportunities will help us to understand why a person acquired one particular bundle of goods rather than another. Alternatively, we might be interested in the opportunities themselves. The approach of rights tends to push us in that direction. Checking whether a person's income is below or above the poverty line has the feature of concentrating on opportunities rather than on the outcome, since a person could have an income higher than the level needed to meet, say, his nutritional norms and nevertheless fail to meet these norms.

Insofar as we are interested in opportunities themselves, a natural extension of Dharm Narain's focus on prices and market opportunities is to look at other types of opportunities that a person has. In the context of poverty, these may include freedom from restrictive ties (e.g., labor bondages), freedom to break caste-specific constraints (e.g., social restrictions imposed by surviving untouchability), freedom from sexual discrimination (e.g., barriers traditionally imposed on women, particularly on widows), or freedom from illiteracy and what Marx called the "idiocy of village life." These issues may seem far removed from Dharm Narain's equations, but Dharm Narain was deeply concerned with these broader questions. The concentration on market opportunities in his equations can be seen as representing only one part of his involvement with poverty and misery. The part—not strangely—is less important than the whole.

Notes

1. Ahluwalia to Narain, 2 January 1980.
2. Ahluwalia is thus quite right to go on to the question of "errors in the price variable" (ibid., 2).

3. Important contributions have come from Anand, Blackorby and Donaldson, Chakravarty, Foster, Greer and Thorbecke, Hamada and Takayama, Kakwani, Kundu and Smith, Osmani, Takayama, and Thon. Some of the variations are discussed in my *Poverty and famines* (1981b), chap. 3 and app. C.

3 A Note on the Price Variable

CHRISTOPHER BLISS

Dharm Narain's concern with the effect of absolute prices on poverty poses a challenge to orthodox beliefs. Poverty is a "real" phenomenon that, according to a simple view of the matter, should not be importantly influenced by "nominal" values. As Amartya Sen remarks, the really interesting feature of Dharm Narain's formulation relates, not to time, but to the use of the price index. I agree, but I also think that there is much truth in the orthodox view that poverty eventually depends on the "real" economy. Therefore, I am surprised that it can be so grossly set aside, in a time-series application, with such apparent success.

As it stands, the equation says that nominal inflation by itself permanently increases poverty. If poverty does not increase in a time of rising prices, it is because of real agricultural growth and the influence of a time trend that is unfavorable to poverty. Attributing this trend to the effects of land reform hardly squares with the facts. In no reasonable reading of postindependence Indian history would land reform be seen as something proceeding steadily, year by year, through the sample period. Perhaps there are other, smoother trend factors, but I wonder what they are.

More plausible in my view is the possibility that the trend in prices has no influence on poverty, while deviations from the trend do. According to this interpretation, the coefficient on time arises largely because, as the equation is formulated, the trend in prices has attracted the positive coefficient attaching to deviations from the trend. The negative coefficient on time corrects for this. A story that is less offensive to reason then emerges. Inflation increases poverty, not because it increases the price level, the latter being a causal component in the determination of the extent of poverty, but rather because deviations from the trend in prices importantly influence the extent of poverty.

One could identify deviations from the trend of prices as the "unanticipated" component of inflation. Dharm Narain's relation then establishes an important example of the nonneutrality of unanticipated inflation, and economic theory and the study of poverty can live in peace.

18

That the Narain relation arises from the nonneutrality of inflation is one idea. I should mention another which has to do with the manner in which price indices figure in the equation. Sen's discussion of this question is not precise; however, I doubt that it matters, because it is unlikely that relative price changes have contributed enough to changes in poverty to explain the findings. Sen refers to *the* price index (as having been brought twice into the equation). There is not *one* price index, but at least *four*. They are:

1. the price deflator for agricultural production;
2. the cost of living index for agricultural workers;
3. the cost index for the critical poverty minimum-consumption basket; and
4. the index of foodgrain costs.

Depending on how the Narain relation is formulated, relative changes in these indices could affect the extent of poverty. Recall that movements into or out of poverty reflected in the relation have to do with the standard of living of people close to the median level of income for rural Indians. The consumption of these people includes many nonfood manufactured products (factory cloth, pots, biddies) the prices of which influence (2) and (3) but not (1) and (4). Equally (1) includes prices of nonfood crops such as cotton, or nongrains such as cooking oil, whereas (4) excludes them.

Relative movements of different price indices reflect real changes in welfare and distribution. They are quite different from the issue raised by Ahluwalia, which has to do with measurement errors in a single price index. This would be an example of what econometricians call "errors in variables." In the example of standard errors in variables, a right-hand variable is measured with an error, and the coefficient on it is biased towards zero. In the present case, the error affects both the right-hand and the left-hand sides in the same direction, and the coefficient on the right-hand side is biased upwards.

Perhaps Sen is too dismissive of the possible importance of errors in variables, but since there are good reasons to believe that inflation will not be neutral with regard to poverty in the short run, there is no compelling reason to look for other explanations.

Why do the poor suffer in periods of inflation? Two reasons are paramount. First, they use money as a store of value because their earnings arrive irregularly during the year. Second, certain money prices, for example, wages, may be "sticky" when compared with prices more quickly affected by changes in supply and demand. A third reason is less important but worth noting: unanticipated inflation typically disturbs relative real exchange rates, and this may influence poverty. An example would be a worker whose wages depend on the price of cotton but who consumes foodgrains. General inflation may generate the different movements in price indices discussed above. In the case of the first effect—the depreciation in the purchasing power of money balances—there may be offsetting influence as inflation lowers the real burden of debt. But this effect is not measured as poverty is normally calculated.

It is clear that Dharm Narain did just what Sen described: he confronted a problem of great richness and complexity and attacked it directly in a manner that immediately yielded results. We must admire this flair but not stop where he began.

4 Determinants of Rural Poverty: The Dynamics of Production, Technology, and Price

JOHN W. MELLOR

Two related dynamic forces—productivity-increasing technological change in agriculture and changing food prices—dominate the current controversy about rural poverty. The interacting effects of these forces vary with the technical characteristics of the land, the institutional controls of rents from land and access to other resources, and the economies of scale associated with the new technology. The dynamics of population growth provide a powerful backdrop.

It is argued that when control of land rents, finance, and inputs such as fertilizer is unequal, the new input-intensive, yield-increasing technology widens income disparities, which leads, in turn, to even greater concentration of asset control. The result is not only a further skewing of income distribution but a possible increase in the proportion of people in extreme poverty (Griffin 1974; Pearse 1975). If there are economies of scale associated with the new technology, they would serve to magnify these unfavorable effects.

A contrasting view is that new technology reduces the cost of food production, thereby lowering real food prices and increasing the demand for labor (Mellor 1968, 1978; Mellor and Johnston 1984; Mellor and Lele 1973). Because food is the principal consumption good for low-income people and because employment is their principal source of income, these effects are considered highly favorable to the poor. In this view, economies of scale in food production are thought either to be negligible or to arise from input supply and marketing functions that are readily dealt with through competition or the countervailing power of government policy.

As rapid population growth puts pressure on the land base, the real per capita income of labor is reduced by the decline of labor productivity and employment as well as by the increase in food prices. The continuing negative force of population growth on the incomes of the poor will overbalance the favorable effects on food prices and employment of weak technological change. This argues for more technological change, not less. What is more important, if poverty increases because of the effects of population growth and is only coincidentally associated with new food-production technology, delays in adopting new technology will result in an even more rapid increase in poverty. Moreover, the argument that adoption of new technology to increase food production should be delayed until needed but uncertain institutional changes, such as radical redistribution of land, have occurred may be harmful to the poor.

Lower food prices reduce the incomes of net sellers of food and raise the incomes of net purchasers.[1] Thus, the urban poor clearly benefit from lower food prices. Rural people in extreme poverty are largely landless or at least net purchasers of food, and hence they also benefit directly from lower food prices. Generally, only those whose income is well above the extreme poverty line can sell a sizable proportion of their food production to finance purchases of nonfood goods and services (Mellor 1978).[2]

It is also argued that lower food prices reduce rural employment (Brown 1979). However, poor people spend 60–80 percent of incremental income on food, and aggregate agricultural production is generally highly inelastic with respect to price. Only when employment in food production is high relative to nonfood crops and when the elasticity of substitution of food crops for nonfood crops is high with respect to price can the lower prices reduce employment, thus overbalancing the indirect effect on income. These conditions are unlikely to be met (Mellor 1978).[3] When there is no change in output, lower prices will certainly reduce the incomes and expenditures of farmers and the derived employment for laborers. This effect may occur through decreased substitution of hired labor for family labor on farms or through decreased expenditures on labor-intensive rural nonfarm goods and services. But for rural laborers to be net losers as a result of lower food prices, the reduction in employment resulting from reduced marginal expenditures by surplus producers would have to exceed the increase in indirect income to the poor resulting from lower prices. Given the high proportion of income spent for food by the very poor, this seems unlikely. Obviously, lower prices accompanying higher output benefit the poor doubly through increased employment and lower food prices.

Much of the controversy about the effects of new technology and price changes on poverty has focused on India, primarily because of the drama of the green revolution in the Punjab and a few other areas. India's size, the availability of data, and the wide range of social, economic, and ecological conditions also have contributed. India's politically vociferous urban population, agriculture dominated by peasant smallholders, substantial rural income inequalities, and massive rural poverty starkly epitomize the poverty-related rural circumstances in much of the Third World. Although the People's Republic of China is thought to be an example of a radical redistribution of land accompanied by improved technology that did not have deleterious income-distribution effects, the paucity of published data and systematic observation makes evaluation of China's experience difficult.[4]

Dharm Narain's work has specific relevance to the controversy about the relation between poverty, food prices, and technology. He uses long-term data from India to show that lower agricultural prices and increased agricultural production tend to reduce rural poverty. These findings make a case for cost-reducing technological change. In contrast to good weather, which comes and goes, the favorable effects of cost-reducing technological change can compound continuously. With technology and weather constant, a growing population, and the diminishing returns characteristic of agriculture, per capita food production can be maintained only with continuously rising prices or falling returns to labor.

Dharm Narain's analysis also shows that in India forces other than food prices and food production have caused poverty to decline somewhat. This finding is more equivocal and complex than his initial work suggests; however, it does seem that forces of growth or of institutional change must have been strong enough to counteract the negative effects of population growth, insufficient increases in agricultural production, and a rise in agricultural prices. This view is supported not only by Dharm Narain's intuitive insight from his lengthy experience with India's agriculture but also by the searching critical examination in the chapters in this volume by Sen and Srinivasan and extension of the analysis to a longer period by Ahluwalia and Desai.

The findings leave unanswered questions. Why is the incidence of poverty so much greater in some circumstances than in others? How do the dynamics of population growth, nonagricultural employment growth, and technological change in agriculture relate to varied background conditions? What policies with respect to technological change in agriculture and agricultural prices will be most effective in reducing absolute poverty?

While historical experience supports Dharm Narain's view concerning the forces at work for India as a whole, we still find major variations at the micro level. State and district data presented by Pranab Bardhan and Hanumantha Rao and his colleagues raise complex questions about the interaction of technology and poverty in different places and under different conditions. At least some of their data appear contrary to Dharm Narain's findings. Also, rural poverty in India is more severe than the subsistence agriculture of the settlement period in the Western United States and in many contemporary developing countries. The basic cause of these differences is the greater population pressure on land resources in India. However, where extreme poverty exists, there is wide variation in the extent of income disparities. Even among areas with similar demographic histories, differences in the incidence of poverty are large.

The Agricultural Production Function and Rural Poverty

The functional relation between production factors and output in agriculture varies with soil, topography, and climate. The importance of these characteristics differentiates the economics of agriculture from that of other sectors. Land differences help determine variations in the relation of labor input to food output. This in turn determines differences in the degree of rural poverty, land rents and the opportunity to concentrate wealth by control of land, the interaction of population growth and new technology, and the labor supply available to nonagricultural activities. Much of the regional variation in rural poverty and its means of amelioration is rooted in the underlying physical relationships.

It is convenient to develop the relations associated with different land types by arbitrarily dichotomizing variability into two situations: the "labor surplus" case and the "hard-working peasant" case. In the former, highly productive agricultural resources provide food for more people than are needed to work the land. In the latter, subsistence is provided only for the laborers who actually work on the land.

THE LABOR SURPLUS CASE

In Asia the roots of extreme poverty lie in rural landlessness and near landlessness. A class of landless poor can arise if the land is highly productive, if population growth is sustained and substantial, and if opportunities for nonagricultural employment are poor. Because the new high-yield crop varieties are generally highly responsive where physical conditions are favorable and input levels are high, they may well be associated with landlessness and high levels of poverty in such areas as the volcanic soils of Java, the Ganges Plain of India, Bangladesh, and the alluvial plains of central Luzon in the Philippines.

The different causes behind the labor surplus case and the hard-working peasant case are best seen through a simple production function relating labor input to crop output.[5] On highly productive land, production rises sharply to a level sufficient to support some multiple of the labor required. Thus, in figure 4.1 the output required for one person to subsist is shown by the horizontal line ab. The labor input of one person (OL_1) provides Oe level of average output, which is nearly four times the subsistence level of output. With that labor input, however, total output (Or) is close to a maximum for the given technology. Since the production function has risen well above the subsistence level, population could expand until

Figure 4.1. Hypothetical relationship between labor input and food output: the labor surplus case (holding inputs of land constant)

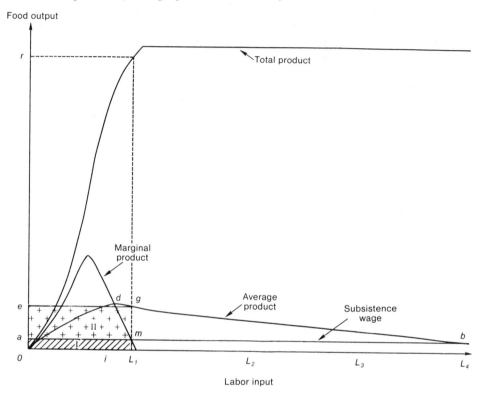

the total production per person declined to the subsistence level. In figure 4.1 this is a population of four (OL_4). Three contrasting situations are presented—one of prosperous equality, one of shared poverty, and one of major inequalities.

If the land resource is abundant, this production function allows a high level of subsistence production; for example, cereals may be fed to livestock, or food may be exchanged for nonagricultural luxuries. As long as land is freely available, additions to the population (that is from OL_1 to OL_2, and so on) will bring new land under cultivation. Labor input per unit area of land will be in effect at point Oi, left of L_1, which is significantly less than a person equivalent, and laborers will have an income well above minimum subsistence, although a portion may be taxed or traded. The exact position of Oi will depend upon the labor-leisure choice by peasants. For the rural population at least, there will be equality of income at a high level. Inequality within the farming class will arise only from differences in labor productivity, management ability, and accumulated capital improvements. This is the case of prosperous equality.

As long as population does not exceed the land available at full employment or nonfarm employment is available at an equivalent level of productivity, there will be no pressures for reduction of per capita income or development of inequality of income among rural people other than those arising from differences in ability, initiative, and parsimony. However, if the land frontier is exhausted and there is no compensating increase in nonfarm employment opportunities, population growth will gradually reduce the average level of living. Presumably, Malthusian forces will stabilize the population when the average income falls to the minimum subsistence level. At that point, three-quarters of the labor force will be in surplus (that is L_1L_4). The underemployed represent zero marginal productivity labor, which is already supported and available for work outside of agriculture. This is the situation that stimulated the labor surplus development literature spawned by W. Arthur Lewis's well-known paper (Lewis 1954).

Under these circumstances, the growing population may share the work to be done or at least the output. We may define this as "shared poverty" (Geertz 1963). Such sharing would occur among members of a family or an extended family or in a system of communal or collective ownership of land. Presumably, the latter has been the objective in the People's Republic of China.

In shared poverty, labor can be released from the farm work force without a decline in output, because its marginal productivity is essentially zero. However, Mellor (1963) and Sen (1966) show that under such circumstances, it is unlikely that labor can be extracted from agriculture without there being a decline in food production because of the positive marginal utility of leisure and the income effects of added employment. In addition, even when labor productivity has declined to a minimal subsistence level, there is always work, including scavenging, that can add to total output. Hence, a situation of zero marginal productivity is unlikely, although returns to such work on a person-equivalent basis may be well below subsistence needs. Nevertheless, we can expect the supply of labor to be highly elastic when the production function is of the type in figure 4.1 and the labor force is larger than OL_1

Figure 4.1 also suggests the possibility of major inequalities in income. If the labor market is such that the wage can be forced to the subsistence level marked by the space I (OL_1ma) in figure 4.1 and "surplus" labor is *not* supported through "shared poverty," then there is a surplus or rent from the land as indicated by space II (*amge*). Presumably, a person owning only the amount of land that would just fully occupy him with the marginal product of his labor at the subsistence level could, if labor

Figure 4.2. Hypothetical relationship between labor input and food output: the hard-working peasant case (for varying levels of land input)

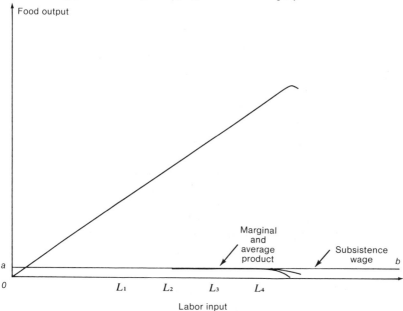

Labor input

became available through population pressure, hire a person at the subsistence level and still have an income several times larger than the subsistence wage. What is most striking, such income could be used to purchase additional land or political power, providing accumulating rents and eventually immense income disparities. Sharecropping and other mechanisms might be used to ease the management problem that might otherwise prevent such vast accumulations. Class differentiation based on asset control and type and amount of physical work done is a logical outcome, leading to a less cohesive rural society.

THE HARD-WORKING PEASANT CASE

Rural areas may have an exceedingly low level of living and still not have a landless class. This is typical of hill and semiarid areas in Asia and large parts of sub-Saharan Africa.[6] This situation occurs if increased labor input provides basic subsistence and no more (the slope of the production function is less steep than in the labor surplus case). In this situation, for varying levels of land input, we get a total product curve of the type shown in figure 4.2, which is simply a straight line from the origin.[7] Since each addition to the labor force must work fully for subsistence (such as at L_1 in fig. 4.2), there is no surplus or basis for rents. The marginal product, the average product, and the subsistence level are all equal. As population increases beyond the point at which the marginal and average products drop below the subsistence level, the surplus labor moves to unsettled land (L_2 in fig. 4.2). Once all the land is taken up (at labor input L_4), the population growth rate stabilizes at a Malthusian equilibrium determined by the pace of technological change. The people work hard at least during seasonal peaks. There is no landless class and little income inequality. There is no surplus to be converted into extreme wealth and inequality. There is some scope for latitude in defining subsistence and in scavenging and other production. Population may grow, income may gradually decline, and the amount of work performed may increase. Microgeographic differences in production functions also offer some scope for differences in income arising from economic rents. Further income differences arise from variations in initiative, skills, and thrift. Given this production function's tendency towards equality, not only is a communal system that divides land according to family size equitable, but it does not interfere with opportunities for wealth accumulation. This is consistent with practices common in much of sub-Saharan Africa.

Population Growth and Off-Farm Employment

In the case of the gently sloping production function, per capita income is low because of innate characteristics of the resource base. Population growth is absorbed by bringing new land under cultivation. Because the level of living is low, population growth is slow and only slowly absorbs the available land area. This is the situation in some parts of Africa. To the extent that the slope of the production function provides any surplus, there will be scope for rents, some differentiation of society by income, movement to poorer land, and a gradual decline in the level of living. This is the dominant situation in Africa. Eventually the land area is used up and a Malthusian equilibrium is reached, with rural population expanding at a rate determined by the rate of technological change.

The steeply sloping production function offers an initially high subsistence level and a gradual decline in the level of living as population expands, even when all comparable cultivable land is utilized. Land with a steeply sloping production function can support a large nonfarm population. This provides the basis not only for economic rents and a prosperous idle class but also for a surplus to exchange for nonagricultural goods and services.[8] The nonagricultural labor force can produce a wide range of consumption goods and provide the basis for capital accumulation and technological change. It can also trade for food from distant areas. One should not expect a large class of landless poor under such circumstances. Such a class would be least likely if there were a concentration of rents, for the rich would seek to mobilize the poor to produce for them, thereby creating demand and hence employment.

Why did a large, rural, underemployed landless class arise, particularly in South Asia and Java? Colonialism occurred after these societies had been considerably differentiated. Colonial regulation of trade not only prevented further development of nonagricultural employment but destroyed much of what already existed. The receivers of rent then traded with the distant colonial power rather than with their own under-employed.[9] Colonial rule may also have reduced death rates through such measures as public health programs and transport of food to avert periodic famine, creating an even larger landless class than otherwise would have existed. The level of living of these classes and their lack of means of subsistence except through access to land would leave them at least temporarily vulnerable to exploitation at even less than subsistence-level wages.

The two types of production functions offer contrasting opportunities for drawing population into nonfarm employment if an exogenous source of capital is available for expanding the nonagricultural sector. In the labor surplus case, labor can be drawn out of agriculture with little or no decline in output. Food for nonagricultural labor can be drawn out of agriculture by trade with the *rentier* class.

For the hard-working peasant case, an exogenous source of capital would push the marginal productivity of labor in nonagriculture above the average income in agriculture. This would draw laborers from agriculture and cause a drop in agricultural production, while the rising incomes of the laborers remaining in agriculture would reduce marketings more than proportionately to output. Thus, increased nonagricultural output must be traded to some other agricultural region for the food needed to maintain the nonagricultural labor force. Nonagricultural growth becomes more difficult, and its relation to improved rural incomes becomes more tenuous. Current history in Nigeria and much of sub-Saharan Africa is fully consistent with this description.

Price Responsiveness of Agricultural Production

The complexities of the processes of labor transfer outlined above are best seen as differences in the price responsiveness of aggregate agricultural output. The more inelastic agricultural output is with respect to price, the less the effect of growth in nonagricultural income on the aggregate income of the poor. This is because an inelastic food supply implies a rising cost of food for transferred labor and rising rents to the *rentier* class. Of course, imports may avert this problem, but they do so without the added employment, income, and income-distribution effects associated with a more elastic supply of domestic agricultural production.

If additional comparable land can be brought into production in response to increased demand, the aggregate supply derived from increased labor input will tend to be elastic with respect to price and a function of labor-leisure trade-offs (Mellor 1963). Assuming initial equilibrium, it is logical to expect the labor-leisure substitution to be relatively elastic for the higher average income of those workers facing the more steeply sloping production function. In the case of the gently sloping production function, labor will be working harder for a given product and hence will be at a point of more rapidly diminishing returns to work relative to leisure (ibid.). What is more important, the marginal propensity to consume food presumably will be higher in the case of average income of the gently sloping production function, so the elasticity of marketings with respect to price will be substantially lower. Thus, for example, one would expect a much higher supply elasticity for Thailand than for a typical country in West Africa. If the production function's slope were exactly that needed to provide subsistence, the elasticity of marketing would be greater than perfectly inelastic only if income rose sufficiently to cause food consumption to decline relative to total income. Even that effect might be overwhelmed by declining marginal utility of additional income. Thus, it is exceedingly unlikely that the rural labor force would benefit from growth in nonagricultural job opportunities except by leaving agriculture. In that event, the consequent drop in food production and rising real food costs would slow the growth of nonagricultural employment. It is no accident that the literature on backward-bending supply curves deals more with the African experience than with the Asian.[10]

If technology is held constant, the aggregate supply will be highly inelastic with respect to price when all available land has been brought into cultivation and average income has been depressed to the subsistence level. The marketed surplus, of course, may be significantly more elastic. Comparing the two types of production functions, growth of nonagricultural employment and incomes will cause a more rapid increase in food prices or imports in the case of the gently sloping function. Drawing labor from agriculture will cause a direct decline in agricultural output. In both cases higher income from increased nonfarm employment will cause a decline in labor input owing to the income effect on labor-leisure choices, but the effect is negligible for the steeply sloping function (ibid.). In the labor surplus case the income effect is likely to be larger than the substitution effect, given that the marginal productivity of labor is minimal.

The foregoing discussion assumes that all production response comes from changes in labor input. With modernization and increased use of fertilizer and other inputs with perfectly elastic supply, the aggregate supply will become more elastic. A more exact generalization cannot be made about that aspect of the relative responsiveness of the two situations delineated.

The Response to Technological Change in Agriculture

Technological change shifts the production function up and normally extends it substantially to the right. This provides a larger output per worker at any given labor input and maintains a positive marginal productivity for a much higher level of labor input.[11] We again continue with the simple dichotomy of two types of land delineated above, and within each, the cases of scarce land and of abundant land. Agricultural labor productivity can be raised only by increasing land productivity through yield-increasing technology if land is fully utilized, the marginal productivity of labor is already at zero, and nonfarm jobs are not growing as rapidly as the population. Figure 4.3 illustrates the situation for the steeply sloping function. The new technology requires additional labor to achieve much of the added output. As output increases from Or_1 to Or'_1, the labor input also has to increase from OL_1 to OL'_1. If the wage has been depressed to the subsistence level, where the marginal product equals the wage (point m), there is no surplus labor. Rents absorb the surplus, and the wage has to rise above the subsistence level to elicit more labor input. Since the marginal utility of leisure can be expected to rise sharply once minimum subsistence is attained, the wage increase may be substantial (ibid.). Incomes of the laboring class will rise with the wage rate and increased employment. On the other hand, if the wage is above the subsistence level and there is surplus labor, the supply of labor can be expected to be highly elastic. The increase in labor income will be determined largely by increased employment. The ideal situation for the *rentier* class would be for the population to expand at exactly the rate of increase in labor absorptive capacity determined by technology. This would keep the wage at the minimum subsistence level and would maximize the increase in rents, as represented by the shaded area ($ee'g'm'mg$) in figure 4.3. Less expansion in the labor force would raise the real wage and lower rents.

If the production function is shifted upward and there is no extension to the right, the new technology simply raises rents. It has the same effect as steepening the slope of the production function. With extension upward, the steeper the slope, the higher the proportion of increments that goes to rent. The empirical evidence on new high-yield technology suggests a steep slope (ibid.; Mellor and Lele 1973).

In this discussion I have assumed a *rentier* class in order to illustrate the least equitable distributional effects of technological change. Obviously, the greater the extent to which the poorest people have rights to land, the

Figure 4.3. Hypothetical relationship between labor input and food output: the labor surplus case with the effect of technological change (Type I) (holding inputs of land constant)

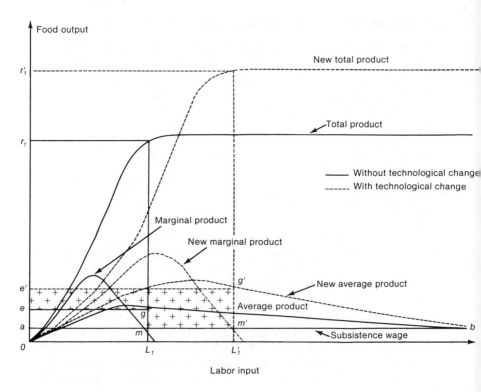

Labor input

more equitable will be the effects of technological change. Where technological change is rapid, a partial land reform that fixes rents, as in the Philippines, in effect appropriates the incremental rents from new technology for the tenant (Ranade and Herdt 1978).

The situation is more complex where the rural population is growing faster than nonagricultural employment. The greater that differential, the more likely it is to overwhelm the favorable employment effects of new technology and to depress net income. For example, if the net agricultural labor force is growing at a rate of 2.0 percent per year and the elasticity of employment with respect to output is 0.6, then yields will have to increase at a rate of more than 3.3 percent per year for real income of the agricultural labor class to increase (2.0 ÷ 0.6 = 3.3). This is an unusually rapid rate to sustain for a period of years. It is clear why the number in absolute poverty increases even as technology improves. The culprit is population growth, not technology. Other things remaining equal, reducing net rural population growth rates by a percentage point would reduce the yield increase requirement to 1.7 percent (1.0 ÷ 0.6 = 1.7). As the economic transformation proceeds, net rural population growth will cease and even become negative (Mellor and Johnston 1984). At this point labor productivity can be further increased by mechanization. With the steeply rising production function, such mechanization is bound to be economic. This may not be true with a differently shaped function, as shown below.

Where the production function slopes more gently, the effect of new technology may be quite different. If the function is shifted upward, which is analogous to increasing the slope, rents are created and the preceding analysis is applicable. If rents have not existed previously, the new rents are much more likely to be widely disbursed among the rural peasantry. However, extending the function, which is analogous to adding land, simply increases the scope to add population at the same standard of living. A small increase in the slope without population growth would provide a small positive income effect to labor. This could well reduce the area cropped, since the income effect somewhat overbalances the substitution effect in production (Mellor 1963). In this case, the average return to labor *employed* would be much lower than for the steeply rising function. It is less certain that even when labor became scarce mechanization would pay, since a given amount of capital would substitute for much less labor value. Thus it may be that yield-increasing technology is a necessary condition for increased mechanization unless the man-land ratio can be increased very greatly (Delgado and McIntire 1982).

To summarize, new agricultural technology is most likely to increase the incomes of the poor when the production function rises steeply. The effect is likely to be greatest when, in equilibrium, landlessness is greatest. For the less steeply rising function, increasing the productivity of labor may be essential to benefiting the poor. In any case, it is new, production-increasing technology, including introduction of improved crops, that must provide the offset to population growth if poverty is not to increase.

The preceding discussion has implicitly assumed equal access to capital at a market rate, so that returns within agriculture are divided between rent to land and labor. The evidence as to access to capital tends to corroborate that assumption. Barker, for the Philippines, and Schluter, for India, are clear on this point (Barker et al. 1972; Guino and Barker 1978; Schluter 1971, 1974). Most striking are the data presented by Raj Krishna, which show that use per acre of credit, fertilizer, and other purchased inputs is greater for small farmers than for large (Krishna 1979). However, if receivers of rent have better access to capital, then rents will be higher relative to labor returns.

The related question of economies of scale also is quickly dealt with. Late-19th-century Russian intellectuals and policy makers held the view—later built into Marxist ideology—that concentration of ownership of land and capital in agriculture was inevitable because of economies of scale and other factors (Shanin 1972). This is simply not true. The example of Japan is perhaps most striking, but the evidence provided by the green revolution is equally strong.[12]

Weather is an important source of change in production relationships. Improved weather is analogous to yield-increasing technology, except, of course, that weather movement in any one direction is only short-run, whereas technology may provide long-run upward trends. In the short run, weather changes are much more important than technological change. The effect on production of a 5–10 percent fluctuation in weather from one year to the next would be much greater than a yield increase from new technology of, say, 2–3 percent. However, over a period of 5 to 10 years, the cumulative effect of technology would far exceed that of weather.

Population growth obscures the effects on poverty of technological changes. This is a source of much of the confusion about the green revolution. Because the short-run effects of weather have been greater than those of either population growth or technology, weather serves as an instructive proxy for technological change. The effects on employment of a major short-run improvement in weather are likely to be concentrated at harvest, and hence they will be smaller than the effects of technologically induced yield increases, which are spread over the season. Good weather leads to increases in output and employment and reduced food prices, all of which serve to raise the real incomes of the laboring class. That is the basis of the relations that Dharm Narain measures. Poor weather, on the other hand, has an effect analogous to a decrease in the land area; it reduces output and the associated demand for labor. It thereby increases the proportion of output paid as rents, since higher prices transfer the reduced income of laborers to landowners.[13]

Indirect Effects on Poverty of Technological Change

The foregoing shows how an increase in agricultural employment consequent to new production technology can reduce poverty. The extent of this reduction depends on the slope of the production function and the degree to which rents exist and are garnered by the already more prosperous. Two indirect but powerful effects of technological change need to be discussed: (1) the effect of food production technology on the substitution of labor for capital in production, operating through the effect on food prices and real wages; and (2) the effect of increased income from technological change on the demand for labor, operating through the increased demand for goods and services. In assessing the effects of new agricultural technology on the poor, it is vital to note that the potential strength of the indirect effects is inversely related to the strength of the direct effects.

SUBSTITUTION EFFECTS

A greater increase in food production than in demand will cause a relative decline in agricultural prices. It has been shown that this price decline is directly favorable to the poor. There are also indirect effects on employment through prices of wage goods. It has been shown that with exogenous capital formation rates constant and with other assumptions at a realistic level, the relative price of agricultural commodities can be expected to decline if technological change is biased towards land (rents) relative to labor (Lele and Mellor 1981).[14] Lower food prices lead to lower relative labor costs and substitution of labor for capital in production. The issue then is the responsiveness of capital-labor ratios to a decline in the price of wage goods and hence to a decline in the price of labor in terms of output of nonagricultural goods and services. This complex question is discussed by Sen in the context of capital-intensive food production (Sen 1968). The answer hinges not only on the choice of technique for the production of any particular good or service but also on the composition of output (Mellor 1976). For this latter reason, the distribution of income working through the effect on the composition of consumption will be an important determinant of the extent to which there can be changes in factor proportions in favor of labor in the context of cheap food. Thus, the following discussion of income effects of food production growth is relevant to discussion of the substitution effects. Policies that increase the technical feasibility of substituting labor for capital are important to equity concerns if direct benefits of new food-production technology are skewed towards high-income people. That the introduction of such technology will be accompanied by lower food prices provides the poor not only a direct benefit but also indirect benefits if capital-labor ratios are responsive to changes in relative food prices and labor costs.

The strength of the substitution effects depends on the extent to which the increase in food marketing and the transaction costs are functions of the production technology. Given the preceding argument, the effects will be relatively weak in the African-type situation owing to a slow growth of agricultural production, the relatively low marketed proportion, and the openness of the trade regimes. This is one more set of factors encouraging high capital-labor ratios in Africa.

INCOME EFFECTS

The more the factor shares from innovation are skewed towards land, for which there is a considerable tendency, the more important are the expenditure patterns of rent receivers in determining the ultimate effect on poverty reduction. In peasant agricultures these patterns tend to be skewed towards expenditures in the local area and to have a large employment content (Hazell, Bell, and Slade 1982; Hazell and Röell 1983; Mellor and Lele 1973). The employment content is particularly large for the substantial expenditures for local services. Household survey data typically show that small farmers and landless workers receive more than half of their family income from nonagricultural sources.

If the rent receivers are absentee or have a high propensity to spend on imported or capital-intensive goods, the effect of agricultural innovation on the alleviation of domestic poverty may be quite small. If imported goods are paid for by exporting the additional agricultural production, the poor will not benefit through reduced prices. These consequences seem to be associated with colonial regimes and extreme concentration of land ownership. These conditions often seem to accompany slow development and application of new technology. Thus, highly skewed distribution of land is deleterious from the point of view of agricultural production, multiplier effects on domestic nonagricultural growth, and distribution of the benefits of growth. Landholdings of the kulak type do not seem to be subject to these problems. This suggests how unfortunate is the failure to distinguish among types of land ownership in analyzing new agricultural technology (see, e.g., Griffin 1974).

The income and employment multiplier effects of new agricultural technology will undoubtedly be largest in areas where the production function is rising steeply. This follows from three factors. First, the likelihood of adopting new technology is higher for reasons discussed above. Second, the factor shares to land will tend to be higher and the skewness of land ownership greater. Third, the steeply rising function is associated with areas of high population densities with more infrastructure and market development. These factors, among others, provide the sharp contrast between northern Nigeria and the Muda Project in Malaysia (Hazell and Röell 1983). The income-specific consumption patterns of the latter provide much stronger linkages between increased income from food production and local employment potentials. We can say generally that the African environment is much less favorable for the secondary effects of agricultural growth.

On a more positive note, public policies such as infrastructure investment and credit facilities can encourage employment-oriented expenditures that enhance the growth and equity benefits of increased incomes (see Mellor 1976).

Because of its large size, agricultural growth's positive multiplier effects can be very large. The increase in employment, particularly in services, may be almost simultaneous with the production increase and would be represented in Dharm Narain's equations as a product of increased food production per capita. When the lags in employment response were substantial, the effect would be caught in Dharm Narain's trend factor or not at all.

Conclusions

Seven key conclusions relating to agricultural growth and equity follow from the foregoing analysis.

First, rural population growth that is not accompanied by commensurate growth in nonagricultural job opportunities is an important source of increasing rural poverty and a major offset to any poverty-reducing measures. It strongly influences time-series measurements of poverty and grossly biases any analysis that does not directly measure its effect.

Second, differences in agroclimatic conditions result in considerable variability in the initial conditions of poverty. These initial conditions interact with new technology and price changes to further increase variability in the incidence of poverty. Neither the incidence of poverty nor the means of its reduction can be understood without reference to these varying underlying agroclimatic conditions.

Third, technological change that increases agricultural production is essential to improve the incomes of poor, laboring people in the context of population growth, limited land, and diminishing returns to labor. Pervasive radical redistribution of assets may substitute in the short run. However, for this to happen, equalization of assets must be virtually complete because of differences among income classes in the marginal propensity to consume food and consequent food-price effects of partial redistributions (Mellor 1978).

Fourth, lower food prices are a significant means of passing on the benefits of increased agricultural production if the direct employment content of that production is low. Lower food prices have a major direct effect on the real income of the poor, and there is a potential indirect benefit of a decline in nominal wages and consequent increased employment.

Fifth, situations in which a greater intensity of poverty is associated with successful introduction of new technology are not surprising. Poverty is likely to be most intensive where the agricultural production function rises most sharply, a situation which also is favorable for new high-yield food-production technology. Thus, new technology may be associated with past levels of intense poverty even while it causes a reduction in such poverty. Similarly, population growth may overpower the favorable effect of new technology. An extraordinarily rapid pace of technological change is needed to overbalance normal population growth if nonfarm employment is not growing. New agricultural technology is at best an imperfect substitute for reducing population growth or accelerating growth of off-farm employment. But it does mitigate the effects of high population growth and may be necessary for increasing off-farm employment.

Sixth, the smaller the direct effects of technological change on poverty reduction, the greater the potentials for the two indirect effects. With the benefits of production-increasing technology going initially to the more well-to-do, demand for food will not increase in proportion to output, and food prices will decline. This situation is favorable both to the real incomes of the poor and to increased employment through substitution of labor for capital. Expenditures of increased income by the rural well-to-do increase demand for goods and services, which creates employment. There is now substantial empirical evidence that in well-differentiated rural societies the service component is large and the response of service employment to increased expenditures also is large and immediate. This potential counterforce to the initial distribution of benefits to landowners makes production-increasing technology vital for improved welfare of the poor. More research is needed in order to devise policies for increasing these favorable effects.

Finally, throughout this analysis the much more difficult problem of development and poverty alleviation in much of sub-Saharan Africa has been underlined. One finds there a less favorable environment for new agricultural technology and poorer conditions for that technology to foster an economic transformation.

Notes

The author is grateful to Raisuddin Ahmed, Christopher Delgado, Gunvant Desai, Peter Hazell, Uma Lele, Yair Mundlak, Chandra Ranade, Ammar Siamwalla, and T. N. Srinivasan for their suggestions. In particular, Chandra Ranade has been helpful not only in this chapter but in checking a number of elements in the equations and text throughout this volume.

1. Dharm Narain's equation is clear as to the positive role of lower food prices in reducing rural poverty. What is referred to in this chapter, and surely what Dharm Narain captures, is a change in food prices owing to shifts of food supply relative to food demand. In the short run, weather is the most important cause of these relative shifts. Weather-induced forces can be expected to be much larger than the monetary-based "inflation" factors in a country with relatively low inflation, such as India. Thus the "real" factors can be expected to overwhelm the "monetary" factors. It is not surprising that an attempt to remove the "monetary" forces through some deflator fails to improve the statistical fit in an economy

where food so dominates consumer price indices. So one may be in essence deflating food prices by food prices and removing "real" as well as "monetary" effects.

2. In a context where average rural incomes are lower than average urban incomes, Adelman and Robinson (1978) argue the favorable effects on income distribution of higher food prices, without pointing out this qualification.

3. For a striking case see Ahmed (1979), which demonstrates that increased rice prices in Bangladesh lower the incomes of the poor by transferring area from jute to rice, with a large net decrease in employment because of the higher labor intensity of jute production.

4. Shifts in China's rural policy in the early 1980s have played havoc among those arguing in favor of major institutional change prior to technological change (see, for example, Khan 1983).

5. This exposition was developed for quite a different purpose in Mellor and Stevens (1956).

6. The export-crop sectors in Africa exhibit production functions more like those of the surplus-producing food-production situation.

7. Note that throughout this chapter, it is assumed that the agricultural production is a linear homogeneous function of land and labor. Holding the land input constant, one can draw the total product curve of labor for which the average product (AP) of labor first rises, then becomes equal to the marginal product (MP), and afterwards begins to decline. If the function is gently sloping in such a way that the peak of the average product is equal to the subsistence required, the farmers will apply that level of labor input on the existing piece of land under cultivation at which $AP = MP$ = subsistence. As the population grows, the farmers will increase the area under cultivation. However, the peak of AP for increased area under cultivation will be the same, since the production is linear homogeneous. Hence we get the long-run total product of labor depicted in figure 4.2 when the land input increases as the population increases beyond L_1. For the derivation of the total-product curve of an input when other inputs change see Fergusson (1969).

8. The rich textile industries of precolonial Asia attest to this potential (Gittinger 1982). See also the contrast in the degree of economic differentiation between the Muda Project (Malaysia) and northern Nigeria in Hazell and Röell (1983).

9. Such a trading relationship could also arise in a highly inegalitarian non-colonial regime, such as prerevolution Ethiopia or perhaps certain Andean countries or in Central America.

10. Berg (1961, 1962) cites literature on this point and provides a refutation, but we show here that there is more to the argument (see also Mellor 1963; and Sen 1966).

11. This description is fully consistent with the green revolution data in works such as Barker et al. (1972); Mellor and Lele (1973); and Rao (1975).

12. For a review of the literature on Japan and the green revolution see Mellor and Johnston (1984).

13. A substantial literature on sharecropping deals with mechanisms for smoothing the erratic distributional effects of weather changes on the poor. These relations might, if left unchanged, leave a larger share of benefits of new technology in the hands of the poor laborer than would otherwise be the case.

14. Stated thus, a closed economy is assumed. In an open economy the effects are similar but more indirect; that is, more food production may still lower domestic food prices owing to saved transaction costs, or foreign exchange is saved, increasing capital formation and hence employment.

5 Agricultural Production, Relative Prices, Entitlements, and Poverty

T. N. SRINIVASAN

Dharm Narain joined the staff of the International Food Policy Research Institute in Washington soon after Ahluwalia had completed his now-celebrated paper (Ahluwalia 1978a). In his inimitable, methodical, unhurried style Dharm Narain applied his mind to the same problem. His familiarity with Indian agriculture, particularly its foodgrain component, led him to believe that in spite of fluctuations, the trend growth in agricultural output of more than 2.5 percent per annum would reduce the extent of poverty but for what was happening outside of agriculture. Quite naturally, he looked at the potential impact on poverty of changes in the relative price of agricultural commodities. He sought to establish the quantitative significance of the impact of terms of trade before delving into the political economy of changes in these terms. It is our loss that he did not live to complete his work. This chapter addresses some of the conceptual and measurement issues that Dharm Narain would undoubtedly have addressed.

The Conceptual Basis and Explanatory Models

In the early 1970s, economists in India were concerned with the conceptual basis of poverty measurement and with empirical estimates of poverty levels. Most of the data came from the household consumption surveys of the National Sample Survey Organisation (NSS). There was also a vigorous debate on whether poverty had increased during the 1960s. Ahluwalia (1978a) was perhaps the first to estimate an explanatory model of changes in the proportion of the poor in the rural population by relating it to the real value added (net) in agriculture per head of the rural population and to time, a catchall variable. Narain added an index of prices as an explanatory variable to the Ahluwalia model.

As A. K. Sen points out in this volume (chap. 2), it appears odd to include a price index (representing changes in *nominal* prices) in a model in which the only other economic variable is *real* value added. Indeed, a more conventional price variable would have been an index of relative prices. But, as is shown below, a formal argument can be advanced to justify Dharm Narain's model.

Consider a consumer whose nominal consumption expenditure, c_t, equals $p_t^c \bar{c} + b(y_t - p_t^c \bar{c})$, where $\bar{c}$ is the "committed" quantity (index) of real *consumption*, p_t^c is the consumer price index, y_t is his nominal or money income, and b is the marginal propensity to spend out of uncommitted income. If c_p represents the poverty bundle, then the current-price poverty line is $p_t^c c_p$, and a consumer with c_t less than or equal to $p_t^c c_p$ is poor by definition. Hence, for the poor,

$$p_t^c \bar{c} + b\,(y_t - p_t^c \bar{c}) \le p_t^c c_p$$

or

$$by_t \le p_t^c [c_p - (1 - b)\,\bar{c}]$$

Suppose now that $y_t = y_t^r \cdot p_t^a$, where y_t^r is "real" income and p_t^a is the price of agricultural commodities. This is plausible, since most rural incomes are generated in kind (rent, wages, etc.).

This means that the rural poor are those whose real income, y_t^r, does not exceed $p_t^c [c_p - (1 - b)\bar{c}] / p_t^a b$. Once again, it is plausible to argue that the distribution of real incomes depends on real agricultural output, q_t^a, p_t^a, and t. The reason for introducing p_t^a is that while q_t^a, the quantity available for distribution, is determined by the past season's resource-allocation decisions, current resource-allocation decisions (which depend on current prices, p_t^a) determine its distribution among the rural population. Thus writing the cumulative distribution function of real income as $F(y_t^r, q_t^a, p_t^a, t)$, the population of rural poor, P_t, is equal to

$$F\,(p_t^c [c_p - (1 - b)\bar{c}] / bp_t^a, q_t^a, p_t^a, t).$$

If in the consumer price index agricultural commodities have a large weight, then p_t^c / p_t^a will be close to unity and can be dropped out of the function. Now c_p, $\bar{c}$, and b are constants. Hence, P_t is a function only of q_t^a, p_t^a, and t. Dharm Narain's relation is a logarithmic approximation of this function.

The above model implicitly assumes a high degree of monetization of the rural economy. The following simple model of the rural economy ignores money and prices altogether. Unlike the Narain relation, which is best viewed as one reduced form equation of an *implicit* structure, its advantage lies in making *explicit* the process that determines the distribution of real incomes. Of course, in such a "real" model, no nominal price variable will appear in any of the relations, and thus the model cannot rationalize the Narain relation. However, it is of interest because it explicitly traces the effect of changes in real output of agriculture on poverty through changes in labor allocation.

The simple model follows: The production function for output of a farm is $F(L, A, \theta)$, where L is the input of labor, A is the size of the farm in hectares, and θ is a technical-change parameter. F is assumed to exhibit constant returns to scale in labor and land with nonnegative marginal products for each factor. The yield per hectare of land can then be expressed as $h(x, \theta) \equiv F(x, 1, \theta)$, where x is the labor intensity (labor per hectare) of cultivation. It will be further assumed that F exhibits non-increasing marginal rates of substitution along any isoquant. Denoting by subscript i the partial derivative of a function with respect to its ith argument, the above assumptions imply that

$$h_i \geq 0, i = 1, 2,$$
$$h - x h_1 \geq 0,$$

and

$$h_{11} \leq 0.$$

For simplicity, let us assume that $\lim_{x \to 0} h_1 = \infty$ and $\lim_{x \to \infty} h_1 = 0$, so that the marginal product of labor declines from infinity to zero as the intensity of cultivation increases from zero to infinity.

At any time, there are three groups of households: those that hire labor at the going wage rate, those that supply labor, and those that do neither. Given its endowments of land, a, and of labor, l, and the going market wage, w, a household for which the *average product* of its labor endowment on its own farm is below the market wage

$$h(l \mid a, \theta) < w \, l/a$$

is assumed to *hire out* part of its endowment while keeping just enough workers on the farm to *raise* their *average* product to the market wage. A household for which the *marginal* product of its labor endowment *exceeds* the market wage

$$h_1 (l \mid a, \theta) > w$$

is assumed to *hire in* just enough labor to *lower* the marginal product to the wage rate. A household for which the average product of its labor endowment *exceeds*, while its marginal product falls short of, the market wage

$$h_1 (l \mid a, \theta) < w < (a \mid l) h (l \mid a, \theta)$$

neither hires in nor hires out. The decision making of households is shown in figure 5.1, where $x_1 (\theta, w)$ is the labor intensity at which the marginal product of labor equals the wage

44   T. N. Srinivasan

Figure 5.1. Labor hiring decision

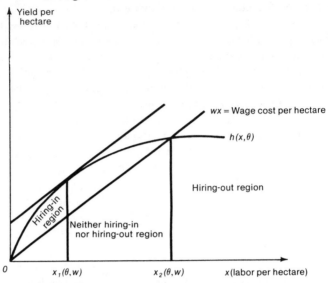

$$h_1 [x_1 (\theta, w), \theta] = w$$

and $x_2 (\theta, w)$ is the labor intensity at which the average product of labor equals the wage

$$h[x_2 (\theta, w), \theta] = wx_2 (\theta, w).$$

Our assumptions on $h (x, \theta)$ ensure that $x_i (\theta, w)$ ($i = 1, 2$) is unique. Also, $x_i (\theta, w)$ is a *decreasing* function of w. All households with labor endowment l exceeding $ax_2 (\theta, w)$ hire out $l - ax_2 (\theta, w)$ units of labor, and those with l falling short of $ax_1 (\theta, w)$ hire in $ax_1 (\theta, w) - l$ units of labor. Those with l lying between $ax_1 (\theta, w)$ and $ax_2 (\theta, w)$ neither hire in nor hire out.[1]

The equilibrium wage, given the technical-change parameter θ and the assumption that land is not traded, is determined by the requirement that demand for hired labor by households hiring in equals the supply of labor by those hiring out. Given the joint density of the land and labor endowments of households, $f(a, l)$, this equilibrium condition can be written as

$$\int da \int_{0}^{ax_1(\theta, w)} [ax_1(\theta, w) - l]f(a, l)dl = \int da \int_{ax_2(\theta, w)} [l - ax_2(\theta, w)]f(a, l)\, dl \quad (5.1)$$

The left side of equation (5.1), representing the demand for hired labor, is *decreasing* in w, while the right side, representing the supply of hired labor, is *increasing* in w, for given θ. Our assumptions on h_1 ensure that x_i (θ, w) tends towards ∞ (0) as w tends towards 0 (∞). This, in turn, means that as w tends towards 0 (∞), demand tends towards ∞ (0) and supply tends towards 0 (∞). The equilibrium wage w is thus uniquely determined as the function $w(\theta)$ of θ. Clearly, the functioning of the labor market in this fashion (i.e., determining the class composition of the rural economy) is not efficient from the point of view of output or income maximization (except for landlord households), since the marginal product of labor does not equal the wage rate for all households. This also means that $w(\theta)$ is not a competitive equilibrium wage. The labor market's functioning, though not competitive, nevertheless may have some descriptive validity. Unlike in the dualistic economy of the Lewis type, in this model dualism applies to the agricultural sector only, the landlords being analogous to the entrepreneurs of the modern sector of the Lewis economy, the peasant and agricultural labor households constituting the pool of labor from which the landlords draw their wage labor either directly (from labor households) or indirectly (when a peasant household moves into the labor category).

If technical change is Hicks-neutral, so that $h(x, \theta) = \theta g(x)$, then it is clear that x_i (θ, w) is homogeneous of degree zero in θ and w, so that x_i depends only on w / θ. Hence, equation (5.1) determines a unique value λ for the ratio w / θ, and the equilibrium wage $w(\theta)$ is equal to $\lambda \theta$. Of course, λ depends on the technology (i.e., the function $g(x)$) and the distribution of endowments (i.e., the function $f(a, l)$). Shifts in θ result in equiproportional shifts in the equilibrium wage with no change in $x_i(\theta, w)$ and hence in the distribution of households among the three classes. An increase in θ raises the income of each household by the same proportion, since (1) a household hiring out has an income of $lw(\theta) = l\lambda\theta[ax_2(\theta, w)]$ from its own farm plus $[l - ax_2(\theta, w)]w(\theta)$ from hired-out labor; (2) a household that neither hires in nor hires out has an income of $ah(l / a, \theta)$ $= a\theta g(l / a)$; and (3) a household hiring in labor has an income of

$$ah[x_1(\theta, w), \theta] - [ax_1(\theta, w) - l]w = \theta\,\{ag[x_1(\theta, w)] - \lambda[ax_1(\theta, w) - l]\}.$$

With the rise in income of every household by the same proportion, the proportion of households, P, below any poverty line fixed in terms of output falls.

If technical change is land-augmenting, so that $h(x, \theta) = \theta j(x / \theta)$, where $j_1 > 0$, $j - (x / \theta)j_1 > 0$, and $j_{11} < 0$, it can be verified that both x_1 and x_2 are increasing functions of θ for given w. This implies from equation (5.1) that $w(\theta)$ is an increasing function of θ as well, the reason being that when the wage rate is unchanged, an increase in θ increases the demand for, and reduces the supply of, hired labor. Since $x_i(\theta, w)$ is a decreasing function of w, the effect of an increase in θ on $x_i(\theta, w)$ is ambiguous. However, in equation (5.1) the demand is increasing as a function of $x_1(\theta, w)$, and the supply is decreasing as a function of $x_2(\theta, w)$. Hence it is clear that the impact on $x_1(\theta, w)$ of an increase in θ is opposite in sign to that on $x_2(\theta, w)$. Now $x_1(\theta, w)$ is the labor intensity that equates the marginal product of labor to the wage rate. An increase in θ raises $x_1(\theta, w)$ when the wage rate is unchanged, because of its yield-raising effect, while an increase in w lowers $x_1(\theta, w)$ when θ is unchanged. Since the equilibrium wage $w(\theta)$ increases with θ, equilibrium $x_1(\theta, w)$ will increase if the yield effect dominates the wage effect at the margin. This, in turn, means that $x_2(\theta, w)$ falls. Together, the rise in $x_1(\theta, w)$ and the fall in $x_2(\theta, w)$ imply that the set of peasant households expands. The reverse will be true if the wage effect dominates the yield effect. In the former case, it is fairly easy to see that the households that hire out labor *after* the increase in θ include *all* of those who hired out, and *some* who were neither hiring in nor hiring out, *before* the increase in θ. Both of these groups experience an increase in income. The group of households who neither hire in nor hire out after the increase in θ is a subset of those who neither hired in nor hired out prior to the increase in θ and hence experiences an increase in income. However, one cannot rule out a fall in income for some households that hire in labor after the rise in θ, such as, for instance, households with negligible endowment of family labor relative to land. It can be shown that the same pattern of income distribution among the three classes of households obtains even if at the margin the wage effect dominates the yield effect. If we assume that households with relatively negligible family labor are predominantly the richer landlord households, we can assert that the poverty proportion will decline with an increase in θ.

If technical change is labor-augmenting, so that $h(x, \theta) = j(\theta x)$, where $j_1 > 0$, $j - \theta x j_1 > 0$, and $j_{11} < 0$, it can be verified that $x_2(\theta, w)$ is an increasing function of θ, while $x_1(\theta, w)$ is an increasing (decreasing) function of θ when the elasticity of $x_1(\theta, w)$ with respect to w is greater (less) than unity. In the former case, equilibrium $w(\theta)$ increases with θ. In the latter case, the effect of a fall in $x_1(\theta, w)$ as θ increases reduces the demand for hired-in labor at any value of w, while the supply is reduced as well with an increase in $x_2(\theta, w)$. Hence, the effect on the equilibrium wage is ambiguous. A sufficiently steep fall in the demand for labor consequent to an increase in θ can bring down the equilibrium wage. If it does, then by reducing the income of relatively poor households that own very little land, such a technical change can increase the poverty proportion. For brevity, a detailed analysis of the impact on income distribution among the three classes of households of a labor-augmenting technical change is omitted.

Up to now, we have not specified the determinants of θ. Let us now specify

$$\theta_t = \alpha + \beta t + u_t \tag{5.2}$$

where u_t is a random disturbance owing to weather assumed to be independently and identically distributed with mean zero. In other words, we are assuming that the *expected* effect of technical change varies linearly over time. This may be owing to, for instance, continuous improvement in cultivation practices or introduction of new high-yield varieties. Given equation (5.2) and assuming that the technical change is either neutral or land-augmenting, it is easy to see that as long as $\beta > 0$, the *expected* value (the expectation being taken over the distribution of u_t) of the poverty proportion $P(\theta_t)$ will have a downward trend, with the *actual* value of $P(\theta_t)$ fluctuating around the trend owing to the weather effect, u_t. It is also clear that if trend term β is small and the variance of u_t is large, then the estimated time trend (approximating $P(\theta_t)$ linearly) from small samples may turn out to be insignificant. For this reason, adding a term such as agricultural output or value added per head of rural population, which in part reflects fluctuation in u_t, may improve the estimates of time trend. This is consistent with the findings of Ahluwalia (1978b).

Although the above model is very simple, one can incorporate several realistic features without affecting the qualitative results. The crucial assumption is that the parameter θ enters the production function as a technical-change factor. To the extent that the use of fertilizers, irrigation, and new crop varieties can be viewed as technical change, it can be reflected in θ. Thus one can introduce in θ terms involving the cost of fertilizers relative to output, the cost of irrigation water relative to output, and so on. A fall in either or both relative costs will increase θ and thus have a favorable effect on poverty reduction, once again assuming that the use of fertilizers and irrigation is land-augmenting. If irrigation is provided through public investment and the cost is not fully passed on to the farmers, only the cost borne by the farmers will enter θ.

The assumption that the distribution of households according to their land and labor endowments does not change may be questioned, though one could argue that the change is likely to be rather slow. To the extent that an exceptionally severe drought induces distress sales of land and other productive assets, and exceptionally good weather does not quite offset such sales, the density function, $f(a, l)$, cannot be assumed to be stationary. Apart from this, the model does not explicitly distinguish differences in inherent fertility of land from embodied fertility in terms of investment in land improvement. If one is willing to postulate that different categories of land are perfect substitutes for each other at specified conversion ratios, the problem is evaded altogether: a is then measured in standard hectares after the conversion ratios are applied to "nonstandard" hectares. Still, the endogenous dynamics of saving and investment in land improvement are ignored in such a formulation. However, the impact of any exogenous change in the distribution $f(a, l)$ can be analyzed once we specify the form of such a change.

As mentioned earlier, the above model is not rich enough to yield the terms-of-trade effect found by Dharm Narain. Indeed, one could argue that in this model such an effect will be opposite in sign to that observed by him in that a favorable shift in the terms of trade towards agriculture owing to a bad harvest will mitigate, rather than exacerbate, the output effect. The reason is, of course, that a poverty line defined in units of agricultural output shifts *downward* with a favorable shift in the terms of trade.

I argued earlier that the process of determining real income distribution and the extent of poverty is implicit in the Narain relation. The above "real" model attempted to make this process more explicit by capturing some stylized features of an agrarian economy in which three modes of production coexist. In contrast to these income-centered approaches is A. K. Sen's "entitlement approach" (Sen 1981a, 1981b). The entitlement of a person in an economy with private ownership and markets is the set of all alternative commodity bundles that that person can acquire in exchange for what he owns.

Sen claims that the income-centered approach offers only a partial picture of the entitlement pattern: "What [one] can earn depends on what [one] can sell and at what price and starting off with incomes leaves out that part of the entitlement picture—the main advantage of the entitlement approach rests—in providing a more comprehensive account of a person's ability to command commodities in general and food in particular" (Sen 1981b, 156). One would have thought that neoclassical welfare theory already supplied a "comprehensive account of a person's ability to command commodities in general."

Be that as it may, it is clear that the distribution of production and consumption among members of a society obviously influences social arrangements, including political, legal, and administrative systems; the system of property rights, or, more broadly, access to resources; the system of markets; and above all, nonmarket arrangements such as contracts and customary ties. It is only slightly less obvious that in a world in which uncertainty is a fact of life, alternative institutional arrangements may imply different consequences for the survival and welfare over time of different individuals and groups. The literature on tenancy and sharecropping, or, more generally, on contractual arrangements, including assignment of property rights, provides ample evidence that the concerns underlying the entitlements approach are already being addressed by the profession.

Measurement of Rural Poverty: Some Conceptual Issues

The conceptual issues relating to the measurement of poverty have attracted the attention of several scholars. There is little that one can add to Sen's (1981b) elegant and admirably lucid discussion of the literature except to draw attention to a couple of points that are often ignored. The first is that even if the proportion of poor in a population does not change over time, this does not mean that any individual (or cohort) who is observed to be poor at one time is poor all of the time. Some individuals move across income classes owing to life-cycle effects, if not for other reasons. However, measurement of poverty is often based on current consumption or income, which ignores life-cycle effects. The second is that in any society there is likely to be a "hard-core" poor who are left out of the income-generation and transfer processes for various reasons. The late Pitambar Pant (Srinivasan and Bardhan 1974, chap. 1) treated the bottom quintile of the population as "hard-core" poor. Whether or not this is correct, life-cycle effects and the "hard-core" problem suggest a lower bound on the extent of measured poverty.

Measurement of Trends in Rural Poverty: Some Statistical Problems

A few remarks are in order regarding the statistical problems associated with the Narain relation. The estimate of the poverty proportion in any year, which is the dependent variable, has been derived from the distribution of the rural population according to per capita consumption expenditure (PCE) at current prices using a current-price poverty line. The latter is obtained by inflating a constant-price poverty level through an appropriate price index. The same price index (or a very close correlate) also appears as an explanatory variable on the right-hand side of the relation in a logarithmic form. If we assume that the conceptually appropriate and empirically correct measured price index is used to derive the current-price poverty line (or to put it in Sen's colorful terminology [chap. 2 above], that "the recovery problem were correctly performed"), introducing this price index or its proxy in the relevant form on the right-hand side when theory suggests that it should not be there creates a "specification bias" in the estimated values of the parameters of the equation, and the same is true if the price index or its proxy is not introduced when theory suggests that it should be. This specification bias is conceptually distinct from the bias that can arise out of errors in measurement in the conceptually appropriate index. The error in measurement creates an error in "recovery," with no bias, at least to a first order of approximation. In other words, as long as the error in measurement of the price index has an expected value of zero, the recovered poverty estimate is also measured with an error that has a zero expectation to a first order of approximation. Suppose, now, that theory suggests that the price index should be on the right-hand side as well. If, for a moment, we ignore the error in "recovery" resulting from the use of an erroneously measured price index, its use on the right-hand side will create the well-known bias owing to errors in the explanatory variable about which Ahluwalia wrote in his letter to Dharm Narain. But if now we reintroduce the "recovery" error on the left-hand side, in the unlikely event of its exactly equaling the error on the right-hand side for *every* observation, the bias owing to errors in the explanatory variable disappears!

Rural Poverty and the "Trickle-Down" Hypothesis

The only precise statement on the "trickle-down" hypothesis in the literature states that rapid growth of per capita income will be associated with a reduction in poverty. A contrasting hypothesis is that underlying the Kuznets curve which postulates that in early stages of growth there will be an increase in the inequality of income distribution and presumably in the extent of poverty as well. Both hypotheses relate to a dynamic process of growth.

In the context of rural India, the trickle-down theory has been interpreted to mean that agricultural growth without major institutional reform will reduce poverty. This theory has been questioned on the grounds that growth need not be poverty-reducing if it does not involve large sections of the population and that the green revolution has been accompanied by an increase in absolute impoverishment.

In chapter 7 of this volume, Ahluwalia extends the data base for his earlier (1978a) analysis. It is obvious from his data for India as a whole that there was no upward trend in the net domestic product of agriculture per head of rural population. In other words, even though the trend value of gross output of agriculture grew a little faster, the value-added component barely kept up with population growth. On this ground alone, any interpretation of Ahluwalia's work as a test of the trickle-down hypothesis must be dismissed out of hand. But Saith (1981) nevertheless regresses the proportion of the rural population below the poverty line against deviations from trend of the index of agricultural production and the consumer price index for agricultural laborers. He estimates seventy regressions in all; fourteen fit simple time trends. The remaining fifty-six bring in the production and/or price indices in the form of deviations from trend, and fourteen of these also include a time trend. Concentrating on the latter group of fourteen, which are comparable to Ahluwalia's, the seven regressions that include the data for 1973/74 do not yield a statistically significant positive trend in poverty, while the seven that exclude the data for 1973/74 do. Thus the basis for Saith's conclusion that the underlying time trend (after allowing for variations in production and prices) indicates rising poverty is the exclusion of just one year's data! Saith's argument for excluding 1973/74 is that the price index with base weights of 1956/57 is extremely likely to understate seriously the importance of groups of commodities whose relative prices rose rapidly from 1970/71 to 1973/74. As Saith himself admits, this argument is not conclusive. In any case, since the commodities in question probably would have had substantial weights in the index anyway, it is not at all certain that there was significant understatement.

Saith further argues that because data for only 1970/71 and 1973/74 during the period 1969/70 to 1973/74 were included in Ahluwalia's regression, the two included years have been given a disproportionately high weight. "It is implicitly assumed that the missing observations would have fallen exactly on the trend fitted without them" (ibid., 199–200). This is not quite correct: exclusion of an observation and inclusion of it, assuming it to be on the fitted trend, are not equivalent. In the latter case, one adds an extra degree of freedom to the residual sum of squares without adding anything to the sum itself, thus reducing the estimated standard error of residuals. Be that as it may, in chapter 7 Ahluwalia shows that inclusion of the observations for 1971/72 and 1972/73 makes no qualitative difference to his earlier conclusions. In any case, the conclusions are largely irrelevant as a test of the trickle-down hypothesis. There was very little to trickle down at the all-India level.

Bardhan (1982) argues that there was some growth in real net value added in agriculture per capita in some states, such as the Punjab and Haryana, but the extent of poverty in these states has not decreased significantly. Whether this contradicts the trickle-down hypothesis depends on its precise specification. One could argue that not only does the growth in income per capita have to be substantial but it has to be sustained for a sufficiently long period for the trickle-down process to operate. Also, migration into the Punjab and Haryana could have slowed the trickle-down process; however, Bardhan quotes a study by Oberai and Singh (1980) to the contrary.

Bardhan uses cross-sectional data in his analysis of poverty. The well-known pitfalls to which cross-sectional data are subject are particularly serious in this case. The levels of economic development and infra-structure at a particular point in time are not necessarily a good indicator of the growth process that led to these levels.

Using household data from West Bengal and a logit analysis, Bardhan finds that the probability of an agricultural-labor or a primarily-cultivator household's falling below the poverty line seems to be higher if the household is in a district where agricultural production has grown at a faster rate. It would be interesting to check whether the qualitative conclusions of a probit analysis would be the same. Bardhan's result would not be inconsistent with trickle-down if the faster-growing districts also had above-average poverty in the initial year. If their growth were not sufficient to offset the initial conditions, Bardhan's terminal-year conclusion would follow.

Bardhan finds that growth of crop production has a significant positive impact on the variation in average per capita monthly expenditure of noncultivating wage-earner households among the fifty-five regions. At the same time, the impact of electric pump sets and oil engines per hectare of cropped area and of larger farm households as a proportion of total rural households on PCE is negative. This leads him to argue that "agricultural growth in general seems to be helpful, but big farmer dominated growth dependent on private ownership need not be" (Bardhan 1982, 18)! Since the number of pump sets and the proportion of large farmer households are two explanatory variables in a multivariate linear regression, it may not be appropriate to draw such inferences about a particular combination of the values of these two variables from the values of their individual regression coefficients.

Bardhan's analysis of cross-sectional data by state is based on the proportion of rural households whose average energy intake falls below a norm of 2,700 kilocalories per consumer unit per day. Use of the same norm for all states need not result in poverty's being under- or overstated to the same extent in all states. If it did, the coefficients of the regression model would be biased to an unknown extent.

Conclusions

Empirical studies testing the trickle-down hypothesis are inadequate, either because they use data that do not indicate significant growth to trickle-down or because they draw inferences from cross-sectional data about dynamic processes. Until better evidence is offered, the conclusion of the late Pitambar Pant (who used data from a cross section of countries) stands.

It is difficult to say a priori what degree of inequality is necessary for growth; but a comparison of the distribution of incomes in different countries is suggestive. It shows that in countries at very different levels of development and with varying socio-political environments, the distribution of incomes follows a remarkably similar pattern, especially in respect of the proportion of incomes earned by the lowest three or four deciles of the population. If this hypothesis can be sustained, the income of the poorest segments as a result of spontaneous economic development may be expected to increase in more or less the same proportion as total income in any country. The attainment of a specified level of minimum income within a given period then becomes purely a function of the rate of development. (Srinivasan and Bardhan 1974, 14)

Even though Pant's conclusion has not been confirmed conclusively, Dharm Narain's unfinished work points in that direction. With appropriate policies to protect the vulnerable sections of the society against food-price inflation, trickle-down may come into its own. If this indeed is the case, the task of accelerating development without inflation gains even greater urgency. Unfortunately, it is too soon to tell whether the stagnation (with inflation for most of the time) that began in 1966 and continued for fifteen years has been broken once and for all.

Notes

I wish to thank Pranab Bardhan, John Mellor, and Amartya Sen for their extensive comments on an earlier draft.

1. See Lele and Mellor (1981) for a similar description of the labor market in a different context.

6 The Income Approach to Measuring Poverty: A Note on Human Welfare below the Line

SHUBH K. KUMAR

Measurements of the prevalence of poverty often provide a starting point for analyzing the welfare implications of policies and programs. The work of Dharm Narain provides a further example of the potential of these measurements to illuminate the development processes that contribute to human well-being.

Generally, two main approaches to measuring the extent of poverty have been used. In the "direct" approach, minimum levels of one or a combination of essential basic needs are specified, and the incidence of poverty is measured in terms of the proportion of the population that falls below these levels. In the "income" approach, poverty is measured in terms of the proportion of the population with less than the minimum income needed to acquire some basic bundle of goods and services. The minimum acceptable income level has been determined in various ways, including the much-debated but widely used approach of Dandekar and Rath (1971). In the work of Dharm Narain and Montek Ahluwalia reported in this volume, no explicit link with any of the basic needs measures has been established for determining the cutoff point. This eliminates the need for making value judgments about other people's needs and also recognizes that when there is a continuum of widespread deprivation, any related basis for setting the line is problematic. Bardhan uses the cost of the average caloric requirements as a basis for determining the poverty line. This is different from the approach of Dandekar and Rath (1971) and Reutlinger and Selowsky (1976), who used reported mean consumption levels across incomes to obtain the upper income level at which average consumption could be considered "unsatisfactory." All three approaches are variants of the income approach, although the last has often been misinterpreted as a basic needs approach.[1]

From a policy or program perspective, the alternative ways of documenting human welfare have a distinct contribution to make. The measurements based on basic needs, such as the incidence and severity of nutritional deficiency, morbidity and mortality rates, water supply and sanitation facilities, housing conditions, and education and health facilities, are most useful in designing programs or policies specifically geared to those problems. They may also be useful in setting priorities, even though this may entail subjective comparisons of the welfare implications of, for example, a poor water supply and a lack of education facilities. On the other hand, the minimum income (poverty line) approach[2] makes it possible to formulate policies and programs that influence employment generation, agricultural production, incomes, and prices.

While the alternative approaches focus on poverty, problems are likely to arise when conclusions about one aspect of poverty are drawn from measurements based on another. Examples are the use of poverty estimates based on the income approach to deduce the magnitude of nutrition problems and the use of estimates of the prevalence of malnutrition to make policy prescriptions for income-generating programs. This is not to say that the two are not linked. Undoubtedly they are, but a great deal of caution has to be exercised when such connections are being made. Since the income approach for measuring poverty has been used in the studies contained in this volume, this chapter will examine the relation of income-based poverty measures to fulfillment of basic needs.

As mentioned earlier, the income approach attempts to determine people's ability to meet some basic needs. Whether or not an individual actually does so can be influenced by a host of factors. This diversity must be recognized in drawing conclusions about actual welfare levels of people in the head count. Nevertheless, the cutoff point is useful if it is based on "average" behavioral characteristics. Some individuals who are below the poverty line may have superior managerial skills, make more efficient use of resources, and achieve the desired basic needs. A case can be made for lowering the poverty line to exclude such individuals. The head count will now have a higher probability of excluding those who through superior efficiency do better than average and those who approximate the "average" behavioral characteristic and hence have a lower than acceptable level of basic needs fulfillment. The head count also will not include individuals with inefficient utilization characteristics who may face severe deprivation. People remaining below the poverty line will now have practically no likelihood of meeting the desired level of basic needs, and their average degree of fulfillment will be below the desired level established earlier.

Problems in relating head-count measures to the actual degree of fulfillment of basic needs are further compounded by variations in tastes, requirements, and access to services that complement the individual resources of households. However, this does not mean that income-based head-count measures have no relevance to the fulfillment of basic needs.

As noted earlier, income-based head-count measures are not used to make value judgments on how people should allocate their resources. However, when the income level is clearly inadequate to meet even basic nutritional requirements, there is a strong presumption that the household's welfare suffers.

An emphasis on calories may not be inappropriate. Before discussing implications of calorie inadequacies, it would be useful to review briefly the basis for establishing calorie requirements. Basic to the existence of any biological organism is energy to fuel all essential processes. The human body uses chemical energy to fuel all its tasks, and the only source of this energy is food. The caloric value of foods consumed represents the maximum amount of energy that is available for the body's physiological processes. After absorption, this energy can be chemically trapped during the biological degradation of carbohydrates, fats, or proteins in intermediary compounds that carry it and then release it by coupling in reactions where the energy is required. The body regulates the process of releasing the energy from food consumed depending on its needs, with excess consumption being stored and stores being depleted if consumption is insufficient for its needs. Because of this controlled storage and depletion process, energy intakes and expenditures can appear to be at variance for prolonged periods. But thermodynamic balance has to be maintained internally. Individuals who maintain a certain body weight over a period of time are in energy equilibrium; that is, energy intake equals energy expenditure.

What is the relation of these mechanisms to the established (but constantly reviewed and updated) standards of energy requirements for a population? The main criteria used for establishing requirements for a population are body weight and activity level. In adults who are in energy equilibrium the main uses of energy are in maintenance of body tissues and for all activities. Energy requirements for both uses are related to body size and activity level. In determining requirements for adults, no reference body size is prescribed; rather, actual body weights are used. First, the energy required for maintenance is calculated using a constant-calories-per kilogram weight factor. Next, the energy required for work is calculated on a body weight basis, which varies with the expected activity level. Accordingly, if correct body weights and activity levels are used, and if the population is in energy equilibrium, then measured intakes *must* equal the estimated requirement.

What does it mean when a low-income segment of a population consumes fewer calories than that estimated to be necessary to maintain the body weight and activity assumed? Since there is no reason why a low-income segment of the population should have requirements lower than those of the rest of the population, one can expect one or more of the following compromises:

1. A reduction in energy expenditures in work or leisure activities. Individual preferences and income levels would largely determine where the cuts took place. There would be a real loss in welfare that might not be measurable in terms of differences in body weight. In children, a reduction in the activity level could impair the development of their mental capacity.
2. A reduction in body weight. This could lead to a new equilibrium between intake and energy expenditure, since energy requirements per kilogram of body weight for both maintenance and activity would be lower. This change would not be without cost. A below- or above- "normal" ratio of body weight to height exposes an individual to additional health hazards. When body weight is too low, the body lacks reserves to draw upon when it is exposed to infection or other forms of stress that raise metabolic activity and energy expenditure.
3. A reduction in nutrients available to children for growth. Growing children require not only more calories per kilogram of body weight than do adults but also proportionately more proteins and other nutrients. Unless foods with a high protein content are provided to children and pregnant women, a calorie deficiency will almost certainly mean a protein deficiency. This may be compounded if rates of energy expenditure are high enough to divert protein or amino acids for providing energy instead of growth.

The compromise in body growth potential has welfare implications. A marginally low body weight at any stage of growth does not appear to be associated with a significant reduction in biological capacity for various functions, such as immune response, that are necessary for survival and work performance. Deprivation of the unborn child is perhaps most critical, since low-birth-weight babies have a low survival probability under usual conditions in most developing countries. Reduction in linear body size is a longer-term deprivation phenomenon that may eventually become incorporated in growth of succeeding generations as an adaptive response to the environment's capacity to provide sustenance. Reduction in body size by dietary deprivation may have survival value, since nutrition requirements will be correspondingly lower for both maintenance and work. Consequently, in an environment with a high degree of uncertainty in food availability, reduction in linear body size could be a most advantageous adaptive response for survival of the species. It is not yet clearly documented whether there is a trade-off here in welfare terms. The cost of such an adaptation may be higher for some population segments than for others. It may be very costly to those who depend for their living on physical capacity and on work requiring a high energy expenditure. On the other hand, those who pursue intellectual endeavors may lose little or nothing and could be the fittest to survive under chronic or repeated acute food scarcities.

The foregoing discussion shows that there are costs to reduction in nutritional energy intake. The cost of this reduction in welfare is likely to be greater for the poor, since they are more likely to be engaged in higher-energy activity and to have a poor sanitary environment with higher morbidity, mortality, and related nutrient losses.

Depending on where the poverty line is drawn, a different standard of basic needs is adjudged as important to a society, given that we could estimate or determine relatively easily the actual conditions of the population below the line.

As mentioned earlier, the main advantage of the income approach is from the policy and program perspective, and hence while we know that different lines can measure different degrees of deprivation, the analysis of factors responsible for reducing or increasing the numbers in poverty is not likely to be affected by the subjective assessment of what poverty constitutes. Over a period of time, one could assume that changes in tastes, efficiencies, and requirements would not affect the basic needs available from a given level of real income. However, the entitlements represented by institutions and services may be significantly altered. This would be particularly true if there were a rapid expansion in services for education, health, water supply, housing, and food subsidies. But this issue relates more to the problem of determining a temporal head-count—or in A. K. Sen's terminology, the recovery problem—and it is less relevant to the command problem, which was the main concern of Dharm Narain and others contributing to this volume.

Notes

1. A major methodological problem arises when nutritional requirements based on "average" population characteristics, such as activity level, body size, and age composition, are applied to individual households. For an ongoing debate on this see Dandekar (1982) and Sukhatme (1982).

2. A more complete measure would include endowments such as physical or human capital assets, which determine the scope of economic opportunities. This measure is described by A. K. Sen (1981b) in his "entitlement approach."

7 Rural Poverty, Agricultural Production, and Prices: A Reexamination

MONTEK S. AHLUWALIA

In his insightful but unfinished work, Dharm Narain drew attention to the behavior of prices as one of the important factors determining the extent of poverty in rural India. His empirical investigations, summarized in Gunvant Desai's contribution to this volume (chap. 1), provide strong prima facie evidence of such influence. Dharm Narain found that rural poverty is not only inversely related to the level of output per head of the rural population, as established in Ahluwalia (1978a), but also positively related to the level of prices. What is equally interesting is that he found that when account is taken of the effect of variations in both output per head and prices, the underlying time trend in rural poverty is negative, a very different conclusion from mine—I reported no underlying trend—and the very opposite of that of Griffin and Ghose (1979) and Saith (1981), who assert a rising underlying trend.

This chapter pursues the issue raised by Dharm Narain using an expanded data base. His results are based on all-India data comprising 12 observations for 1956/57 to 1970/71. An additional estimate is available for the year 1958/59, and the period can be extended by including data for 1971/72, 1972/73, 1973/74, and 1977/78 (see table 7.1).

Rural Poverty in India, 1956/57 to 1977/78

A complete assessment of trends in rural poverty should take account of several dimensions of poverty, of which income or consumption levels per head is only one. Equally relevant are factors such as longevity, access to health and education facilities, and perhaps also security of consumption levels from extreme shocks. However, time-series data on all of these dimensions are not available. Data from a series of consumption surveys conducted by the National Sample Survey Organisation (NSS), are available, and these data have been used in most of the studies of rural poverty in India. In this paper, I use NSS data on the distribution of

Table 7.1. Rural Poverty and Agricultural Income

	Percentage of Population in Poverty (Head-Count Measure)	Sen Index	Rural Population (Millions)	NDP Agriculture (Rs. crores, 1970/71 Prices)
1956/57	54.1	0.23	329.47	11,953
1957/58	50.2	0.22	335.63	11,321
1958/59	46.5	0.19	341.80	12,604
1959/60	44.4	0.17	347.96	12,364
1960/61	38.9	0.14	354.13	13,143
1961/62	39.4	0.14	360.29	13,234
1963/64	44.5	0.16	376.04	13,204
1964/65	46.8	0.17	383.92	14,429
1965/66	53.9	0.21	391.79	12,279
1966/67	56.6	0.24	399.67	12,084
1967/68	56.5	0.24	407.55	14,043
1968/69	51.0	0.20	415.42	14,121
1970/71	47.5	0.18	431.17	16,354
1971/72	41.2	—	439.05	16,209
1972/73	43.1	—	445.34	15,118
1973/74	46.1	0.17	451.63	16,298
1977/78	39.1	0.14	476.79	19,045

Note: Estimates of the percentage of the population in poverty (col. 1) for the years 1971/72 and 1972/73 are from data provided in Government of India, Department of Statistics, National Sample Survey Organisation (1981a) and Rao (1979). All other estimates are based on fitting a Lorenz curve to the data, as described in Ahluwalia (1978a). Sen indices for 1971/72 and 1972/73 could not be computed because the sources cited for these years do not provide the full information needed.

consumption expenditure in nominal terms, combined with poverty lines in current prices, to compute two indices of poverty; the percentage of the rural population in poverty (the traditional head-count measure) and the Sen Index, which takes account of extent of poverty within the population below the poverty line (table 7.1). The poverty line for each year corresponds to a constant-price poverty line of 15 rupees per capita in 1960/61 prices adjusted using the consumer price index for agricultural laborers (CPIAL). The numerous deficiencies in these estimates have been well documented.[1] Nevertheless, they present a unique picture of changes in rural poverty over more than 20 years (fig. 7.1). No comparable time series for such a long period are available for any other developing country.

The movements in rural poverty over two decades are shown in figure 7.1. The expanded data set bears out my (1978a) conclusion that there is no underlying time trend in poverty for the period as a whole. The percentage of the population in poverty declined through the fifties, rose

Figure 7.1. Rural poverty in India

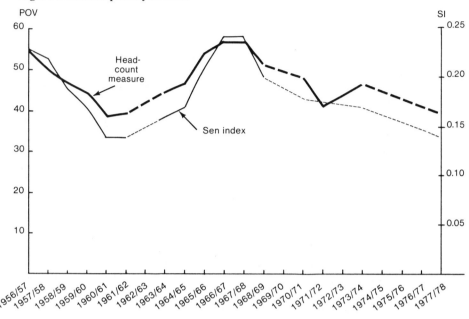

to a peak in 1967/68, and then declined substantially, though unevenly, through the seventies. The Sen Index shows an almost identical pattern. The absence of any time trend is confirmed by the following results (figures in parentheses are t ratios).

$$POV = 48.97 - 0.19\,t \qquad R^2 = 0.04$$
$$\qquad\qquad (0.8)$$
$$SI = 1.63 - 0.007t \qquad R^2 = 0.04$$
$$\qquad\quad (0.8)$$

Both indices show great variation in the extent of poverty. This could have been expected with the head-count measure, which takes no account of the intensity of poverty. When there is a substantial concentration of the population at the poverty line, as in India, small changes in the level of consumption can shift large numbers of people above or below it. This would show up as large changes in the measured incidence of poverty even though the changes in real consumption levels were marginal. This problem does not arise with the Sen Index, which gives due weight to the extent to which the consumption of individuals falls below the poverty line. It is therefore significant that the Sen Index also shows a coefficient of variation of 0.18 compared with that of only 0.12 for the head-count measure. Clearly, the variations in the measured degree of poverty over time reflect substantial variation in the measured levels of real consumption. It is important to explain these changes and to study their implications for policy.

The addition of data for the seventies materially affects some assessments of the underlying trends in rural poverty in India. For example, Griffin and Ghose (1979), in their critique of Ahluwalia (1978a), argued against the use of data from the fifties. They argued that the impact of the green revolution on rural poverty could be assessed only by focusing on the period after 1960/61. Using data for 1960/61 to 1973/74, they concluded that there was a significant trend increase in rural poverty in the period despite the downtrend from the 1967/68 peak. However, as shown in figure 7.1, the trend completely reversed in the 10 years following 1967/68. There is no basis whatsoever for asserting that the incidence of rural poverty in India has been rising from the sixties onwards.

My own assessment that there were movements in both directions, with no underlying trend, needs to be qualified in the light of two observations by Tyagi (1982). The first relates to Tyagi's argument that CPIAL, which is used to compute the poverty line in various years, exaggerates the extent of the rise in prices because it is based on 1956/57 weights. Tyagi points out that prices of wheat, production of which has increased rapidly, rose somewhat less than prices of items such as barley and gram (chickpeas), whose production growth has been more modest. Consumption patterns have changed in favor of items whose prices rose less. Tyagi does not present an alternative price series for rural consumption, but he shows that a composite index of cereal prices for 1973/74 using CPIAL weights is 2.6 percent higher than one using weights derived from the 1973/74 consumption pattern.[2] However, cereals account for only about 50 percent of total consumption expenditure in the rural expenditure classes, and unless there is a similar weighting problem for other food items, the overstatement of the rise in overall prices would be less than for cereals. Thus, this particular bias may well be small. However, any upward bias in the price index would lead to some overstatement in the extent of poverty in the seventies.

Tyagi also questions the accuracy of the NSS consumption estimates for 1960/61 and 1961/62. He shows that NSS estimates for these years show much higher levels of foodgrain consumption by households than do the official estimates of total foodgrain availability, a discrepancy that narrows considerably in the seventies. Tyagi argues that the most plausible explanation is that the NSS overestimated foodgrain consumption in 1960/61 and 1961/62. If this is indeed the case, the NSS consumption estimates for 1960/61 and 1961/62 may need to be revised downwards, which would raise the estimates of poverty in these years. An upward adjustment in the estimates of rural poverty in 1960/61 and 1961/62, combined with a downward adjustment in the seventies to correct for the exaggeration of the rise in prices by the base weighted price index, would have the effect of showing a modest trend improvement in rural poverty. It is not possible to resolve these questions satisfactorily with the data available. We can only note that even when there is a profusion of apparently comparable data, our assessment of trends can only be tentative. This also qualifies any attempt to explain observed trends.

The Narain Equation and Some Alternatives

Dharm Narain's analysis of the determinants of rural poverty was based on an equation that both expands and restricts the equation used in Ahluwalia (1978a), in which rural poverty is shown as a function of agricultural income per head of the rural population y and time t. Dharm Narain expanded this specification to include p, the consumer price index for agricultural laborers, as an explanatory variable reflecting the prices faced by the rural poor as consumers. He restricted the Ahluwalia formulation by using current agricultural income per head, while the Ahluwalia equation used income not only in the current year but also with a one-year lag.[3] A further difference is that in Dharm Narain's formulation all variables (including time) are entered in logarithmic form.

Table 7.2 presents the Narain equation as estimated from the expanded data set and compares it with the Ahluwalia equation, which includes lagged income but not prices. It also presents results from a composite specification which includes both prices and lagged agricultural income. All equations are in logarithmic form.

The effect of extending the period under study on the estimated co-efficients of the Narain equation can be seen by comparing equations (3) and (4) in the table, which relate to the full period, with equations (1) and (2), which relate to the shorter period covered by Dharm Narain.[4] The explanatory power of the equation is considerably less for the full period than for the shorter period, but the results are qualitatively similar and statistically impressive. The coefficient on the agricultural income variable is negative, and on price positive, and both are highly significant. The coefficient on time is also negative and significant. These conclusions hold whether we use the head-count measure of poverty or the Sen Index as the dependent variable.

An interesting aspect of the comparison is that the coefficient on prices for the shorter period is reduced by half in the full period. On the other hand, the income coefficient doubles in the full period. Clearly, in the Narain equation the role of prices is substantially reduced when data for the seventies are included, while variations in income per head become

Table 7.2. Determinants of Rural Poverty

Constant		log y	log y (−1)	log p	log t	R^2	Number of Observations
A. *Narain Equation*							
1956/57 to 1970/71							
1) log POV	3.42	−0.58		0.58	−0.18	0.94	13
	(4.4)	(3.7)		(9.1)	(8.0)		
2) log SI	−2.19	0.91		0.88	−0.31	0.96	13
	(2.6)	(4.4)		(10.6)	(10.6)		
1956/57 to 1977/78							
3) log POV	7.27	−1.22		0.23	−0.12	0.62	17
	(4.7)	(4.0)		(2.2)	(2.4)		
4) log SI	3.24	−1.85		0.42	0.22	0.74	15
	(2.0)	(4.5)		(3.0)	(3.3)		
B. *Ahluwalia (1977) Equation*							
5) log POV	10.75	−0.99	−0.93		−0.03	0.68	17
	(5.9)	(3.4)	(2.7)		(1.4)		
6) log SI	8.80	−1.46	−1.45		−0.08	0.70	15
	(3.4)	(3.2)	(2.5)		(2.0)		
C. *Composite Equation*							
7) log POV	9.63	−1.04	−0.76	0.17	−0.10	0.74	17
	(5.3)	(3.8)	(2.3)	(1.7)	(2.2)		
8) log SI	6.39	−1.60	−1.01	0.32	−0.20	0.81	15
	(2.7)	(4.2)	(2.2)	(2.4)	(2.3)		

Note: Figures in parentheses are t statistics. The variables are defined as: POV, head-count measure of poverty; SI, Sen Index; y, NDP in agriculture in constant prices per head of the rural population; y (−1), the one-year lagged value of y; p, the consumer price index for agricultural laborers; and t, time.

much more important. One possible reason for this could be that the vulnerability of the poor to sharp increases in prices declined in the seventies owing to the expansion and extension of public distribution into rural areas, which helped the poor protect their consumption in periods of rising prices.

The explanatory power of the Narain and Ahluwalia equations is broadly comparable. The explanatory power of the Narain equation is lower when the head-count measure is the dependent variable but higher when the Sen Index is used.[5] These comparisons suggest that the effect of lagged agricultural income on rural poverty is at least as important as prices if we are concerned with explaining variation in poverty. What is more, this is not, as might be supposed, a case where lagged income per head acts as a proxy for prices. The correlation between y_{-1} and p is only 0.17, and the correlation between the logarithms of these variables is only 0.20. The low correlation may appear counter intuitive, but it is not surprising when one considers that p is heavily time-trended, whereas y_{-1} is not. The significance of y_{-1} as an explanatory variable is therefore clearly independent of prices and is much more plausibly explained in terms of the cushioning effect through borrowing or sale of assets mentioned in note 3. The effect on consumption, and therefore poverty, of a fall in income in one year can be cushioned by borrowing or sale of assets, a cushion that is exhausted if there are two successive bad years. For this reason, a decline in income in one year does not lead to as large an increase in poverty as when there are two bad years in succession. Equally, a rise in income levels immediately following a bad year does not reduce poverty as much as might be expected, since consumption loans undertaken in the previous year would have to be repaid, and assets sold replaced, before consumption levels could recover fully. Lagged agricultural income is therefore an important explanatory variable in its own right.

The composite equation in table 7.2 includes both y_{-1} and p as explanatory variables. The composite equations (7) and (8) have a higher explanatory power than either the Ahluwalia or the Narain equation. They explain three-fourths or more of the variation in rural poverty, depending upon the measure used. The coefficient on p is positive, but the significance level declines. It is below acceptable levels when the dependent variable is the head-count measure of poverty but remains highly significant when the Sen Index is used.[6]

To summarize, the expanded data base for 1956/57 to 1977/78 confirms that rural poverty, agricultural income, prices, and time are related broadly as indicated in Dharm Narain's results, but with important differences. Rural poverty appears inversely related to income per head in the rural areas, and the relation is considerably strengthened if agricultural income is also lagged. The addition of lagged agricultural income somewhat weakens the significance of the coefficient on prices but does not negate it entirely. However, the absolute size of the coefficient on prices is considerably reduced in the extended period and is further reduced if lagged agricultural income is included.

Problems of Interpretation

Interpretation of the estimated equations reported above is not as easy as it may seem at first. Aggregate relationships of this type are often consistent with more than one underlying causal mechanism, and it is important to subject them to close scrutiny before accepting them as evidence for one or another point of view. This applies to both the observed positive relationship with prices and also the inverse relationship with agricultural income.

THE ROLE OF PRICES

The positive coefficient on the price variable in the Narain equation has been interpreted as confirming the hypothesis that inflation tends to accentuate rural poverty independent of the level of agricultural output per head. The hypothesis is entirely plausible on a priori grounds, but this does not mean that the equation as specified is appropriate to test it.

The a priori case is easily established. Sen's (1981b) model of a rural economy illustrates the plight of wage earners when there is a sharp rise in food prices. Such a rise could take place without any change in production per head in the rural economy because of a general inflation in which food prices move up with other commodity prices. Food prices also could rise owing to developments outside the rural economy, such as a rise in export demand or reduced imports of food. In either case, if rural money wages do not rise sufficiently to offset the increase in prices, the real incomes of the poor decline.[7] Such real wage effects are not the only mechanism through which price changes may affect rural poverty. Even if the rural poor are self-employed peasant producers who produce goods other than those they consume, a rise in food prices could accentuate rural poverty if it is not matched by a rise in the prices they receive.[8]

The specification used by Dharm Narain is not appropriate to test for such price effects, because the explanatory variable used is the level of prices, whereas it should be a relative price variable. The vulnerability of the poor arises from the fact that the prices they pay as consumers may rise more than those they receive as wage earners or producers. The misspecification leads to considerable difficulties in interpretation. If the price variable in the Narain equation should have been a relative price variable p/p^*, where p^* is some appropriate index of prices received by the poor, then the underlying relationship is of the following form:

$$\log \text{POV} = \alpha + \beta \log Y + \delta \log p^* + c \log t + u$$

Inclusion of p^* in the equation is necessary because an increase in p increases poverty only if p^* does not rise *pari passu*. In many situations, a sharp upsurge in inflation may mean a rise in p, the prices paid by the poor, without an immediate corresponding rise in p^* (especially when p^* refers to money wages). This, of course, can be expected to have an adverse effect on poverty. However, as p^* catches up, the initial adverse effect is presumably overcome.[9] The Narain equation does not allow for any catching up—a higher level of p has a perpetually adverse effect on poverty, which is clearly misleading.

This misspecification also introduces a bias in the estimated equation. Since the excluded variable p^* is bound to be highly correlated with time (because of the inevitable trend element in prices), its exclusion from the estimated equation biases the estimated coefficient on t. In effect, the expected negative coefficient on p^* will be reflected in the estimated coefficient on t, which is biased downwards. It is because of this bias that in spite of the high t ratio, we cannot take the estimated negative coefficient on t at face value. This brings into question Gunvant Desai's interpretation, in chapter 1 of this volume, of the negative coefficient on time in the Narain equation as indicative of the operation of other processes tending to reduce rural poverty apart from the effect of changes in income levels per head.

A second problem with the Narain specification is the possibility of bias in the estimated coefficient on prices. This was the subject of an extensive correspondence between myself and Dharm Narain and is also referred to in the chapters in this volume by Sen (chap. 2) and Srinivasan (chap. 5). The problem arises because (1) the estimate of poverty is derived from the distribution-of-consumption expenditure in nominal terms combined with a current-price poverty line based on the price index p; and (2) as I mentioned earlier, the price variable is likely to be measured with an error. These two factors mean that there is an error in our measure of poverty, the dependent variable, which is correlated with the error in p, an explanatory variable. Since the two errors have a positive covariance, this will produce an upward bias in the estimated coefficient on p. It must be emphasized that the problem does not arise solely because p figures on both sides of the equation. As Sen points out, there can be no objection to "recovering" real consumption levels by dividing nominal consumption by prices and then relating real consumption thus measured to prices. If there is a relationship between real consumption and prices, it should certainly surface in the estimation. The problem arises because the error in p leads to a corresponding error in the measure of poverty. It should be noted that if poverty were independently measurable, an error in the explanatory variable p would not lead to the same bias. The familiar problem of errors in variables would, of course, arise, as pointed out by Sen. This would produce biased least-squares estimates, with the slope on p being underestimated. However, the error problem we have been discussing is quite different; it arises because the error in the explanatory variable p also produces an error in the dependent variable, and the two errors are correlated. This introduces a positive bias in the estimated coefficient on p. The existence of such a bias makes it difficult to take the estimated positive and significant coefficient on p at face value.

In view of these difficulties, it is worth considering whether other specifications of the estimated equation would overcome these problems. One approach would be to construct a variable that directly measures changes in prices paid by the poor as consumers relative to those they receive as producers. Unfortunately, data needed to construct an appropriate relative price variable are not available. There is no reliable series for rural money wages, nor is there an acceptable index reflecting prices received by the poor as producers. Since the poor are both wage earners and producers, we should examine the effect of price increases on the rural poor in terms of a relative price variable in which the prices received by the rural poor are measured by a composite index of both money wages and relevant farm-gate prices. It would be better still to

Table 7.3. Alternative Price Specifications

A. *Logarithmic Form. Dependent Variable: log POV*

Constant	log y	log $y(-1)$	log (p/p_d)	log p	log p_d	log t	R^2
1) 8.48	−1.0	−0.87	0.45			−0.01	0.69
	(3.4)	(2.5)	(0.8)			(0.3)	
2) 7.85	−1.01	−0.85	0.57				0.69
	(3.5)	(2.6)	(1.6)				
3) 9.50	−1.05	−0.72		0.54	−0.38	−0.08	0.75
	(3.7)	(2.1)		(1.0)	(0.7)	(1.5)	
4) 10.02	−1.04	−0.77		0.88	0.82		0.70
	(3.6)	(2.2)		(1.6)	(1.7)		

B. *Linear Form. Dependent Variable: POV*

Constant	y	$y(-1)$	(p/p_d)	$\dot{P}$	$\dot{P}(-1)$	t	R^2
5) 111.5	−1.39	−1.24	0.29				0.72
	(3.8)	(2.9)	(1.8)				
6) 95.6	−1.48	−1.17	0.43			0.18	0.73
	(3.8)	(2.6)	(1.8)			(0.8)	
7) 139.4	−1.32	−1.27		0.04		−0.13	0.67
	(3.0)	(2.5)		(0.3)		(0.8)	
8) 117.6	−0.90	−1.08			0.22	−0.16	0.70
	(1.7)	(2.2)			(1.2)	(1.0)	
9) 116.4	−0.89	−1.06		0.03	0.22	−0.17	0.70
	(1.6)	(2.0)		(0.2)	(1.1)	(1.0)	

Note: Figures in parentheses are t statistics.

conduct a separate analysis for the incidence of poverty in each group. This is beyond the scope of this chapter.

A crude alternative, though perhaps the only feasible one, is to treat p_d, the national accounts deflator for agricultural gross domestic product (GDP), as a proxy for prices received by the rural poor and then use the relative price variable p/p_d as an explanatory variable. The results are presented in table 7.3. The coefficient on the relative price variable p/p_d is positive but not significant in the logarithmic form, especially when t is included. However, it is positive and significant in the linear form. When p and p_d are separately entered in the logarithmic equations (equations [3] and [4] in table 7.3), we obtain the expected positive coefficient on p and the negative coefficient on p_d, but the significance levels are low. Removing the time term improves the significance level of these coefficients, but they still remain below the conventional limits.

A second way around the specification problem is to test for the impact of prices by using the rate of inflation, rather than the level of prices, as the explanatory variable. There is considerable a priori justification for this. If the problem arises because of the stickiness of money wages, then we can expect poverty to increase in periods when prices rise, but once prices stabilize, money wages can be expected to catch up, so that in time the initial adverse effect of inflation would be corrected, even though the level of prices remained high. Thus it is not the level of prices but the fact of rising prices that is important. This hypothesis is tested in equations (7), (8), and (9) in table 7.3, in which the current year's rate of inflation, $\dot{p}$, and the previous year's rate of inflation, $\dot{p}_{-1}$ are used as explanatory variables, first separately and then jointly. It is somewhat surprising that there is no significant coefficient on these variables in any of these cases.

AGRICULTURAL PRODUCTION AND POVERTY

The rationale for using agricultural income per head of the rural population as an explanatory variable affecting rural poverty is self-evident. If the distribution of income remained constant and there were no adverse terms-of-trade effects, then an increase in agricultural production should raise income levels for all sections of the rural population, thus pushing some individuals above the poverty line. We cannot, of course, assume that the distribution of income would remain constant or that terms-of-trade effects would not occur. Nevertheless, a significant negative coefficient on the agricultural income variable tests whether the net effect of rising income per head after allowing for these other considerations is a reduction in poverty to some extent. This is the so-called trickle-down mechanism, about which much has been written. The existence and strength of such mechanisms is clearly important for policy. They hold out the hope that strategies for raising agricultural production would tend to reduce poverty even if they were not accompanied by radical institutional changes such as land reforms, which, desirable though they are, have proved extremely difficult to implement in practice.

The equations in tables 7.3 and 7.4 confirm that rural poverty is inversely related to income levels per head. This is so whether we look at Dharm Narain's or Ahluwalia's formulations or the composite equation, all of which show negative and significant coefficients on the income variables. Can we interpret this inverse relationship as some sort of confirmation of trickle-down mechanisms?

To begin with, we must recognize the difference between saying that trickle-down mechanisms exist and saying that trickle-down has worked. To assert that trickle-down mechanisms exist is only to say that the rural economy works in such a way that a rise in agricultural production and income levels per head would lead to some decline in rural poverty. This is quite different from saying that trickle-down has worked in the sense that it has actually led to a decline in poverty over time. Such an outcome would require not only that trickle-down mechanisms exist but also that agricultural growth has been sufficiently rapid for income levels per head

Table 7.4. Agricultural Production and Rural Poverty

Logarithmic Form

	Constant	log y	log y(−1)	d	d.log y	d.log y(−1)	R^2
log POV	10.49	−1.07	0.77	1.25	0.18	−0.61	0.97
		(8.9)	(6.2)	(1.0)	(0.8)	(2.0)	
log SI	7.87	−1.51	−1.21	−10.68	−1.15	4.30	
		(1.7)	(1.3)	(0.5)	(0.4)	(0.6)	0.36

Linear Form

	Constant	y	y(−1)	d	d.y	d.y(−1)	R^2
POV	142.25	−1.57	−1.12	0.16	0.59	−0.62	0.67
		(2.8)	(2.0)	(0.003)	(0.6)	(0.5)	
SI	0.74	−0.009	−0.007	−0.68	−0.005	0.02	0.64
		(2.4)	(1.9)	(0.8)	(0.4)	(0.8)	

Note: Figures in parentheses are *t* statistics.

to rise over time. The estimated inverse relationship does indeed suggest that trickle-down mechanisms do exist. But it is also true that growth was not fast enough to achieve the desired reduction in poverty over the period as a whole. Real agricultural income, measured in terms of net domestic product (NDP) in agriculture, grew about 2 percent per year from 1956/57 to 1977/78, which was only slightly faster than rural population.[10] As a result, agricultural NDP per head of the rural population showed no significant growth trend. Year-to-year fluctuations reflect the effect of weather on total agricultural production, but these variations are around a near-stationary level.

$$\text{Log } y = 5.85 + 0.0026\, t \qquad R^2 = 0.08$$
$$(1.4)$$

As Srinivasan points out in chapter 5 in this volume, there simply was not enough growth for trickle-down mechanisms to have a significant trend impact on poverty.

Even this interpretation of the estimated equations as indicating a limited *potential* for trickle-down has been challenged. Some believe that while agricultural expansion may have had strong links with income generation for the poor in the first half of the period, this linkage weakened considerably in the second half. It has been argued that agricultural growth up to the mid-sixties resulted principally from area expansion, which favored increased use of labor and therefore benefited the poor. Growth in the second period was mainly the result of higher yields, which resulted from the new technology. It is argued that adoption of this technology was associated with changes in the rural economy that limited the downward flow of benefits. The concentration of increased yields in certain regions is relevant in this context. Equally important is the fact that the new technology depends heavily upon intermediate inputs such as pump sets and tractors, which may have reduced the use of labor in agriculture. In addition, the high credit requirement may have limited benefits to smaller and marginal farmers.

The hypothesis that the linkage between higher agricultural production and the alleviation of rural poverty weakened after the mid-sixties needs to be studied intensively. The case for it is certainly not established a priori. While some technological changes, such as combine harvesters, probably were labor-displacing, others were not necessarily so. The spread of irrigation, high-yield varieties, and application of fertilizers calls for a more labor-intensive production. Even the use of tractors, insofar as it permits more effective multiple cropping, is not necessarily a net displacer of labor. Similarly, while it may well have been more difficult for small and marginal farmers to benefit from the new technology, there was a conscious shift of policy in the seventies aimed at overcoming these difficulties. There was a considerable expansion in rural development programs and employment-generating schemes aimed at supporting productive activity and income levels in precisely these "weaker groups."

Table 7.4 presents a crude test of whether the relationship between agricultural production and rural poverty weakened in the second half of the period. A dummy variable d is specified which takes the value zero for 1967/68 and is set at unity for 1968/69 and thereafter. Using this variable in conjunction with y, we can introduce the product term dy as an additional explanatory variable into the equation along with y. A significant positive coefficient on the new variable would indicate that the inverse relationship between rural poverty and income per head dampened in the second period. In no case is there a significant positive coefficient on either d or dy, which we would expect if the trickle-down mechanism had become weaker. Similar equations have been estimated using slightly different cutoff points from the dummy variable but with essentially the same results.

These results suggest that trickle-down mechanisms exist in the sense defined above and also that there is no evidence that they have weakened in the later period. However, this conclusion should not be interpreted as an endorsement of trickle-down strategies to the exclusion of other policies or strategies directly aimed at helping the poor. The need for devising strategies of growth to ensure adequate flows of benefits to the poor, or more modestly, for supplementing the general strategy of raising agricultural production with more target-oriented programs aimed at the weaker sections, remains urgent. Trickle-down processes alone would probably take an inordinately long time. The estimated equations certainly bear this out. Even if we take the elasticity of our head-count measure of poverty with respect to income per head to be 1.2 (the highest level obtained in table 7.2), the objective of reducing the extent of rural poverty from 40 percent of the rural population to about 20 percent would require an increase in per capita income of about 42 percent. Since our ability to raise the rate of growth of agricultural NDP is limited, an increase of this order takes time. If agricultural NDP per head of the rural population were to rise by 1 percent per year—a modest improvement over past performance—it would take 35 years to reduce the percentage of the population in poverty to 20 percent by trickle-down alone. If the growth rate were raised to 2 percent—a very substantial improvement over observed rates of growth—it would take 18 years. Growth certainly makes a difference, but it must be conceded that even on optimistic assumptions, the process would be slow if we relied on growth alone.

Conclusions, Qualifications, and Speculations

The implications of my results for the important issues addressed by Dharm Narain, with their limitations and qualifications, can now be summarized. To begin with, I must put things in perspective by emphasizing that a critical limitation of my analysis is the use of a unidimensional measure of poverty in terms of consumption levels. A comprehensive assessment of the living conditions of the poor, and changes over time, must encompass not only consumption levels but also health, longevity, security in both health and consumption levels, and, of course, access to public goods such as drinking water and education. Rural development policy in India has been shaped consciously to improve conditions in all these aspects, and we need to assess progress in terms of changes in these dimensions as well as changes in consumption per head. Time-series data on all of these dimensions are scarce, although the available evidence points to considerable improvement in health, longevity, and education. An interesting feature of recent experience is the establishment of institutions such as the public distribution system and rural employment programs, both of which add to the security of income and consumption by insulating the population to some extent from the worst effects of drought and inflation. Unfortunately, it is not possible to assess the impact of these developments on the living conditions of the rural population in a comprehensive manner. Therefore, the indices that we have used, although clearly inadequate, probably provide the best possible basis for studying the issues considered in this chapter.

The first issue that I have considered relates to the long-term trend in rural poverty. The NSS data permit the firm conclusion that there is no basis for the view that the incidence of rural poverty has increased over time, especially in the period after the green revolution. The data for 1956/57 to 1977/78 show no significant trend, and the data for the period after the green revolution show a more or less steady decline. The measured incidence of rural poverty in 1977/78 seems to be about the same as that observed in 1960/61 and 1961/62, but this may be misleading, because of the biases pointed out by Tyagi (1982). These may result in understatement of the extent of poverty in 1960/61 and overstatement of it later. Whether these biases exist is far from definitely established, but if they do, the corrected long-term trend may well show a slight decline in rural poverty. What is more important, however, is whether the improvements observed in the seventies will continue. The NSS has switched from annual consumption surveys to 5-year surveys. The data for 1982/83, when they become available, will help to throw light on this all-important issue.

The second issue considered in this chapter is the relationship between rural poverty and agricultural income levels per head. Three conclusions have emerged: (1) There is fairly strong evidence of an inverse relationship between agricultural income per head and the incidence of rural poverty, especially if account is taken of lagged effects; (2) there is no evidence that this relationship has weakened since the green revolution; and (3) reliance on growth alone will not bring about a large reduction in the incidence of poverty in the near future. These conclusions underscore the need for rural development programs aimed especially at the rural poor.

Because of the highly aggregative nature of my analysis, these conclusions must be qualified. Differences among states may arise because of variations in agricultural conditions and patterns of growth. The analysis also assumes a common structure over time in the model to be estimated. Yet it could be argued that important changes have taken place that cannot be captured in the regression equations by using dummy variables. The effect of rising agricultural production on rural poverty depends upon a very wide variety of factors. Some of these are essentially exogenous, such as developments in the land-man ratio and the nature of the technology underlying the rise in production. Others depend upon policy towards agricultural development. For example, programs designed to increase the ability of small and marginal farms to benefit from available improvements in technology and irrigation help to widen the spread of production gains. Equally important are factors affecting the state of rural labor markets, which determine the ability of labor to command an appropriate wage. Labor organization can be particularly important in this context, as shown by the experience of Kerala. Also, rural employment programs—which add to labor demand in rural labor markets, to the advantage of landless laborers—have been an important element of rural development policy in the seventies. The state of urban labor markets and the possibilities for migration are also relevant. The impact and interaction of these factors on rural poverty cannot be analyzed through aggregate analysis alone.

Finally, a word on the issue of inflation and its impact on the rural poor, which was the particular focus of Dharm Narain's inquiry. The a priori case for arguing that the poor are especially vulnerable to inflation is extremely strong, and Dharm Narain was undoubtedly right to focus attention on this phenomenon. There are technical difficulties with the particular specification he used, and alternative specifications that are free of these defects do not yield clear evidence of a significant relationship between the rate of inflation and the degree of rural poverty. This is somewhat surprising. One reason may be that our measure of poverty aggregates across two socioeconomic groups that constitute the bulk of the rural poor—landless laborers and marginal farmers—and inflation affects these two groups somewhat differently. Landless laborers may be hard-hit by inflation because money wages lag behind price rises, but small farmers may not be similarly affected, since they consume what they produce, so that with given production levels, they are not adversely affected if the rate of inflation is higher. Indeed, where there is a small surplus, they may even benefit from inflation if it turns the terms of trade in their favor.

It may well be that a disaggregation of the poor into separate socio-economic groups might provide strong support for Dharm Narain's hypothesis. This, together with the other disaggregations mentioned above, provides promising lines for further inquiry.

Notes

The author is grateful to Bagich S. Minhas, chairman of the NSS Governing Council, for permission to use preliminary NSS tabulations of consumer expenditure for 1977/78 to estimate rural poverty for that year.

1. See, for example, the debate between Bardhan (1973) and Minhas (1971) on the appropriate choice of a deflator. For a more general critique of NSS-based poverty lines see Tyagi (1982).

2. The weights were based on the expenditure patterns of the first nine expenditure classes of Rs. 34.43 per capita, in the 1973/74 NSS consumption survey. The upper end of this group is the monthly expenditure class. The current-price poverty line in 1973/74 using CPIAL was Rs. 43.50.

3. The rationale for the two-period distributed lag, with both y and y_{-1} as explanatory variables, is that poverty is defined in terms of consumption, and consumption can be protected from a decline in income in any one year by borrowing or sale of assets. This cushion is exhausted, however, if there are two bad years in succession, since borrowing capacity is limited and assets sold have to be replaced.

4. The estimate coefficients in equation (1) (table 7.2) differ slightly from the Narain results reported by Desai (chap. 1) for two reasons. First, we have 13

observations for the period covered by Dharm Narain instead of his 12. This is because Dharm Narain based his work on an earlier version of Ahluwalia (1978b), in which only 12 observations were reported for this period. Second, the data relating to the net domestic product in agriculture per head of the rural population shown in table 7.1 are based on revised data.

5. When the equations are estimated in linear form, the Ahluwalia equation has a higher explanatory power in both cases, but the difference is negligible in the case of the Sen Index.

6. It is interesting to note that when the equations are estimated in linear form, neither the coefficient on prices nor the coefficient on time is statistically significant.

7. The existence of a lagged response of money wages to price increases in rural economies has been documented in the case of Bangladesh by Papanek and Dey (1982).

8. This point is particularly relevant for the small and marginal producers, who often are forced to sell at low prices immediately after the harvest and to buy at high prices during the remainder of the year. This gap between prices received and prices paid may well increase substantially.

9. Papanek and Dey (1982) find that in Bangladesh, rural wages catch up with prices over a two-year period.

10. The trend growth rate of agricultural production is higher—about 2.5 percent—but, of course, it is value added, and not production, that is relevant as a measure of total income from agriculture.

8 Poverty and "Trickle-Down" in Rural India: A Quantitative Analysis

PRANAB K. BARDHAN

For those who find radical institutional changes politically disturbing or infeasible, the so-called trickle-down hypothesis is comforting. The evidence (mostly indirect) from rural India, however, is mixed and not unambiguously comforting. In three articles written near the end of the 1960s, I showed that aggregative evidence suggested that the percentage of the rural population below a defined per capita expenditure level increased during the 1960s[1] in spite of moderate agricultural growth. Since then, in a widely quoted paper, Ahluwalia (1978a) has raised the hopes of the comfort seekers. Using data for the 1960s with those for some years in the earlier decades and a few years in the subsequent decade, he found no significant trend increase in poverty. He also observed an inverse relationship between poverty and agricultural performance for rural India as a whole. His results for individual states were somewhat less hopeful. In *none* of the six states in which growth in agricultural output per capita had been significant (Punjab-Haryana,. Uttar Pradesh, West Bengal, Tamil Nadu, Kerala, and Orissa) was there any significant decline in the percentage of poor people. In fact, West Bengal showed a significant trend rise.

Ahluwalia's exercise has been criticized and modified by several authors. The particular context of the discussion on the trickle-down hypothesis was centered largely on the effects of the new agricultural strategy that the government of India adopted in the early sixties, which emphasizes the promotion of agricultural growth by increasing the profitability of cultivation (particularly on larger farms and in better-irrigated regions) through subsidization of inputs and price support of outputs. From this point of view, it is meaningful to concentrate only on the period subsequent to the early sixties. Griffin and Ghose (1979) and Saith (1981) have shown that such a truncated time series of poverty does not bear out Ahluwalia's conclusions. Both Dharm Narain (1979) and Saith (1981) have found a very strong positive association between rural poverty and the consumer price index for agricultural laborers.[2] Since in recent years prices of some major foodgrains in India have been determined more by the strength of political lobbying than by market forces, this positive association suggests one possible influence on poverty of the political forces strengthened by the new agricultural strategy.

In regard to Ahluwalia's observation of a negative relation between poverty and agricultural performance, it has been pointed out, particularly by Kohli (1980), that one should be careful in interpreting this observation. If all it means is that in years of better rainfall (or other acts of mercy by nature) rural poverty tends to decline, it will be an acceptable proposition to most people on both sides of the debate (although some may regard this trickle-down as not enough). What is controversial is the other interpretation, which some participants have jumped to, namely, that this observation means that the particular type of growth process unleashed by the new agricultural strategy has contributed significantly to the mitigation of rural poverty. Ahluwalia's exercise is not enough to support this latter interpretation.

Any growth of output (strictly speaking, value added) in agriculture in excess of the rate of growth of the rural labor force is, of course, likely to generate some forces that tend to improve the incomes of small farmers and wage laborers, who constitute the bulk of the rural poor. How is it, then, that the new strategy of agricultural growth may have counteracted these forces and even immiserized some people? Some of the possible ways may be listed as working through the following:

1. the effects of adoption of labor-displacing machinery;
2. the increased profitability of self-cultivation by large landlords, leading to eviction of small tenants;
3. the increased dependence of agriculture on purchased inputs and privately controlled irrigation, driving some small farmers, with limited access to resources and credit, out of cultivation and into crowding the agricultural labor market;
4. a similar crowding of the agricultural labor market by displaced village artisans, as the demand pattern of the new rural rich shifts away from local handicrafts and services to mass-produced urban consumer goods and services;
5. growth-induced in-migration of agricultural labor from backward areas;
6. the use of pump sets, enabling richer farmers to appropriate communal groundwater, resulting in a possible drop in water tables and making the traditional lift irrigation technology even less effective than before for poorer farmers without pump sets;
7. a decreased interest on the part of the village leadership, largely dominated by the large farmers who have acquired their own irrigation

equipment, in the maintenance of old irrigation channels, hurting the poorer farmers who depend on them;

8. a decline in the participation of women in the agricultural work force, particularly those women helpers on the erstwhile small family farms, who cannot now offer themselves in the wage labor market on account of various social and economic constraints; and

9. the increased political bargaining power of the rural rich, resulting in higher administered prices of foodgrains (of which the rural poor are net buyers), while typically wages lag behind the price rises (and as monetization of wage payments increases with agricultural progress).

Not all of the above-mentioned processes are equally likely, and even when operative they may not constitute a case against the new technology as such. The intent here is to focus on the consequences of the institutional framework in which the changes in technology have come about.

Unfortunately, the immediate prospect of constructing a long time series of poverty data that would allow us to isolate the effects of these processes is not very good. Since 1973/74 (the last year in Ahluwalia's data set), the NSS has stopped collecting consumption survey data every year, opting instead to conduct such surveys at five-year intervals. For the last quarter of this century we shall have only five annual estimates from this source.[3]

The Rural Labor Enquiry reports recently published data bearing on poverty in rural India during the period 1964/65 to 1974/75. Average daily earnings in agricultural operations by men in agricultural-labor households, deflated by the consumer price index for agricultural laborers, *declined*, by 12 percent over this 10-year period for rural India.[4] It also declined in all states except Punjab-Haryana, Uttar Pradesh, and Jammu and Kashmir (where it rose) and Karnataka (where it stayed the same). The rural labor enquiry reports do not provide estimates of total annual earnings of the agricultural-labor households for this period. But there is enough scattered information in the reports for an estimate of the total annual wage income of all the earning members in an average agricultural-labor household.[5] This is computed for each state in table 8.1. Using the consumer price index for agricultural laborers as a deflator, we find that between 1964/65 and 1974/75, annual wage income per agricultural-labor household declined in all states (including Punjab-Haryana) except Uttar Pradesh. For rural India as a whole, it declined by 16 percent.

The decline in Punjab-Haryana is particularly striking. It is often suggested that in-migration of rural labor from the backward districts of Bihar and Eastern Uttar Pradesh has kept the growth of wage income in check. However, it is doubtful that in-migration was substantial enough

Table 8.1. Annual Wage Income per Agricultural-Labor Household in India

State	Y_w 1964/65	Y_w 1974/75	ACPI with 1964/65 as 100	Y_w 1974/75 at 1964/65 Prices	Col. 4 as Percentage of Col. 1
	Rs.	Rs.		Rs.	%
Andhra Pradesh	434.97	999.43	258	387.38	89
Assam	987.27	1,933.22	261	740.70	75
Bihar	475.76	1,094.49	261	419.34	88
Gujarat	845.12	1,495.65	240	623.19	74
Jammu and Kashmir	616.06	1,414.30	253	559.01	91
Karnataka	506.40	1,183.16	236	501.34	99
Kerala	664.41	1,440.08	290	496.58	75
Madhya Pradesh	620.19	1,152.14	299	385.33	62
Maharashtra	630.91	1,214.01	241	503.74	80
Orissa	498.39	780.98	278	280.93	56
Punjab-Haryana	992.38	2,146.00	242	886.78	89
Rajasthan	617.17	1,552.13	280	554.33	90
Tamil Nadu	445.89	1,005.58	293	343.20	77
Uttar Pradesh	385.12	1,081.85	230	470.37	22
West Bengal	767.23	1,252.32	249	502.94	66
All-India	536.53	1,164.59	257	453.15	84

Sources: Values for column 1 have been computed on the basis of data from Government of India, Labour Bureau (1975), tables 2.1, 2.6, 3.2, 3.3, 4.4, 8.4, 8.8, 9.4, and 9.8, as well as the tables in app. 5. Values for column 2 have been computed on the basis of data in Government of India, Labour Bureau (1980), tables 2(a).1, 3(a).1.1, 3(a).1.2, and 3(a).1.3; and in Government of India, Labour Bureau (1979), table 2.9(a).1.

Note: Y_w is the total annual wage income earned by all usually occupied workers (men, women, and children) in the agricultural-labor household. ACPI is the agricultural laborer consumer price index: the index using 1964/65 as the base year is as given in Government of India, Labour Bureau (1979), table 3.4.

by 1974/75 to have significant effects. A study by Oberai and Singh (1980) shows that in a 1977 survey of 2,124 rural households in 26 villages in Ludhiana District in the Punjab there were 92 agricultural-laborer in-migrants and 79 out-migrants, so that there was net in-migration of only 13 agricultural laborers in the whole sample.

More recently, the NSS tabulation of the results of the 32d Round (1977/78) employment and unemployment survey has provided some information on the distribution of agricultural-labor households by expenditure class (see table 8.2). The last year for which this percentage distribution data had been available was 1963/64, from the Rural Labor Enquiry reports. Using Rs. 15 at 1960/61 prices as the poverty line,[6] the agricultural-labor consumer price index as the deflator (which increased from 118 in 1963/64 to 323 in 1977/78), and applying the standard linear

Table 8.2. Percentage Distribution of Agricultural-Labor Households by Expenditure Class in Rural India, 1963/64 and 1977/78

1963/64		1977/78	
Annual Per Capita Expenditure Class in Rs. at Current Prices	Percentage of Total Number of Agricultural-Labor Households	Annual Per Capita Expenditure Class in Rs. at Current Prices	Percentage of Total Number of Agricultural-Labor Households
0–50	0.32	0–119.9	0.16
51–100	5.19	120–239.9	2.36
101–150	18.98	240–359.9	13.49
151–200	23.17	360–479.9	22.41
201–250	17.59	480–599.9	20.34
251–300	13.02	600–839.9	23.68
301–350	6.78	840–1,199.9	12.28
350+	14.95	1,200–1,799.9	4.09
		1,800–2,399.9	0.78
		2,400+	0.41

Sources: The 1963/64 data are from Government of India, Labour Bureau (1975); the 1977/78 data are from Government of India, Department of Statistics, National Sample Survey Organisation (1981b).

interpolation method to find a point between two discrete expenditure group limits, our estimates suggest that between 1963/64 and 1977/78 the proportion of agricultural-labor households below the poverty line for rural India as a whole *increased*, from 52 percent to 56 percent. Over this period the net domestic product from agriculture (at 1960/61 prices) increased by about 43 percent.

All of this evidence of decreasing total wage income or increasing poverty for agricultural-labor households between the mid-sixties and mid-(or even late) seventies would have been of somewhat less concern if agricultural-labor households themselves had been declining in proportional importance in rural areas. The evidence suggests quite the contrary. Between 1964/65 and 1974/75 agricultural-labor households as a proportion of total rural households increased from 21.8 percent to 25.3 percent for rural India as a whole; by 1977/78 this proportion had climbed to about 30 percent, according to the NSS tabulation.

One problem with the preceding discussion, as with most of the literature on the subject, is that it uses data at a much too aggregative level. What one really needs is an intensive micro-level analysis of the effects unleashed by various types of agricultural growth processes under different institutional settings. There are a few scattered micro-level village case studies on this question, but usually they are more descriptive than analytical. Besides, their extremely small-scale nature inhibits wider generalization. This is a general problem with micro-level field studies in social or economic anthropology. Such studies often capture the nuances and qualitative aspects of the interaction of technology and institutional relations with a perspicacity and richness of detail that is impossible to attain in large-scale sample surverys. But when it comes to assessing the empirical importance of alternative findings in these studies, it is a question of the evidence in "my" village against that in "yours," that in "my" tribe against that in "yours"; the result is rather chaotic inconclusiveness. Yet, on issues central to public policy and political programs, generalizability, with all its sweeping crudity, is an important necessity.

Analytical studies of rural poverty in India that are sufficiently intensive at the micro level and yet yield results that are statistically generalizable are clearly lacking. In the rest of this chapter, I make a limited attempt to analyze the NSS cross-sectional data on rural poverty, but at a disaggregated level, and to explain variations in the extent of poverty in terms of a multivariate model.[7] Since our variables are necessarily confined to those defined and collected by the NSS (supplemented by other secondary sources of data that we could lay our hands on), quite often they cannot capture the finer variations and intricacies in technological and institutional determinants of poverty, and the analysis has to make do with crude proxy variables—and on some key determinants, no variables at all. Since NSS data do not provide a long enough time series on poverty, deeper probes into the disaggregated NSS cross-sectional data may still be worthwhile, in spite of the obvious constraints of the NSS data-collection framework.

I analyze the NSS cross-sectional data at three levels of disaggregation: (1) at the level of the individual household in about 550 sample villages of West Bengal in 1977/78;[8] (2) at the level of 55 NSS regions (below the state level) covering almost all of rural India in the early 1970s; and (3) at the more aggregative state level for 1971/72.

My analysis of poverty in the 1977/78 West Bengal sample households deals separately with agricultural-labor households and primarily-cultivator households (described by the NSS as "self-employed in agricultural occupations"). Starting with the agricultural-labor households, I again take the poverty line as a monthly per capita expenditure level of Rs. 15 at 1960/61 prices.[9] (For an explanation of how I derived an approximate district-level price index to deflate the current-prices expenditure data see the notes to table 8.3.) The mean per capita monthly expenditure at 1960/61 prices (PCEXPR) in these households was Rs. 12.54 (with a standard deviation of Rs. 5.66).

The results of a logit analysis of the probability that an agricultural-labor household falls below our poverty line are reported in table 8.3. The

Table 8.3. Logit Analysis of the Probability of an Agricultural-Labor Household's Falling below the Poverty Line in Rural West Bengal, 1977/78

Explanatory Variable	Estimated Coefficient	Standard Error
1. Area cultivated by the household in acres (CULTIVAT)*	−0.6094	0.1113
2. Number of dependents in the household (NDEP)*	0.4005	0.0362
3. Number of men with above-primary education level in the 15–60 age group (EDM)*	−0.8066	0.1901
4. Number of men in the household usually occupied in nonfarm work NFM)*	−0.6549	0.2142
5. Distance of the village from nearest town, in km. (DIST)*	0.0085	0.0034
6. Village irrigation level (VILIRR)*^{a}	−0.1669	0.0565
7. Average daily wage rate in Rs. for male agricultural labor in the village in the reference week (VWAGEM)*^{b}	−0.3041	0.0494
8. Dummy for male wage employment in public works in or near the village (PUBWORKM)	−0.3753	0.2610
9. Dummy for January–March quarter (SBRND3)	0.2727	0.1577
10. Dummy for the household belonging to schedule caste (SCHCASTE)*	0.3073	0.1222
11. Normal annual rainfall in the district where the village is located (RAIN)*	−0.3005	0.0879
12. Nitrogenous fertilizer (in kg.) used per hectare of area under foodgrains in the district where the village is located (NHA)*	−0.0485	0.0079
13. Rate of growth in agricultural production in the district where the village is located (GROWTH)*^{c}	0.2804	0.0933

Sources: The data for variables 1, 2, 3, 4, 5, 6, 7, 8, 9, and 10 are from Government of India, Department of Statistics, National Sample Survey Organisation (1981b). The data for variable 5 are from Government of India, Registrar General (1971). The district-level variables—11, 12, and 13—are from various issues of the *Statistical Abstract*, published by West Bengal, State Statistical Bureau.

Note: The likelihood ratio index was 0.3020; the number of observations was 2,127.

The poverty line has been assumed to be given by a monthly per capita expenditure level of Rs. 15 at 1960 prices. Finding a suitable deflator to convert the current-prices expenditure data was a problem. As an approximation, I have used the food price index for the bottom expenditure class of households (Rs. 1–100 per month *per household*) for different regional centers, as regularly published by the State Statistical Bureau of West Bengal. I have taken simple averages over the price index figures of different regional centers within a district, and used this district-average price index to deflate the consumption expenditure of a household located in that district.

* All variables marked by an asterisk are significant at less than the 5 percent level.

^{a} VILIRR represents four levels of irrigation in the village cultivated area: (1) not irrigated at all; (2) a positive percentage but not more than 10 percent; (3) 10–25 percent; and (4) more than 25 percent.

Table 8.3 (*Continued*)

b VWAGEM has been computed by taking the total wage earnings on casual farm male labor by all the NSS sample households in the village divided by the corresponding total number of casual farm-male-labor days.

c GROWTH has been estimated by fitting a regression line on the annual time-series data on agricultural production over a period of 18 years (1960/61 to 1977/78) for each of rural West Bengal's 15 districts.

explanatory variables are of different kinds and are derived from the NSS as well as the Census Bureau and State Statistical Bureau sources. Some of the variables are specific to each individual household—area cultivated (CULTIVAT), number of nonearning dependents (NDEP), number of men aged 15 to 60 with education above the primary level (EDM), number of men usually occupied in nonfarm work (NFM), membership in a scheduled caste (SCHCASTE), and the NSS subround in which the household was visited (SBRND). Some variables are specific to the village where the household is located—village male wage rate for farm work in the reference week (VWAGEM), village irrigation level (VILIRR), distance of the village from the nearest town (DIST), and whether adult males in the village got any wage employment in public works in or near the village in the reference week (PUBWORKM). The other variables relate to the district in which the sample village is located (in the absence of village information on these)—normal annual rainfall (RAIN), level of nitrogenous fertilizer use (NHA), and rate of growth of agricultural production (GROWTH).

Most of the variables have highly significant coefficients (except for PUBWORKM and SBRND3, though they have expected signs). As expected, the probability of falling below the poverty line is *lower* for an agricultural-labor household with a larger area to cultivate for its own, a smaller number of dependents, greater participation in nonfarm work, and a higher education level (the last two increasing the nonagricultural opportunities available to the household) or for an agricultural-labor household that belongs to a village where the wage rate is higher, the cultivated land is in general better irrigated, there is more rainfall and more fertilizer use, and there are alternative opportunities to work on public works programs. The probability of falling below the poverty line is *greater* if, again as expected, the village is remote (and hence there are fewer alternative opportunities for the labor household), the household belongs to a scheduled caste (there are fewer "connections" and greater deprivations in access to resources and job opportunities, and lower bargaining power), and the current period is in an agriculturally slack season (subround 3—January through March—is largely a slack period in most parts of West Bengal).

An unexpected finding is the highly significant positive coefficient of the variable GROWTH[10] in table 8.3. *Other things remaining the same, the probability of an agricultural-labor household's sliding below the poverty line seems to be higher if it is in a district where agricultural production has grown at a faster rate.* To what extent this result is owing to the various possible adverse effects of the agricultural growth process that I discussed earlier (particularly those effects owing to the crowding of the agricultural-labor market resulting from growth-induced tenant eviction and smaller farmers' being driven out of cultivation by the increased costliness and credit intensity of cultivation) is difficult to estimate. It is certainly consistent with (1) the trend increase in poverty in rural West Bengal, which has one of the better agricultural growth records in India in recent years; (2) the significant rise in the proportion of agricultural-labor households to total rural households; and (3) a finding in a survey of 110 randomly selected villages in West Bengal in 1975/76 (Bardhan and Rudra 1978) that 81 percent of the villages in the highly advanced areas reported an increase in tenant eviction, compared with 19 percent in backward areas.

An alternative explanation of the relation between growth and poverty could be associated, as Srinivasan has pointed out, with the usual problem of deriving time-series conclusions from cross-sectional data. If the faster-growing districts in West Bengal also happened to be the ones with above-average poverty in the initial year and if their growth was not sufficient to offset those initial conditions, one could arrive at a relation such as ours. While this is technically possible, empirically it is a very unlikely explanation. Looking at the district data, it is clear that the growth rate has been faster in those districts (including the Intensive Agricultural District Program [IADP] districts) that were relatively better off right from the beginning (i.e., in the early sixties).

Table 8.4 presents results of an ordinary-least-squares (OLS) analysis of the variations in PCEXPR in the same agricultural-labor households in West Bengal. Results are similar to those of the logit analysis,[11] except that two variables, PUBWORKM and SBRND3, which were not statistically significant in the latter, are now quite significant in the OLS analysis. Again, the variable GROWTH seems to have a highly significant association with *lower* levels of living in the agricultural-labor household, other things remaining the same.

For the primarily-cultivator households in West Bengal in 1977/78, the mean value of PCEXPR is Rs. 20.59, with a standard deviation of Rs. 13.87. Table 8.5 presents the results of a logit analysis of the probability that a primarily-cultivator household falls below our poverty line. Most of the explanatory variables are similar to those in table 8.3, except for the following: there are now two irrigation variables, one for the percentage of the household cultivated land that is irrigated (IRRCULT) and one for

Table 8.4. Linear Regression Analysis of Determinants of Per Capita Monthly Expenditure (at 1960 Prices) of Agricultural-Labor Households in Rural West Bengal, 1977/78

Explanatory Variable	Regression Coefficient	Standard Error	Significant at Percentage Level
1. CULTIVAT	1.9011	0.2294	0.0%
2. NDEP	−1.0305	0.0641	0.0
3. EDM	2.3801	0.4123	0.0
4. NFM	2.3575	0.4689	0.0
5. DIST	−0.0183	0.0063	0.4
6. VILIRR	0.4429	0.1152	0.0
7. VWAGEM	0.7900	0.1008	0.0
8. PUBWORKM	1.2075	0.5360	2.4
9. SBRND3	−0.6449	0.2587	1.3
10. SCHCASTE	−0.7436	0.2499	0.3
11. RAIN	0.6028	0.1810	0.1
12. NHA	0.1227	0.0155	0.0
13. GROWTH	−0.7602	0.1715	0.0
Constant term	9.8718	1.7585	0.0

Note: R^2 = 0.2013; F = 29.5; number of observations = 2,127; mean (PCE×PR) = Rs. 12.54; standard deviation = Rs. 5.66.

the proportion of the village cultivated area that is irrigated by canals and tubewells (CTIRRP), which are less dependent on the vagaries of local rainfall than most other irrigation sources; a dummy variable to represent households belonging to scheduled tribes (SCHTRIBE); and a variable to represent the population of the village (VPOP).[12] I have dropped the village wage and public works variables, VWAGEM and PUBWORKM, which are less relevant for primarily-cultivator households.

All the variables that appear in both table 8.3 and table 8.5 have highly significant coefficients with similar signs. Note that the quadratic term, (CULTIVAT)², has a significant positive association with the probability of poverty, while CULTIVAT itself has a negative coefficient. This may imply that even though a larger amount of land to cultivate provides more steady income and better access to other resources, a point may be reached at which larger size may have a negative effect on productivity, all other factors remaining the same. This is much discussed in the size-and-productivity literature. As expected, IRRCULT and CTIRRP and the busy agricultural season of October–December (SBRND2) have a negative association with the probability of poverty, while in the slack season of April–June (SBRND4) and with the household belonging to a scheduled tribe (SCHTRIBE), poverty is more likely. What sign to expect for the coefficient of VPOP is not clear: a higher density may

Table 8.5. Logit Analysis of the Probability of a Primarily-Cultivator Household's Falling below the Poverty Line in Rural West Bengal, 1977/78

Explanatory Variable	Estimated Coefficient	Standard Error
1. CULTIVAT*	−0.3745	0.0406
2. (CULTIVAT)²*	0.0072	0.0018
3. Percentage of household cultivated and irrigated (IRRCULT)	−0.1889	0.1774
4. NDEP*	0.2306	0.0248
5. EDM*	−0.6629	0.0950
6. NFM	−0.4303	0.2266
7. DIST*	0.0118	0.0033
8. Proportion of total cultivated area in the village irrigated by water from canals and tube wells (CTIRRP)*	−0.6456	0.2373
9. Dummy for October–December quarter (SBRND2)	−0.0903	0.1485
10. Dummy for April–June quarter (SBRND4)	0.2233	0.1510
11. SCHCASTE*	0.7687	0.1304
12. Dummy for household belonging to scheduled tribe(SCHTRIBE)*	0.7246	0.2404
13. Population size of village in thousands (VPOP)	0.0211	0.0113
14. RAIN*	−0.1720	0.0791
15. NHA*	−0.0566	0.0073
16. GROWTH*	0.4113	0.0879

Note: Likelihood ratio index = 0.2290; number of observations = 2,041. Apart from the variables already introduced in table 8.2, the new variables are IRRCULT, SCHTRIBE, SBRND2, SBRND4, VPOP, and CTIRRP; of these the first four are derived from Government of India, Department of Statistics, National Sample Survey Organisation (1981b), and the last two from Government of India, Registrar General (1971). Again, the variables marked by an asterisk are significant at less than 5 percent level.

lower per capita income, other things remaining the same; on the other hand, a larger population may also be associated with more commercialization and nonagricultural opportunities, which lower the likelihood of poverty. In table 8.5, VPOP has a positive but insignificant association with poverty. Apart from VPOP, the coefficients of IRRCULT, SBRND2, and SBRND4 are not statistically significant; all the other variables are significant at less than the 5 percent level. Again GROWTH is very significantly associated with the likelihood of poverty. What I have said about the possible growth-induced mechanisms of pauperization of small farmers may be relevant for primarily-cultivator households.

Table 8.6 presents the corresponding OLS analysis of variations in PCEXPR in primarily-cultivator households. Results are similar to those of the logit analysis, except that IRRCULT is now highly significant,

Table 8.6. Linear Regression Analysis of Determinants of Per Capita Monthly Expenditure (at 1960 Prices) of Primarily-Cultivator Households in Rural West Bengal, 1977/78

Explanatory Variable	Regression Coefficient	Standard Error	Significant at Percentage Level
1. CULTIVAT	1.6971	0.1837	0.0%
2. (CULTIVAT)²	−0.0283	0.0081	0.1
3. IRRCULT	3.6871	0.9377	0.0
4. NDEP	−1.2679	0.1204	0.0
5. EDM	2.9100	0.3719	0.0
6. NFM	1.1396	0.9183	21.5
7. DIST	−0.0486	0.0176	0.6
8. CTIRRP	3.7141	1.1369	0.1
9. SBRND2	0.6574	0.6627	32.1
10. SBRND4	−0.7444	0.6957	28.5
11. SCHCASTE	−1.8965	0.6905	0.6
12. SCHTRIBE	−3.9474	1.3220	0.3
13. VPOP	0.1063	0.0627	9.1
14. RAIN	0.2726	0.4478	54.3
15. NHA	0.2053	0.0358	0.0
16. GROWTH	−1.3232	0.4668	0.5
Constant term	17.2501	1.3059	0.0

Note: $R^2 = 0.2027$; $F = 34.3$; number of observations = 2,041; mean (PCEXPR) = Rs. 20.59; standard deviation = Rs. 13.87

while NFM and RAIN are no longer statistically significant (although the coefficients of all of these have similar signs, as before). VPOP is now marginally significant but with an opposite sign. Our expectation for the sign of the coefficient of this variable is, in any case, rather ambiguous. Again, the variable GROWTH has a highly significant association with a lower level of living in the cultivator households, other things remaining the same.

The next level of disaggregation covers most of rural India. The NSS sample design divides the rural area of the country into sixty-six agricultural regions,[13] grouping within each state (or union territory) districts having similar crop patterns and population densities. On the average, each region includes 4 or 5 homogeneous districts. There were sufficient data for all subsequent variables for only 55 regions.[14]

A major problem of analyzing variations in poverty at the regional level is the lack of regional data on distribution of consumer expenditure and a consumer price index for the rural poor. Thus, I used two alternative surrogate indicators of poverty, the per capita monthly expenditure level of the noncultivating-wage-earner households (estimated from NSS 25th Round data on the "weaker sections" of the rural population [see

Government of India, Department of Statistics, National Sample Survey Organisation n.d.])[15] and the proportion of rural households that were poor in terms of the value of assets owned (estimated for the All India Debt and Investment Survey of the Reserve Bank of India [see Reserve Bank of India 1972]).

I obtained the expenditure level at 1960/61 prices[16] by deflating the per capita monthly expenditure of noncultivating-wage-earner households in each region in 1970/71 by the consumer price index for agricultural laborers (for the state as a whole). For the 55 regions, the mean value was Rs. 14.84, with a standard deviation of Rs. 3.68. Table 8.7 presents the results of a linear regression analysis of the regional variations in per capita monthly expenditure of noncultivating-wage-earner households (EXPWR). As expected, it is higher in regions with better rainfall, more irrigation, greater use of wells as a source of irrigation (possibly indicating the productivity impact of private control of irrigation), lower density of population (usually associated with less crowding in the rural labor market), a greater proportion of workers in manufacturing (indicating alternative opportunities for farm workers), and a smaller proportion of scheduled-caste and scheduled-tribe households (suffering from special social disadvantages in access to opportunities).

Unlike in West Bengal, GROWTH, the rate of growth of crop production in the region, seems to have a positive impact on the level of living of the wage-earning households. However, one should also note the *negative* coefficient of PUMHA, the number of oil engines and electric pump sets per hectare of cropped area in a region. This may indicate possible adverse effects associated with certain *types* of growth.[17] The proportional importance of large farmers in the region also has a negative effect, as indicated by the negative coefficient of LFARMP.[18] Agricultural growth in general seems to be helpful, but large-farmer-dominated growth dependent on private ownership of modern equipment may not be.[19]

This is confirmed also by the results of table 8.8, which uses my alternative surrogate variable for poverty, ASTPOOR, the proportion of rural households in each region that are poor in terms of the value of assets owned. The usefulness of this variable may be limited, since poverty is usually defined in terms of consumption, not wealth, and I do not have state-level price indices that reflect variations in asset prices. But since I have defined the asset-poor to be those households that have Rs. 1,000 or less in assets, I have probably captured at least the poorest households in each region. Only the lowest 18 percent of households in rural India had assets of Rs. 1,000 or less on 30 June 1971. Table 8.8 indicates that the proportion of asset-poor is lowest in better-irrigated (particularly well-irrigated) and high-growth regions and in regions where the scheduled-caste households make up the lower percentage of total

Table 8.7. Linear Regression Analysis of Determinants of Per Capita Monthly Expenditure (at 1960/61 Prices) of Noncultivating-Wage-Earner Households in 55 Regions in Rural India, 1970/71

Explanatory Variable	Regression Coefficient	Standard Error	Significant at Percentage Level
1. Annual normal rainfall in the region in meters (NRAIN)	2.0369	0.7005	0.6%
2. Proportion of area irrigated (IRRP)	0.1058	0.0365	0.6
3. Area irrigated from wells as a proportion of total area irrigated (WELLIRR)	0.0442	0.0187	2.3
4. Average annual rate of growth of agricultural output (GROWTH)	0.4896	0.1436	0.1
5. Electric pump sets and oil engines used per hectare of cropped area (PUMHA)	−18.4191	10.9018	9.8
6. Large-farmer households as a proportion of total rural households (LFARMP)	−0.0921	0.0440	4.2
7. Density of population per square kilometer (DENS)	−0.0207	0.0041	0.0
8. Proportion of (male) population belonging to scheduled castes (MSCHCASTE)	−0.1045	0.0567	7.2
9. Proportion of (male) population belonging to scheduled tribes (MSCHTRIBE)	−0.1051	0.0290	0.1
10. Proportion of working population in the region in manufacturing, repairing, and services (MFGP)	0.1111	0.0864	20.5
Constant term	15.7150	1.9398	0.0

Note: $R^2 = 0.6207$; $F = 7.2$; number of observations = 55; mean (EXPWR) = Rs. 14.84; standard deviation = Rs. 3.68. The dependent variable (EXPWR) is taken from Government of India, Department of Statistics, National Sample Survey Organisation (n.d.), for each region, and the deflator is the agricultural-labor consumer price index for the state where the region is located. The region-level estimates for NRAIN and WELLIRR were worked out after taking simple averages of district-level data in Government of India, All States (1970/71). IRRP for each region is the area of owned irrigated land as a percentage of total owned land as of 30 June 1971, as reported in Reserve Bank of India (1972). From the same source I have taken LFARMP, the proportion of total rural households operating land above 7.5 acres. The region-level estimate of GROWTH has been computed after taking simple averages of district-level data on the annual compound growth rate of output of 19 major crops over the period 1962–65 to 1970–73, as given in Bhalla and Alagh (1979). PUMHA has been estimated by taking the data on electric pumps and oil engines from Government of India, Ministry of Food and Agriculture (1971) and using the Bhalla-Alagh estimates of area under 19 crops in each region. The data for DENS, MSCHCASTE, MSCHTRIBE, and MFGP are all from Government of India, Registrar General (1971).

Table 8.8. Linear Regression Analysis of the Proportional Importance of Asset-Poor Households in 54 Regions in Rural India, 1971

Explanatory Variable	Regression Coefficient	Standard Error	Significant at Percentage Level
1. IRRP	−0.1715	0.0881	5.8%
2. WELLIRR	−0.1342	0.0335	0.0
3. GROWTH	−1.9350	0.4086	0.0
4. PUMHA	137.0665	25.1567	0.0
5. MSCHCASTE	0.3734	0.1438	1.2
Constant Term	19.6031	2.5380	0.0

Source: The regionwise data are from Reserve Bank of India (1972).

Note: $R^2 = 0.5879$; $F = 13.7$; number of observations = 54; dependent variable = proportion of rural households in each region who possess assets of Rs. 1,000 or less, as of 30 June 1971 (ASTPOOR); mean = 18.32 percent; standard deviation = 10.28 percent.

households. Again, PUMHA, the number of oil engines and electric pump sets per hectare of cropped area, has a significant positive association with poverty.

Tables 8.9 and 8.10 present state-level data and regression results. The state-level estimates were taken directly from the NSS 26th Round for 1971/72, which defines poverty in terms of the proportion of rural households whose average calorie consumption, based on data on quantities of food consumed, falls below a calorie norm[20] of 2,700 *per consumer unit per day* (which comes to a norm of roughly 2,160 calories per capita per day).[21] This dependent variable I have called CALPOOR. Table 8.10 indicates that it is negatively associated with the value of agricultural production per male worker and positively associated with the concentration ratio of rural asset ownership and (weakly) with the consumer price index for agricultural laborers. In other words, there is less rural poverty in more productive regions but more in areas with more unequal distribution of asset ownership and higher consumer prices for the poor. It was not possible to try out other important technological, institutional, or demographic independent variables, since with data for only 15 states, the degrees of freedom are rather low.

Summing up the results of (1) the two time-point comparisons of annual wage income or poverty of agricultural-labor households, (2) the logit and OLS analyses of household-level cross-sectional data for about 550 NSS sample villages in West Bengal, (3) the OLS analysis of cross-sectional data for 55 regions covering most of rural India, and (4) the OLS analysis of cross-sectional data for 15 states, it seems possible to say that the evidence on trickle-down effects of growth on poverty are at best rather mixed and occasionally quite negative. Agricultural growth and

Table 8.9. Cross-sectional Data in India, by State, 1971/72

State	(1) Percentage of Rural Households Consuming below a Calorie Norm in 1971/72	(2) Average Value of Annual Agricultural Production per Male Agricultural Worker, in Rs., 1970/73	(3) Consumer Price Index for Agricultural Laborers in 1971/72 with 1960/61 as Base	(4) Concentration Ratio of Assets Owned by Rural Households on 30 June, 1971
Andhra Pradesh	54%	1,674	183	0.703
Assam	55	1,350	212	0.556
Bihar	51	861	207	0.672
Gujarat	45	2,091	183	0.634
Haryana	22	3,504	205	0.629
Karnataka	51	1,925	192	0.655
Kerala	74	2,349	211	0.661
Madhya Pradesh	37	1,656	208	0.589
Maharashtra	59	1,656	207	0.649
Orissa	57	1,445	223	0.598
Punjab	27	4,170	205	0.683
Rajasthan	38	1,677	176	0.559
Tamil Nadu	64	1,950	187	0.711
Uttar Pradesh	32	1,328	192	0.592
West Bengal	71	1,539	210	0.660

Note: The data in column 1 are from the NSS 26th Round estimates (see Government of India, Department of Statistics, National Sample Survey Organisation 1976), where the calories derived from food consumption were estimated from consumption quantity data and the calorie norm was taken at 2,700 calories *per consumer unit* per day (which comes to a norm of roughly 2,160 calories per capita per day). The data in column 2 are from Bhalla and Alagh (1979), and those for column 4 are estimated from Reserve Bank of India (1972). Since the consumer price index data in column 3 are not available separately for the Punjab and Haryana, the same figure has been used for both states.

productivity improvements in general tend to help raise incomes all around, but certain *types* of growth processes generate negative forces for the poor, particularly in an institutional setting of highly unequal distribution of assets and access to resources. To fully trace the specific impact of particular types of growth processes, one needs a sufficiently large number of intensive microstudies and time-series data from carefully monitored panels.

It is futile to attempt to settle the controversial issues of this literature at the level of aggregation on which most of the discussion has been conducted so far.

Table 8.10. Linear Regression Analysis of Determinants of the Percentage of Calorie-Poor Households in 16 States in Rural India, 1971/72

Explanatory Variable	Regression Coefficient	Standard Error	Significant at Percentage Level
1. Value of annual agricultural production per male agricultural worker in Rs., averaged over 1970–73 (OPL)	−0.0113	0.0039	1.4%
2. Consumer price index of agricultural laborers in 1971/72, with 1960/61 as base (ACPI)	0.3489	0.2374	17.0
3. Concentration ratio of assets owned by rural households on 30 June, 1971 (CONCASS)	168.7547	68.4289	3.1
Constant Term	−106.1175	67.6018	14.5

Note: $R^2 = 0.5357$; $F = 4.2$; number of observations = 15; dependent variable = percentage of rural households consuming below a calorie norm of 2,160 calories per capita per day on an average in 1971–72 (CALPOOR); mean (CALPOOR) = 49.13 percent; standard deviation = 15.47 percent.

Notes

The data processing for this paper was helped by Tom Paynter and Dilip Dutta and supported by a grant from the National Science Foundation. I am also grateful to M. L. Dantwala, A. K. Sen, and T. N. Srinivasan for comments on an earlier draft. Remaining errors are, no doubt, attributable to my obduracy.

1. See Bardhan (1970a, 1970b, 1973). In none of these papers did I suggest a *trend* rise in the percentage of rural poor. I only gave some evidence for a rise in poverty *over the sixties*, which has now been confirmed by Ahluwalia's time series. Even though my papers used only head-count estimates of the poor, the directional results were confirmed even with the use of the more appropriate Sen Index of poverty (Sen 1973).

2. This was also suggested in my analysis of the state-level poverty estimates in Bardhan (1970a, 1973).

3. Apart from this, an additional problem with the time-series data is changes in the coverage, concepts, and methods of estimation in NSS consumption data, which affect their comparability over time.

4. The year 1974/75 was not a good agricultural year. Nevertheless, between 1964/65 and 1974/75, net production of foodgrains rose by 20 percent, and the net domestic product from agriculture (at 1960/61 prices) rose by 11 percent.

5. The estimated total annual wage income excludes income from self-employment, which represents only a very small proportion of the total employment of the average agricultural-labor household.

6. This is the poverty line that I have used in earlier articles; Bardhan (1973) provides detailed justification for this line on the basis of nutritional norms. Sukhatme (1978) has since pointed to problems of assuming average nutritional

norms on account of interpersonal variability of nutritional needs and the existence of adaptive mechanisms over time. Sukhatme's critique of the poverty literature on this ground has, however, been seriously questioned in several articles in recent issues of the *Economic and Political Weekly*. In any case, for assessing the trickle-down effects of growth, a finding to the effect that the proportion of people whose incomes are inadequate for buying the *average* nutritional minimum for the group has increased in spite of growth is of considerable interest (see Sen 1980).

7. For a multiple-classification analysis of household per capita expenditure in terms of some characteristics of households and of the household head for rural Maharashtra and Gujarat on the basis of disaggregated NSS 1972/73 data see Visaria (1980).

8. I am grateful to V. M. Dandekar for access to the detailed household-level NSS data tapes for West Bengal.

9. Since in 1960 the cost of living in rural West Bengal was higher than that for rural India, this poverty line is in effect lower than the all-India poverty line of Rs. 15 at 1960 prices.

10. As for any possible multicollinearity problem, with GROWTH being correlated to other independent variables, let me note here that the correlation coefficients of GROWTH with VILIRR and NHA are significant but not very high—0.37 and 0.51, respectively; the correlation coefficient of GROWTH with VWAGEM is negative but not significant.

11. Since the dependent variable is now the level of per capita expenditure rather than the probability of poverty, the signs of the coefficients of all the variables are, of course, exactly reversed.

12. These last two variables, SCHTRIBE and VPOP, were also tried for the equations in tables 8.3 and 8.5, but they turned out to be highly insignificant.

13. This was the number of regions at the beginning of the 1970s; it has increased somewhat in recent years.

14. The excluded regions are: Manipur, Meghalaya, Nagaland, Tripura, Pondicherry, Goa, Daman, and Diu, Delhi, Himachal Pradesh, Chandigarh, and one (the mountainous) out of the three regions in Jammu and Kashmir.

15. I have not used the per capita monthly expenditure of the bottom decile of cultivator households in each region as an alternative indicator of poverty (even though data were available to me), because in different regions the bottom decile refers to different levels of living.

16. I should note here that use of this deflator ignores the problem of regionally different costs of living in 1960/61.

17. The correlation of PUMHA with the other irrigation variables is not high; in particular, the correlation coefficient between PUMHA and WELLIRR is only 0.27. So it seems that the positive coefficient of WELLIRR indicates more the effect of other kinds of wells, not necessarily fitted with pumps, which still predominate in the total number of wells. It is striking that in the whole of rural India the use of pump sets is heaviest in Tamil Nadu. It was with respect to a study of a Tamil Nadu district (North Arcot) that Chambers and Farmer (1977) noted the serious adverse effects of irrigation by privately owned pump sets, which lowered the water table for poorer farmers, sometimes driving their land out of irrigated cultivation.

18. Of course, regional variations in the quality of land make the uniform cutoff line of 7.5 acres for defining large farms very arbitrary, but since the effect of LFARMP is considered, after controlling for regional variations in some of the irrigation variables, the distortion introduced by this arbitrariness may not be large.

19. In a broadly similar interregional regression exercise, Rao et al. (chap. 9 in this volume) find that poverty is negatively associated with crop output growth rate and the irrigated percentage of land and positively associated with the proportion of scheduled castes and scheduled tribes and the consumption of fertilizers per hectare. Clearly, my results are consistent with theirs.

20. Apart from the problems raised by Sukhatme (1978), this all-India norm also overlooks the possible differences in minimum calorie requirements in different parts of India in view of differences in climatic conditions, average body weights, and so on.

21. This estimate of poverty has at least the advantage of bypassing the problem of defining an appropriate consumer price index to deflate expenditure data for the poor.

9 Infrastructural Development and Rural Poverty in India: A Cross-sectional Analysis

C. H. HANUMANTHA RAO, DEVENDRA B. GUPTA, and P. S. SHARMA

Our discussions with Dharm Narain for over two decades on the impact of infrastructural development on agricultural growth and rural poverty and inequality have resulted in the pursuit of a number of useful ideas. Here we present results from a study of the impact of selected infrastructural, institutional, and technological variables on rural poverty and inequality in consumer expenditure, based on 1972–73 data for 59 National Sample Survey (NSS) regions.

Recent studies on the extent and trend of poverty in India have been based on different methods and have not resulted in general agreement. Most relevant to the present study are those by Montek Ahluwalia (1978a) and Ashwani Saith (1981), which try to analyze rural poverty and its relation to agricultural performance. Ahluwalia deals primarily with trends in rural poverty from 1956/57 to 1973/74 and tries to explain them by agricultural performance as measured by agricultural net domestic product (ANDP) per person. He obtained his data from various NSS rounds. His work indicates no significant all-India trend, though he finds an inverse relation between the incidence of poverty and the change in agricultural output per head. State-level data do not show a consistent pattern.

On the contrary, Saith has found different results with "essentially the same set of data." Saith uses agricultural performance (in ANDP per person) and prices (the consumer price index for agricultural laborers, CPIAL) as well as the time variable t in his equation. The inclusion of price as an explanatory variable is justified by the "command" approach implied in Dharm Narain's work (Desai 1981). Saith's results show that the price variable is considerably more important than the production variable. In addition, he found that after price and production fluctuation effects were taken into account, the incidence of poverty increased over time. Unlike in Ahluwalia's study, agricultural performance only "partially" affected the incidence of poverty.

Lakdawala (1978) tried to connect the incidence of poverty in rural areas and agricultural performance through "employment" variables. His paper emphasizes the importance of understanding the mechanisms involved in the agricultural growth process.

The foregoing suggests that to explain poverty, not only growth of agricultural output but the factors that determine the pattern of that growth should be analyzed. The present study tries first to separate out the influence of institutional, infrastructural, and technological factors that seem to underlie agricultural performance and then to capture the effect of different variables by cross-sectional analysis of the NSS regions.

Data and Variables

Infrastructural development through public investment in irrigation, rural electrification, roads, and so on, is expected to distribute the gains from agricultural growth widely by providing opportunities to the less-developed regions and to small and marginal farmers. Public investment in canal irrigation, for example, can be expected to benefit farmers of all classes roughly in proportion to the size of their holdings. Because of the complementarity between public and private investments, public investments also reduce the cost of private investment for individual farmers and thus contribute to increasing private investments, even by the less-advantaged.

An outline of infrastructural, social, and institutional variables relating to rural poverty in India follows:

A. Institutional variables
   1. Scheduled-caste and scheduled-tribe population in rural areas, expressed as a percentage of the rural population (1971 census).
   2. Urban population related to total population (1971 census).
   3. Rural literacy, the number of literate and educated persons in the rural areas as a percentage of the total rural population (1971 census).
B. Infrastructural-technological variables
   1. Road density, total road mileage, including national highways, state highways, other Public Works Department roads, *Zila Parishad* roads, *Panchayat Samitis* and Village *Panchayat* roads, and project roads but excluding urban roads, for 1975/76. For each geographical area, road mileage is expressed as the total per 100 square kilometers.
   2. The gross irrigation ratio, the relation of the average gross irrigated area to the average gross cropped area during 1970/71–1972/73.
   3. The canal irrigation ratio, the area irrigated through canals expressed as a percentage of the total net irrigated area for 1972/73.

4. The proportion of villages electrified, derived by relating the number electrified to the total number on 31 March 1974.
5. Consumption of fertilizers per hectare, computed as the ratio of the fertilizer consumption to the gross cropped area in 1970/71–1972/73.
C. Variables pertaining to growth and productivity
   1. Crop output (percentage per annum), derived by relating the gross value of output of 19 major crops in 1970/71–1972/73 to the corresponding gross value of output of these crops in 1962/63–1964/65 and compounding annually.
   2. Productivity per hectare, obtained by dividing the gross value of output of 19 major crops in 1962/63–1964/65 by the cropped area in the same triennium.
   3. The consumer price index for agricultural laborers; since this index was not available at the regional level for 1972/73, state figures were used to represent the regions.
D. The poverty ratio, the dependent variable, broadly defined in two ways
   1. Calorie intake. Using the data collected under the 27th Round of the NSS and a calorie norm of 2,200 kilo-calories per capita per day, the percentage of persons in each region whose actual intake was less than or equal to the desired minimum was computed. Since the calorie intakes are presented in terms of averages for expenditure intervals, the number of people whose intake was less than or equal to the minimum was computed by linear interpolation.
   2. Consumer expenditure. Following Bardhan, the poverty ratio was derived on the basis of Rs. 15 per capita per month at the 1960/61 price level. The consumer price index for agricultural labor at 1972/73 prices was used to adjust for the price level. Since prices for the regional level were not available, state prices were used for regions within the states.

Using calorie intake as the basis for deriving the poverty ratio mitigates to some extent the problems connected with using prices as a deflator. Gini coefficient ratios pertaining to consumer expenditure were computed and used to assess the expenditure inequalities of regions and their relation to independent variables of the study as well as poverty ratios. All the variables defined above are at NSS regional levels. Poverty ratios are based on 1972/73 data or, if data for that year are not available, on data for as close to that year as possible.

FIELD OF INQUIRY

As mentioned above, the present paper covers 59 NSS regions (see app. 9.1 for definitions of these regions). To assess the impact of regional factors, we also have estimated the above equations for each of four broad geographical areas—the Hills, the Great Plains, the Deccan Plateau, and the Coastal Areas. The principal reason for doing this is that the level of infrastructure may have a different impact on poverty in some areas than it does in others. For example, the rainfed regions would require fewer irrigation facilities than the other regions.

Empirical Results: All India

The regression results shown in tables 9.1–9.3 are somewhat sensitive to the definition of poverty. For example, literacy turns out to be positive and significant when a calorie-intake definition of the poverty ratio is used, but it is negative and nonsignificant when the poverty ratio is based on per capita expenditure corrected with prices (table 9.1). Calorie-intake definitions of poverty abstract from price variations. But price changes result in shifts in consumption from one type of food to another. Indeed, the 26th Round results of the National Sample Survey indicate that some persons well below the poverty line have a calorie intake far above the minimum norm.

Two factors have to be borne in mind when interpreting the impact of rural literacy on the rural poverty ratio. First, the overall literacy rate is still very low, and the majority of the literate probably belong to the population above the poverty line who can afford to send their children to school. Second, education at the primary and secondary levels does not have a clear vocational bias. One cannot expect an immediate relation between literacy rate and income generation for the poverty population. A nonsignificant or even a positive relationship of this variable with the rural poverty ratio is not surprising.

The rural poverty ratio is greater in regions where the proportions of scheduled-caste and scheduled-tribe population and of agricultural labor are highest. Persons in these sections of the population generally lack assets and have poor access to resources and gainful opportunities. The rate of urbanization is negatively related to the rural poverty ratio. This may be owing to migration of the rural poor to urban areas because of better income-earning opportunities (Mohan 1982).

The development of irrigation and rural electrification seems to be associated with a lower poverty ratio (table 9.2). That irrigation, particularly canal irrigation, should result in the reduction of the rural poverty ratio is to be expected in view of the rise in employment and wage rates associated with such development. Also, the benefits from canal irrigation can be expected to be distributed widely among different classes of farmers. The negative sign of the variable representing the percentage of villages electrified, though not significant, reinforces the above inference in regard to the impact of irrigation *as such* on the rural poverty ratio.

Table 9.1. Regression Coefficients for the Rural Poverty Ratio (1972/73) and Selected Institutional (Independent) Variables: All India

Dependent Variable	Constant	Percent Scheduled-Caste and Scheduled-Tribe Population (X_2)	Rural Literacy Rate (X_4)	Percent Agricultural Labor (X_5)	Percent Urban Population (X_3)	$\bar{R}^2$
Rural poverty ratio (calorie intake)	1.01	0.1159* (1.88)	0.3258* (1.67)	0.2416** (2.01)	−0.2341 (−1.37)	0.2189
Rural poverty ratio (per capita expenditure corrected for prices)	1.68	0.0113 (0.25)	−0.1098 (−0.77)	0.2149** (2.4)	−0.2107* (−1.69)	0.0803

Note: The number of regions is 59. The equations are in log linear form. Figures in parentheses are *t* values.

* 10 percent level of significance

** 5 percent level of significance

Table 9.2. Regression Coefficients for the Rural Poverty Ratio (1972/73) and Selected Infrastructural-Technological Variables: All India

Dependent Variable	Constant	Gross Irrigation Ratio (X_7)	Fertilizer Consumption per Hectare (X_8)	Percent Villages Electrified (X_{10})	Canal Irrigation Ratio (X_{13})	Road Density (X_{17})	$\bar{R}^2$
Rural poverty ratio (calorie intake)	1.98	−0.4729*** (−4.24)	0.5696*** (4.53)	−0.1706 (−1.55)	−0.0738 (−1.63)	−0.0104 (−0.14)	0.2445
Rural poverty ratio (per capita expenditure corrected for prices)	1.54	−0.0728 (−0.82)	0.696 (0.70)	−0.0243 (−0.28)	−0.0079 (−0.22)	0.0644 (0.12)	−0.0403

Note: The equations are in log linear form. Figures in parentheses are *t* values.
*** 1 percent level of significance

One cannot overlook the high intercorrelation between irrigation variables and rural electrification ($r = 0.95$).

The relation between road density and the rural poverty ratio is not significant at the all-India level. The positive relation of the poverty ratio with fertilizer consumption is puzzling. It needs to be interpreted with considerable caution because the intercorrelation between fertilizer consumption and the gross-irrigation ratio and with rural electrification is as high as 0.97 and 0.98, respectively. Available empirical evidence indicates that the employment generated per unit of output from the use of fertilizers is lower than from irrigation and that the consumption of fertilizers has grown faster among large farms than among small and marginal farms (Rao 1975). There is no evidence, however, that the use of fertilizers in any region has been associated with a reduction in employment and wages or dispossession of small and marginal farmers.

Growth of agricultural output is associated with a lower rural poverty ratio under both definitions (table 9.3). This supports the view that agricultural growth *as such* contributes to the reduction of poverty by raising employment and wages and increasing output by the small-farm sector. Table 9.3 also indicates that the hectare productivity in the base period had a positive and significant relation with the poverty ratio across the regions in 1972/73. This finding is in line with the general observation that the areas of high productivity per hectare are characterized by high density and, therefore, greater poverty (Sundaram and Tendulkar 1982). Rural poverty defined in terms of calorie intake does not seem to bear a significant relation to either inequality in consumer expenditure or the consumer price index for agricultural workers. Where expenditure is deflated by the consumer price index across the regions, however, both coefficients are positive and significant. In interpreting these results, one needs to take into account the possibility of spurious correlation between errors in the variables.

Empirical Results: Regions

Although each NSS region is relatively homogeneous, the number of observations was limited—for example, only 9 in the Hills and 22 in the Deccan Plateau. Therefore, as expected, many of the regression coefficients are not statistically significant. Nevertheless, their signs are in the same direction as for all India.

Table 9.4 presents the results relating to infrastructural-technological variables at the regional level, with two definitions of the rural poverty ratio. As in the case of all-India results, increases in the irrigation ratio are associated with a reduced poverty ratio, although the coefficients are significant only in the Hills and the Coastal Plains. The canal irrigation and rural electrification ratios generally point in the same direction.

Table 9.3. Factors Affecting Rural Poverty: Regression Results, All India

Explanatory Variable	Dependent Variable: Rural Poverty Ratio (Calorie Intake)			Dependent Variable: Rural Poverty Ratio (Minimum Expenditure)		
	Constant	Regression Coefficient	$\bar{R}^2$	Constant	Regression Coefficient	$\bar{R}^2$
Group output growth rate (X_9)	1.5901	−0.0791*** (−3.36)	0.1506	1.5612	−0.0336* (−1.99)	0.0492
Per-person agricultural productivity (X_{11})	1.6578	−0.004 (−0.20)	−0.0168	1.5526	0.0082 (0.62)	−0.0108
Per-hectare agricultural productivity (X_{12})	1.6382	0.0011*** (5.95)	−0.0175	1.5468	0.0085 (0.69)	−0.0091
Gini coefficient of consumer expenditure (X_{14})	1.5375	−0.1858 (−0.33)	−0.0156	2.0752	0.8667** (2.40)	0.0761
Consumer price index for agricultural workers (X_{22})	2.1518	−0.2162 (−0.15)	−0.0171	−5.1151	2.85*** (3.16)	0.1338

Note: The equations are in log linear form. Figures in parentheses are *t* values.

   * 10 percent level of significance

  ** 5 percent level of significance

 *** 1 percent level of significance

Table 9.4. Regression Coefficients for Rural Poverty Ratios (1972/73) and Selected Infrastructural-Technological Variables: Regions

Dependent Variable	Constant	Gross Irrigation Ratio (X_7)	Fertilizer Consumption per Hectare (X_8)	Percent Villages Electrified (X_{10})	Canal Irrigation Ratio (X_{13})	Road Density (X_{17})	$\bar{R}^2$
Hills (9 regions)							
Rural poverty ratio (calorie intake)	2.11	-0.9936** (-2.57)	1.0899** (2.47)	-0.4927 (-0.86)	-0.0362 (-0.16)	0.0575 (0.17)	0.5709
Rural poverty ratio (per capita expenditure corrected for prices)	1.31	-0.4545 (-1.59)	0.535 (0.65)	0.7974 (1.91)	-0.1496 (-0.87)	-0.2807 (-1.14)	0.3685
Great Plains (15 regions)							
Rural poverty ratio (calorie intake)	1.95	-0.2788 (-0.54)	0.0098 (0.028)	-0.5572 (-1.65)	0.0545 (0.22)	0.3655 (1.39)	0.5212
Rural poverty ratio (per capita expenditure corrected for prices)	1.51	-0.278 (-0.42)	0.2129 (0.47)	-0.0307 (-0.07)	0.0042 (0.013)	0.1509 (0.45)	-0.2943
Deccan Plateau (22 regions)							
Rural poverty ratio (calorie intake)	0.41	-0.1386 (-0.75)	-0.5606 (-1.78)	0.5606** (2.34)	-0.0749 (-1.59)	0.8427** (2.69)	0.4866
Rural poverty ratio (per capita expenditure corrected for prices)	1.78	-0.0028 (-0.031)	-0.3928** (-2.55)	0.1255 (1.07)	-0.0163 (-0.71)	0.0639 (0.42)	0.5816
Coastal plains (13 regions)							
Rural poverty ratio (calorie intake)	1.62	-0.1014* (-1.97)	0.1603** (2.78)	-0.0373 (-0.63)	-0.0197 (-0.67)	0.129* (2.10)	0.6060
Rural poverty ratio (per capita expenditure corrected for prices)	1.28	0.0033 (0.020)	-0.0812 (-0.45)	0.0129 (0.071)	0.0632 (0.69)	0.1591 (0.83)	-0.3523

Note: The equations are in log linear form. Figures in parentheses are *t* values.
* 10 percent level of significance
** 5 percent level of significance
*** 1 percent level of significance

However, the two rural electrification coefficients that are statistically significant show positive signs. They relate to the Hills and the Deccan Plateau.

A decline in the poverty ratio normally occurs when irrigation facilities are installed, because the area can be sown more than once a year. With greater cropping intensity and higher yields per acre, employment per acre is significantly higher. Higher productivity—per acre as well as per capita—results in higher wage rates in irrigated regions (Mehra 1976).

Relations between poverty level and road density are positive in most cases, and the coefficients relating to the Deccan Plateau and the Coastal Plains are statistically significant. The effect of roads on poverty levels in the region is complex. While a developed road network would improve opportunities for people of the region to get fair prices for their produce, this could reduce supplies and push prices up in local areas. Mechanization of transport and of agriculture through introduction of tractors could adversely affect the landless agricultural labor and possibly small and marginal farmers. Roads also may help rich farmers more than small ones. On the other hand, by contributing to the modernization and growth of agriculture and facilitating the migration of labor, roads may reduce poverty.

The relation between road density and poverty in a cross-sectional framework for a large country like India is difficult to test. Road density—mileage per 100 square kilometers of area—would generally be greater in the densely populated plains, where there is more poverty. Nothing definite can be inferred until more information about land concentration and the intensity of transport is available.

The relation of the poverty ratio to fertilizer consumption also is complex. Consumption of fertilizers depends on the availability of irrigation facilities, as well as the responsiveness of farmers to the new technology. The regression coefficients for fertilizers in the Deccan Plateau are negative and significant, whereas those for the Hills and the Coastal Plains are positive and significant. The evidence from this study does not permit firm conclusions.

The relation of the growth rate of agricultural output to poverty is negative for both definitions of poverty and is statistically significant in the Coastal Plains and the Deccan Plateau. Similarly, an increase in agricultural productivity per person is associated with a reduction in the poverty ratio except in the Coastal Plains, where both are positively associated (calorie-intake definition). The position with regard to per-hectare agricultural productivity is somewhat different. The relation to the poverty ratio (calorie-intake definition) seems to be positive in all regions except the Hills and is statistically significant in the Coastal Plains (table 9.5).

The relation between poverty and employment rates indicates that except in the Hill region, where out-migration of labor and remittance

Table 9.5. Factors Affecting Rural Poverty: Regression Results, Regions

Explanatory Variable	Dependent Variable: Rural Poverty Ratio (Calorie Intake)			Dependent Variable: Rural Poverty Ratio (Minimum Expenditure)		
	Constant	Regression Coefficient	$\bar{R}^2$	Constant	Regression Coefficient	$\bar{R}^2$
Hills (9 regions)						
Crop-output growth rate (X_9)	1.42	-0.082 (-0.94)	-0.02	1.46	-0.0178 (-0.31)	-0.147
Per capita agricultural productivity (X_{11})	1.54	-0.0388 (-0.86)	-0.087	1.49	-0.0084 (-0.29)	-0.151
Per-hectare agricultural productivity (X_{12})	1.55	-0.339 (-0.84)	-0.043	1.49	-0.0071 (-0.28)	-0.152
Great Plains (15 regions)						
Crop-output growth rate (X_9)	1.72	-0.563*** (-3.25)	0.3896	1.66	-0.2342 (-1.4)	0.061
Per capita agricultural productivity (X_{11})	7.25	-1.317*** (-3.28)	0.3944	2.69	-0.2596 (-06366)	-0.041
Per-hectare agricultural productivity (X_{12})	-0.83	0.4643 (1.05)	0.0066	-0.29	0.3747 (1.09)	0.013
Deccan Plateau (22 regions)						
Crop-output growth rate (X_9)	1.61	-0.088*** (-3.17)	0.3113	1.62	-0.039** (-2.39)	0.191
Per capita agricultural productivity (X_{11})	2.47	-0.173 (-0.24)	-0.0494	2.43	-0.173 (-0.45)	-0.042
Per-hectare agricultural productivity (X_{12})	-1.44	0.6463 (1.67)	0.0824	2.41	-0.1516 (-0.68)	-0.027
Coastal Plains (13 regions)						
Crop-output growth rate (X_9)	1.83	0.0082 (0.50)	-0.061	1.52	-0.0272 (-1.03)	0.005
Per capita agricultural productivity (X_{11})	1.73	0.0221 (1.75)	0.137	1.57	-0.0079 (-0.34)	-0.073
Per-hectare agricultural productivity (X_{12})	1.71	0.0246** (2.26)	0.241	1.25	-0.0015 (-0.067)	-0.083

Note: The equations are in log linear form. Figures in parentheses are t values.
** 5 percent level of significance
*** 1 percent level of significance

Table 9.6. Rural Poverty and Unemployment in India, by Geographical Area

Dependent Variable	Overall	Hills	Great Plains	Deccan Plateau	Coastal Plains
Rural poverty ratio (calorie intake)	−0.00008 (−1.00)	−0.0440 (−1.6)	0.0421* (2.31)	0.0155 (1.50)	0.0059 (1.66)
Rural poverty ratio (per capita expenditure corrected for prices)	0.0088* (1.78)	0.0054 (0.28)	0.0267* (1.78)	−0.0042 (−0.57)	0.0106* (1.79)

Note: The equations are in log linear form. Figures in parentheses are *t* values.
* Significant at least at the 10 percent level

income are probably more important, high unemployment would be generally associated with high poverty levels (table 9.6).

Conclusion

The relations between various infrastructural variables and poverty levels are complex. Canal irrigation facilities tend to reduce poverty levels, and rural electrification appears to be a useful means of dealing with poverty problems. The effects for roads and fertilizer use are not conclusive and need further investigation. The evidence presented does not, however, refute the view that opening up of areas through roads and the use of fertilizers contribute to raising employment and wages. The real incomes of the poor would increase, despite the possibility of higher prices of essential commodities in certain situations.

Both poverty and inequality in consumer expenditure are found to rise with the increase in the proportion of agricultural labor and of population belonging to scheduled castes and scheduled tribes. Clearly, both of these groups need to be given special emphasis in any antipoverty program.

Our analysis implies that higher prices lead to higher poverty by depressing purchasing power and altering the patterns of consumption. Also, regions with high growth rates in agriculture and high agricultural output per person have a low poverty ratio. Productivity per hectare, on the other hand, generally is positively related to rural poverty.

Notes

The authors thank Sunil Bhargava for building regional-level estimates of various indicators and K. K. Nagar, D. T. Bhavani, M. Kannan, and S. J. Savanur for computer programming and analysis. The authors are indebted to John Mellor for his helpful comments and suggestions on the original draft.

Appendix 9.1. Geographical Coverage of Fifty-nine National Sample Survey Regions

State	Region
A. Hills	
1. Assam	Hills
2. Himachal Pradesh	Himachal Pradesh
3. Jammu and Kashmir	Mountainous outer hills
4. Jammu and Kashmir	Jhelum Valley
5. Manipur	Hills
6. Meghalaya	Meghalaya
7. Tripura	Tripura
8. Uttar Pradesh	Himalayan
9. West Bengal	Himalayan
B. Great Plains	
1. Assam	Plains
2. Bihar	Northern
3. Bihar	Central
4. Haryana	Eastern
5. Haryana	Western
6. Punjab	Northern
7. Punjab	Southern
8. Rajasthan	Western
9. Rajasthan	Northeastern
10. Uttar Pradesh	Western
11. Uttar Pradesh	Central
12. Uttar Pradesh	Eastern
13. West Bengal	Eastern plains
14. West Bengal	Central plains
15. West Bengal	Western plains
C. Deccan Plateau	
1. Andhra Pradesh	Inland, northern
2. Andhra Pradesh	Inland, southern
3. Bihar	Southern
4. Madhya Pradesh	Inland, eastern
5. Madhya Pradesh	Eastern
6. Madhya Pradesh	Inland, western
7. Madhya Pradesh	Western
8. Madhya Pradesh	Northern
9. Maharashtra	Inland, western
10. Maharashtra	Inland, northern
11. Maharashtra	Inland, central
12. Maharashtra	Inland, eastern
13. Maharashtra	Eastern
14. Karnataka	Inland, eastern
15. Karnataka	Inland, southern
16. Karnataka	Inland, northern
17. Orissa	Southern
18. Orissa	Northern
19. Rajasthan	Southern

20. Rajasthan	Southeastern
21. Tamil Nadu	Inland
22. Uttar Pradesh	Southern
D. Coastal Areas	
1. Andhra Pradesh	Coastal
2. Gujarat	Eastern
3. Gujarat	Plains, northern
4. Gujarat	Plains, southern
5. Gujarat	Dry areas
6. Gujarat	Saurashtra
7. Kerala	Northern
8. Kerala	Southern
9. Maharashtra	Coastal
10. Mysore	Coastal ghats
11. Orissa	Coastal
12. Tamil Nadu	Coastal, northern
13. Tamil Nadu	Coastal, southern

Source: Government of India, Department of Statistics, National Sample Survey Organisation (1976).

Note: Districts included in the NSS regions are the ones listed in NSS publications.

Appendix 9.2. Correlation Matrix

	X_1	X_2	X_3	X_4	X_5	X_7	X_8	X_9	X_{10}	X_{11}	X_{12}	X_{13}	X_{14}	X_{17}	X_{19}	X_{22}
X_1																
X_2	0.126															
X_3	0.128	−0.172														
X_4	0.165	−0.101	0.525													
X_5	0.182	−0.074	0.507	0.955												
X_7	−0.080	−0.144	0.494	0.922	0.909											
X_8	0.061	−0.120	0.576	0.964	0.943	0.974										
X_9	−0.334	−0.119	0.382	0.713	0.652	0.832	0.788									
X_{10}	0.087	−0.130	0.554	0.979	0.960	0.954	0.975	0.752								
X_{11}	−0.165	−0.128	0.262	0.012	0.143	0.178	0.150	0.151	0.131							
X_{12}	0.309	−0.180	0.309	0.245	0.254	0.307	0.328	0.246	0.259	0.287						
X_{13}	−0.351	−0.257	−0.074	0.033	0.036	0.174	0.069	0.307	0.061	0.161	0.291					
X_{14}	−0.025	0.073	0.093	−0.067	0.045	−0.066	−0.045	−0.138	−0.040	0.290	0.240	−0.025				
X_{17}	0.310	−0.122	0.083	0.182	0.108	0.080	0.139	0.149	0.138	−0.130	0.615	0.188	0.166			
X_{19}	0.171	0.349	−0.186	−0.095	−0.034	−0.146	−0.116	−0.232	−0.101	0.002	0.044	−0.143	0.283	0.035		
X_{22}	−0.049	0.155	−0.247	−0.316	−0.259	−0.376	−0.366	−0.409	−0.346	0.116	−0.252	−0.120	0.369	−0.310	0.447	1.000

Note:

X_1 = Rural poverty ratio (calorie intake)
X_2 = Percent scheduled-caste and scheduled-tribe population
X_3 = Percent urban population
X_4 = Rural literacy rate
X_5 = Percent agricultural labor
X_7 = Gross irrigation ratio
X_8 = Fertilizer consumption per hectare
X_9 = Crop-output growth rate per annum

X_{10} = Percent villages electrified
X_{11} = Per capita agricultural productivity
X_{12} = Per-hectare agricultural productivity
X_{13} = Canal irrigation ratio
X_{14} = Gini coefficient in consumer expenditure
X_{17} = Road density
X_{19} = Rural poverty ratio (per capita expenditure corrected for prices)
X_{22} = Consumer price index for agricultural workers

10 Technology, Growth, and Equity in Agriculture

M. L. DANTWALA

Dharm Narain's (1965) interest in agricultural prices predates his appointment as chairman of the Agricultural Prices Commission. But it probably was his involvement in the determination of agricultural prices for the Indian government's price policy that revealed to him the critical relevance of foodgrains prices to the incidence of poverty. It is therefore not surprising that at the first opportunity, which the International Food Policy Research Institute provided, he put his hunches and intuitive insights to rigorous statistical analysis. I, too, had speculated on this relationship and in a freewheeling mood had characterized lowering of food prices as "instant socialism," transferring, as it does, real income from surplus producers to poor consumers. Thus, apart from mutual affection, this theme of prices and poverty led to our academic affinity.

This paper examines the impact of the new technology associated with high-yield varieties (HYVs) of seeds on agricultural growth and food production. If food prices are to be kept low without becoming unremunerative to producers, a technology that induces higher returns to inputs like irrigation and fertilizers must be used. This is precisely what the HYVs did.

India's agricultural performance since independence, and particularly since the introduction of HYVs, has been faulted on the following grounds:

1. The growth of agricultural production has been unimpressive. Foodgrain production has barely kept ahead of population growth, and per capita availability has remained stagnant.

2. Growth has been uneven. Since technology associated with HYVs favored better-endowed regions and large farmers, interregional and interclass disparities have widened.

3. Agricultural development has failed to alleviate rural poverty and unemployment, and both probably have intensified.

This paper examines whether preoccupation with technology was responsible for the blemishes in agriculture's performance and whether more attention to "institutional" change would have had better results. Or to put it differently, did agricultural development sacrifice equity to growth?

No single sector of the economy can fulfill all development objectives. Other sectors have to play supporting roles. Blame for failure should not be placed on any single sector. For example, a working group headed by Sukhomoy Chakravarty (ICSSR 1980, 5) stated that a 2.7 percent per annum growth rate of agricultural output between 1949/50 and 1973/74 was impressive compared with the secular rate of some developed countries or with the Indian economy's virtual stagnation during the first half of this century. Net domestic production of foodgrains nearly doubled between 1951 and 1971. But per capita availability from domestic production changed little because of population growth. Had the population growth rate expected in the First Five Year Plan been achieved, the nutritional level of India's population would have risen.

Similarly, the ICSSR group reported that the proportion of the labor force engaged in agriculture remained at over 72 percent of the country's total throughout the period of planning (ibid., 17). While the number of workers in agriculture (including animal husbandry, fishery, and forestry) increased by 64 percent between 1951 and 1971,[1] the cropped area increased by only 26 percent and per capita crop land dropped from 0.33 hectare to 0.25. The average size of an operational holding declined from 2.30 hectares in 1970/71 to 2.0 hectares 6 years later. A much faster decline in operational holdings is in prospect, since the labor force is likely to increase more than either the net or the gross cropped area. Noting that the number of agricultural-labor households increased from 15.4 million in 1964/65 to 20.77 million in 1974/75, the ICSSR report stated: "When this feature is read in conjunction with significant increase in the proportion of small owners and their declining position in per capita land, *one notices an unmistakable trend towards gradual proletarianisation of the agricultural economy*" (ibid., 39; emphasis added).

Agricultural strategy cannot be blamed for this progressive shrinkage in per capita crop land and the bulge in landlessness. The slow growth of the nonagricultural sector failed to relieve the population pressure on the land. Historically, the process of development has meant a growing absorption of the labor force from the primary sector by the secondary and tertiary sectors. The Second Five Year Plan (1956-61) had envisaged that the proportion of the labor force in agriculture would be lowered from 70 percent at that time to 60 percent over a 20-year period. This, however, did not happen.

In contrast, in Japan the total number of farm households remained remarkably stable—5.52 million in 1974, 5.49 million in 1939, and 5.51

million in 1908. Thanks to rapid industrialization, the number of permanent agricultural laborers *declined* from 1 million in the mid-Meiji period to 380,000 in 1920 and 165,000 in 1941 (Ishikawa 1981).

Production

Although the ICSSR working group considered the 2.7 percent growth rate of agricultural production from 1949/50 to 1973/74 impressive, it also observed that growth was accompanied by increasing instability and a slackening of agricultural income growth since the early sixties.

Studies bearing on the stability of agricultural production and its relation to the new technology show mixed results. Sarma, Roy, and George (1979) observed that the coefficient of variation in aggregate foodgrain production decreased from 0.14 in 1949/50–1964/65 to 0.08 in 1967/68–1976/77, the post-HYVs period. *The Economic Survey, 1981–82* seems to confirm this.[2] However, studies by Mehra (1981) and Hazell (1982) reach a contrary conclusion. Mehra attributes most of the variation to fluctuations in yield. In his foreword to this study, John Mellor suggests that "there may well be a *causal relationship* between the observed instability and rapid application of new food production technologies," since the standard deviation for nonfoodgrain crops did not increase. On the other hand, Mehra observed that "wheat and rice show only a small increase in absolute yield variability." These are the crops on which use of the new technology has been widespread. In the Punjab, where the use of tube wells has increased dramatically, the yield variability of all of the six crops examined remained constant or declined, although HYVs were used extensively.

Hazell's study (1982) confirms that the coefficient of variation of total cereal production increased from 4.03 percent during 1954/55–1964/65 to 5.85 percent during 1967/68–1977/78. He found "enormous variability in production risks between crops and states." The increase in risk was least for wheat (a 2.1 percent increase in the coefficient of variation) and highest for bajra (225.2 percent). Among the states, production variability decreased in the Punjab (– 30.3 percent) and Bihar (– 21.1 percent), and changes were marginal in Uttar Pradesh and Madhya Pradesh. All the other states showed increases. For all India the coefficient of variation in total cereal output increased 45.2 percent, but the yield increased by only 20.4 percent.

Hazell rejects Mehra's hypothesis of a causal link between the new seed-cum-fertilizer technology and increased production and yield instability. According to his findings, only part of the increases in yield variances might be attributed to the widespread adoption of improved seed-cum-fertilizer technologies since the mid-1960s. Other important sources of increased production have been more positive correlations between the yield fluctuations of different crops in the same and in different states and an increase in the variability of crop areas sown, which is itself now more positively correlated with yields. These fundamental shifts probably have less to do with the new technologies than with changes in weather patterns, the spatial allocation of cereal crops, and the more widespread development of irrigation.

The evidence for a slackening of the agricultural growth rate since the early sixties is far from conclusive, and various studies have not produced a consensus. However, it is clear that foodgrain production has fluctuated sharply in recent years, rising from 111 million tons in 1976/77 to 126 in 1977/78 to 132 million tons in 1978/79. It then fell disastrously to 110 million tons in 1979/80 but jumped to 130 million tons in 1980/81. Between 1978/79 and 1981/82—both years of good monsoons—foodgrain production increased by no more than 1.2 million tons. Although past performance belies a prophecy of catastrophe, it must not induce complacency, particularly in view of the fact that the nutritional requirements of the vast number of people living below the poverty line have yet to be met. There can be no doubt that agricultural production, particularly of pulses and oilseeds, has to grow much faster over the coming decade if it is to wipe out the nutritional gap and supply the raw materials needed by industry.

Disparities

The unevenness of agricultural growth is a major problem. The Jawaharlal Nehru University-Perspective Planning Division (JNU-PPD) study (Bhalla and Alagh 1979) revealed vast differences in yields across the country. Of 282 districts studied, 69 accounted for 20.5 percent of cultivated area in 1970/73 but contributed 36.4 percent of the national output. At the other extreme, 83 accounted for 31.74 percent of total cultivated area but produced only 15.68 percent total output. During the period 1962/65–1970/73, output grew from 4.5 to 7.5 percent in 48 districts, from 1.5 to 4.5 percent in 102 districts, and from 0.0 to 1.5 percent in 62. The remaining 70 districts had growth rates of from − 1.5 to − 3.0 percent and covered more than a quarter of the cultivated area.

A noteworthy feature of the 1962/65–1970/73 period, however, is a decline in the number of low-productivity districts and in the area covered by them, the number dropping from 106 to 85 and the area, from 39.5 percent to 31.36 percent.

Certain patterns emerge from the JNU-PPD study. First, areas with high agricultural productivity levels are significantly associated with areas of high rainfall and assured irrigation. The opposite is the case in areas where the productivity is lowest. Similarly, high rates of growth are very positively associated with high productivity levels and/or increased irrigation. Negative rates have been recorded in the central and southern dry parts of India.

The JNU-PPD study has identified 49 districts that had a negative to 1.5 percent growth rate between 1962/63 and 1970/73 and productivity of less than Rs. 700 per hectare at the 1970/73 yield level. A majority of these were either drought-prone or preponderantly tribal. While every effort should be made to upgrade their agricultural potential, research should ascertain the comparative cost of alternative development.

Of the approximately 142 million hectares of land cultivated every year, 104 million hectares have a mean rainfall ranging from about 350–1,400 mm. Most of the region is semiarid, but a substantial area in Rajasthan, Gujarat, and between Sholapur in Maharashtra and Anantpur in Andhra Pradesh is arid, with rainfall of 500 mm. or less falling in just one or two months. The soils are also unresponsive. It is in this area that research and extension need to be concentrated. Fortunately, the endeavors of the International Crops Research Institute for the Semi-Arid Tropics (ICRISAT) are beginning to yield promising results. According to Swindale (1981), director general of ICRISAT, "It is not difficult to believe that the low yields (below 800 kg./ha. in the rainfed region) can be increased by 50 to 100 percent, with the technologies that exist." Results from five separate experiments at ICRISAT over a four-year period are highly promising. Use of improved seeds and fertilizers with improved management, not beyond the capability of an average farmer, increased gross returns by Rs. 3,086 per hectare. Average added costs amounted to Rs. 327, yielding a benefit-cost ratio of 9.4. The use of supplementary water increased profits by an additional Rs. 570. The technology is bullock-powered and based upon the concept of a small watershed as the basis of the resource management unit. Pilot-scale testing is being done in farmers' fields. ICRISAT has demonstrated that rainfed areas "can be major contributors to growth, and to *increasing employment and to the rapid reduction of rural poverty*" (ibid; emphasis added).

Such technology would necessitate some structural changes, as well as adjustments in farmers' aptitudes. To reap the full benefit from the ICRISAT technology, it is necessary to remove field boundaries to permit shaping the land into graded broadbeds and furrows to facilitate cultivation and surface drainage and building a common pond—within a small watershed of about 12 hectares. Traditionally, the farmers in this area do not cultivate during the rainy season and take only a *rabi* crop from the residual post-monsoon moisture. ICRISAT technology has demonstrated the feasibility of harvesting two crops, and the farmers will have to learn to cultivate during the *kharif* season.

The HYVs technology favors well-endowed regions, particularly in regard to rainfall and irrigation, and the better-off farmers who could bear—through their own resources or borrowing—the higher per-acre cost of cultivation and invest in fixed capital assets. Even in regions like the Punjab, where the yield per acre on small farms matched that on large farms, the larger land base of the latter resulted in inequality in income. Given this fact, the relevant questions to ask are, Did the Indian policy maker make a mistake in encouraging the adoption of this technology *at the time when he did so*? What options were available at that time? Would it have been possible to mitigate the adverse effects of this technology? Did the Government of India take adequate measures to do so?

For satisfactory answers, one has to review the situation between 1961 and 1965, when it was decided to adopt the HYVs and associated technology. For four consecutive years, from 1960/61 to 1963/64, foodgrain production remained stagnant at the start and then began to decline. The excellent harvest of 1964/65 revived hopes of resurgence, but the two subsequent droughts dashed them again. The situation was desperate. Per capita availability of foodgrains was diminishing, despite imports of four million to six million tons a year. The index of foodgrains prices rose by 30 percent in five years. Observers abroad questioned the country's ability to feed itself.

In such a situation, the first priority for the Indian policy maker was to grow more food as quickly as possible. Fortunately, around this time high-yield varieties of seed became available. No apology is needed for the government's decision to seize the opportunity offered by the HYVs to quickly and sharply augment food production. The wisdom of that decision was affirmed when two consecutive, unprecedented drought years—1965/66 and 1966/67—resulted in a drop of 17 million tons in foodgrain production. Without the green revolution, it would have been impossible to lift the production potential of Indian agriculture. There was no alternative production strategy available *at that time*. Even awareness of the likelihood that gains from the new technology would not be distributed equally would not have justified a decision to forgo adoption of the new technology, which offered an opportunity to avoid widening food scarcities and the humiliation of accepting the conditions of U.S. food aid.

If production and prices of foodgrains are considered in relation to poverty, the equity aspect of the adopted strategy was not as negative as has been made out. This is precisely what Dharm Narain was struggling to establish. Only a quick and substantial increase in foodgrain production or large imports could restrain the upsurge in prices occurring at that time. The production upsurge provided by the HYVs averted the crisis predicted by many.

In chapter 8 in this volume, Bardhan cites eight means by which the new strategy might have counteracted forces—such as high growth of output—that tend to improve the income of small farmers and wage laborers. I have examined some of these forces, relying mostly on empirical data for the Punjab, where the new strategy has been adopted most widely and most intensively.

1. The labor-displacing effect of adoption of machinery induced by the new technology. The Punjab probably makes the most extensive use of labor-saving machinery, especially tractors and pump sets. Yet there is clear evidence that labor input has increased phenomenally and that the wage rate in real terms has improved since the adoption of the new strategy. According to a recent study (BISR 1981), the "intensity of human labor used per unit of area was about 66 percent higher in 1976–77 than in 1967–68." The increase was shared by family members and hired laborers. Another significant development has been the diversification of the Punjab economy. Bardhan refers to the "displacement of village artisans." The Punjab is perhaps the only state in which the share of workers in the secondary and tertiary sectors, which was declining until 1971, increased, rising from 37.32 percent in 1971 to 40.85 percent in 1981. The productivity of these workers is much higher than that of the "displaced artisans." The adoption of labor-saving machinery is not an inevitable concomitant of the new strategy, though in certain situations it may become necessary in order to take full advantage of the new technology. In fact, expenditure on draught cattle is equal to 49 percent (61 percent in one region) of the total material cost of marginal farmers in the Punjab (Bhalla and Chadha 1981).

2. The increased profitability of self-cultivation by large landlords, leading to the eviction of tenants. Eviction of tenants is not peculiar to the post-HYVs-technology era. Probably a much larger number were evicted (legally and illegally) in the wake of early land reforms (the Zamindari Abolition) and other measures. It is alleged that even Operation Barga in West Bengal is inducing evictions. The increased profitability of self-cultivation under the new strategy offered great temptation to resume tenanted land and acquire land on lease from weak landholders. This resulted in a rather curious situation in which small farmers became "landlords" and large farmers became tenants. However, resumption of land and eviction of tenants does not appear to be universal. According to the Bhalla-Chadha study (1981), in the Punjab and Haryana the percentage of operated area leased in *declined* from 40 percent in 1953/54 to 26 percent in 1971/72, with all size classes sharing in the decline. Furthermore, the percentage of total area owned by large farmers (25 acres and above) declined from 37 percent in 1953/54 to 23 percent in 1971/72.

3. Increasing dependence of small farmers on purchased inputs. The

proposition that increasing dependence on purchased inputs has driven small farmers with limited access to resources and credit out of cultivation and into a crowded agricultural labor market needs to be examined from several angles. First, with the growth of population, small-farm families became marginal farmers, and marginal-farm families, practically landless laborers. To what extent the inability to purchase (modern) inputs drove them into the ranks of landless laborers is a matter of conjecture. In the Punjab, small farmers do not seem to have had much difficulty obtaining purchased inputs. Bhalla and Chadha show that differences by size class in total bio-chemical inputs per acre are not significant. As a result, for the Punjab as a whole, farm business income per acre does not show any significant size-class differences.

4. The preemption of underground water by large farmers. I share Bardhan's concern about the preemption of underground water by large farmers. More than a decade ago, I suggested socialization of underground water. The Gangetic belt has a large, unexploited underground water potential. Neither the rich nor the not-so-rich are exploiting it. Here is an area ripe for a multidisciplinary probe.

5. Poor maintenance of old irrigation channels. It is somewhat far-fetched to suggest, as Bardhan does, that the upsurge in tube-well irrigation, as an offshoot of HYVs technology, is responsible for the poor maintenance of old irrigation channels. Neglect of irrigation channels and the resulting waterlogging and salinity of soil is an old story. It is not fair to blame the new technology. As a matter of fact, the dependence of HYVs technology on controlled water input has enhanced awareness of the importance of water management. The HYVs have increased the profitability of all irrigation.

6. The decline in female participation in the agricultural work force. NSS data do not suggest a significant decline in female participation in the agricultural work force (Visaria 1984). In fact, Sheila Bhalla's study (1981) on Haryana reports that "the number of female labor supplied per household is relatively greater in the three more technologically advanced regions."

7. Pressure by the rural rich for higher administered prices of foodgrains. The rural rich (farmers) have persistently put pressure on policy makers to raise support and/or purchase prices not only of foodgrains but of all farm commodities. However, not all of the pressure comes from rural rich. The Communist party of India (CPM) and other leftist groups also support the agitation by farmers' organizations for higher administered prices. It is a matter of pride that Indian economists associated with the Agricultural Prices Commission did not succumb to the pressure and exercised a restraining influence. And at least a part of the credit for this goes to the polite stubbornness of scholars like our dear-departed friend

Dharm Narain, who served as the chairman of the Agricultural Prices Commission during the period when the pressures from the farm lobby were gathering force.

To repeat, the question that we are examining is not whether the proletarianization of Indian agriculture is accelerating—in all probability it is—but simply whether the new agricultural strategy is responsible. Every size class of landholders/operators has felt the pressure of population. This would be evident if studies of the process related to the same set of families over time. The stock profiles at different points of time do not fully reveal this position. For example, if the size distribution in, say, 1953/54 and 1971/72 indicates that the middle peasantry (with 5 to 25 acres), retained its share in total area, this does not mean that some families did not retrogress. Rather, it means that some families joined the ranks of "small" farmers, while some in the high size class joined the middle group. The stock profiles would not fully reveal this process, since they would show retrogression only at the top and the bottom. The top class becomes smaller, the bottom becomes larger, and the middle remains the same, gaining from the top and losing to the bottom.

Land Reforms and the Agrarian Structure

A comprehensive appraisal of the land-reform measures of the Government of India is beyond the scope of this paper. The following discussion is limited to the equity aspect of agrarian development.

With all of its limitations, the Zamindari Abolition was a bold land-reform measure. That the constitution was amended to protect the legislation from protracted litigation testifies to its genuineness. Absentee landlordism was abolished on over 173 million acres of land, though some large landlords retain large chunks of *sir*, or "self-cultivated" land. The tenancy legislation also was a progressive measure. While it led to resumption of land, resulting in authorized and unauthorized eviction of subtenants, it also conferred occupancy rights on the statutory tenants. The ceiling legislation, though seemingly progressive, was probably never meant to be implemented, at any rate not by the political leadership at the state level.

The literature on India's agrarian structure is replete with reference to the inequitable concentration of ownership and operational use of land. Some scholars are unable to resist the temptation to draw the Lorenz curve and prove inequity despite the fact that data on size distribution of owned and operated land do not take into account variations in productivity owing to soil and climatic conditions or availability of irrigation. This data deficiency cannot be wholly overcome, but more rigorous analysis of available data would reveal that the concentration ratio derived from the Lorenz curve greatly exaggerates the inequity.

The last available sample data on landholdings—for 1976/77—at first sight seem to confirm concentration. In that year, 2.44 million large operational holdings (10 hectares and above), or just 3 percent of the total, occupied 42.82 million hectares, or 26.3 percent of operated area. At the other extreme, 44.53 million marginal holdings (less than 1 hectare) constituted 54.6 percent of the total but operated only 17.50 million hectares, or less than 10 percent of the total (Government of India, Ministry of Agriculture and Rural Reconstruction 1981).

To determine whether such a distribution is inequitable, it is necessary to take into account the soil and climatic conditions under which the large holdings are operated. District information on this is not available, but the All India Agricultural Census for 1970/71 (Naidu 1975) provides circumstantial evidence that permits reasonable inferences.

In 1970/71, 2.6 million holdings, or 4 percent of the total, were of 10 hectares and above and covered 50 million hectares, or 31 percent of the total. Of these, 1.6 million holdings (58 percent), covering 22.74 million hectares (46 percent), were wholly unirrigated. This group held 23 percent of the wholly unirrigated area. By contrast, holdings of less than 1 hectare constituted 51 percent of the total but had only 9.5 percent of the wholly unirrigated land. The average size of holdings in the category of 10 hectares and above was 18.10 hectares, but the irrigated component was only 1.8 hectares. Its share in the net irrigated area was only 17.3 percent. Fifty-two percent of the wholly unirrigated land was in Rajasthan (13 percent), Gujarat (7.7 percent), Maharashtra (15.4 percent), and Madhya Pradesh (15.8 percent).

The All India Agricultural Census for 1970/71 makes the following observations: The largest spread of the unirrigated areas is in the western and central areas of the country, characterized by semiarid conditions. This vast region comprises the states of Rajasthan, Gujarat, Maharashtra, and Madhya Pradesh, along with the adjoining areas of the southern states of Karnataka and Andhra Pradesh. These states together account for 71 million hectares of unirrigated area, constituting about two-thirds of the country's total unirrigated area (Naidu 1975, 57). Of the 12.4 million hectares of land available for cultivation but not being cultivated, one-half (6.4 million hectares) are in large holdings (ibid., 40).

The above data clearly indicate that much of the land under large holdings is of poor quality or in a poor ecological environment. Though I support unequivocally a ceiling on excessive ownership of land, I would like to destroy the illusion that redistribution of land alone will make a significant contribution to the eradication of poverty in rural areas.

The arithmetic of the land-man ratio compels this conclusion. As mentioned earlier, per capita crop land has been declining as the rate of increase in cropped area has fallen and the work force in agriculture has increased. Since these trends are likely to continue, obviously it will be impossible to accommodate gainfully the growing work force on the available crop land either as cultivators or laborers. That viable holdings can be provided to marginal farmers and landless laborers by ceiling legislation that would limit maximum net income from farming to, say, Rs. 25,000 per year—equivalent to the remuneration of a junior executive in a nationalized bank or a semiskilled worker in a factory—is an illusion. At best, ceiling legislation if rigorously enforced may make available enough land to provide house sites to the landless.

Granting the inexcusable laxity by state governments in the implementation of land reforms, there is no evidence to support Joshi's view (1982a) that giving priority to the production approach has resulted in a lower priority for land reforms. This view implies that food prodution is less important than reducing poverty. The lower priority of land reforms was evident before the new technology appeared and persisted even after the food crisis. It is unfair to blame this on the new technology. Are we to believe that prolongation of the food crisis would have spurred a more sincere land-reform movement?

Joshi's claim that the increase in production coincided with increases in inequality and poverty is at best a half-truth. In a particular region, the incidence of poverty may go up in spite of a high agricultural production growth rate. Sheila Bhalla has observed that "the high average incomes of the 'prosperous' Region II mask the serious incidence of grave poverty among the landless labor households there." She hastens to add, however, that "this must not be taken to imply that in Region II poverty is now worse than it was before the Green Revolution. That is almost certainly not the case" (Bhalla 1981, 71). It may also be conceded that since the landless poor have no proprietary claim in the increased production, they may not benefit directly from it. But there is no evidence of either reduced absorption of hired labor in agricultural production or reduced real wage under the new technology. The more likely explanation for the increased incidence of poverty is that prosperity led to in-migration from backward regions. If poverty has increased in spite of higher food production, nonagricultural factors, such as inflation, demographic pressure, and failure to diversify the rural economy and reduce the dependence of the growing labor force on farm land, should be held responsible. By increasing production, the new technology lifted many small farmers from subsistence farming. Further gains are possible with a more effective input delivery system (Vyas 1982) and community action. To reduce my (painful) disagreement with Joshi, I fully endorse his statement that "development of irrigation and of water management system, small farmer-oriented land reforms with strong support for community rather than private rights in resources structure necessary for modern agriculture, the pursuit of private gains within the limits of community welfare as the guiding motivation—these are the indispensable requirements of dynamic agriculture in labor surplus Asian countries including India" (Joshi 1982a).

Equity

India's agricultural price policy has been severely criticized for keeping prices deliberately low, thus providing a disincentive to production. This has been dubbed as urban bias in the mistaken belief that the poor and the net purchasers of food live only in urban areas. The literature on the adequacy of agricultural prices, the effectiveness of higher prices in augmenting production, and the propriety of procurement at support prices or below market prices is abundant. My impression is that few Indian scholars accept the view that policy makers deliberately kept prices of farm products low. The terms of trade have not been adverse to agriculture except since the oil crisis. Farm prices have rarely, if ever, been fixed in the sense that it was an offense to sell farm products in the open market at whatever prices they could fetch. Throughout the decades of planning, the prices of *manufactured* goods—cement, steel, coal, paper—have been subjected to severe controls, giving rise to a flourishing black market. There has been no black market in agricultural commodities.

My plea has been that if you cannot provide employment to the unemployed poor or fair remuneration to the larger number of the "under employed," give them food at lower prices, which would give a higher purchasing power to their rupee. And the only way to do this without adversely affecting the incentive to produce is to adopt cost-reducing technology or to subsidize consumption, which the Government of India has been doing on an increasing scale.

To the best of my knowledge, the only alternative to the HYV technology is more rapid expansion of public irrigation. No one would question the critical importance of expanded public irrigation and water conservation. Lack of funds does not appear to be a major constraint on the expansion of irrigation; however, there is evidence that lack of cement, steel, and bricks (coal) has hampered completion of irrigation projects. But in the absence of fertilizer-responsive varieties of seed, the contribution that irrigation can make to augmentation of production is limited. The spurt in tube-well irrigation resulted largely from the introduction of HYVs technology. Water conservation also is remunerative if appropriate technology with drought- and pest-resistant seeds is available, as demonstrated by ICRISAT.

In addition to redistribution of crop land, land-reform measures that promote equity include social control of ground water, providing tenancy rights if not ownership to sharecroppers, consolidation of fragments, and equal distribution of gains from land improvement and development. These measures greatly strengthen the status of small farmers. Measures previously adopted—the Small Farmers Development Agency (SFDA), the Integrated Rural Development Programme (IRDP), the National Rural Employment Programme (NREP), Minimum Needs, and so on— are in the right direction but need conceptual refinement and more faithful implementation.

If by equity we mean simply equal access to land, given the pressure of population nothing short of collective or cooperative ownership of land can provide such access to everyone currently engaged in agriculture, either as small or large owners, tenants, sharecroppers, or landless laborers. But to suggest such a solution would be highly unrealistic. Equity measures probably would be more acceptable politically if more emphasis were placed on more equitable allocation of noncrop land assets and inputs such as irrigation, fertilizer, and, for the weaker sections, credit and "reservation" of further developments in sectors allied to the agricultural sector. Further, all policy measures should be directed towards ensuring that the bulk of additional production in agricultural and allied industries is generated by small and marginal farmers. This would mean preemption of allocation of public expenditure for agricultural and rural development—whether in irrigation, land reclamation, animal husbandry, forestry, or fisheries—largely in favor of weaker sections of the population (Dantwala 1979).

While gains from redistribution of crop land assets might be limited, those from the generation of additional assets and income from allied industries would be considerable. But even these might not significantly reduce poverty. Further action would be necessary to diversify the rural economy through generation of nonagricultural employment.

To Sum Up

A substantial increase in agricultural/food production is a necessary but not sufficient condition for alleviation of poverty. The impact of higher production must be reflected in lower consumer prices. The success of agricultural policies also depends, in large measure, on supporting policies in other sectors of the economy.

The adoption in the mid-sixties of the new technology, despite some adverse side effects, helped to overcome chronic food shortages. This restrained the rise in food prices which was reducing the purchasing power of the poor. Of no less significance was the restoration of belief in the capacity of Indian agriculture to free its growing population and spare the country the humiliation of continuing dependence on food aid.

Even with labor-intensive, small-farm technology, Indian agriculture will not be able to absorb gainfully the growth in the agricultural labor force—more than 100 million in the last three decades.

The difficult task of diversifying the rural economy through the encouragement of allied industries—forestry, animal husbandry, and so on—and village industries will have to be undertaken.

To ensure that the gains of diversification are not preempted, some sort of "reservation" of development in favor of the weaker section would be necessary. If the political leadership is reluctant to so favor the weaker section, which is quite likely, there is no alternative for the poor but to form a solidarity front and use their numerical strength to claim not only a larger share of existing assets and current income flows but a preponderant share in the additional assets and incomes generated through public expenditure and development programs.

Notes

1. The Planning Commission, in its Draft Five Year Plan for 1978–83, estimated that the labor force in agriculture would be 213.8 million in 1983 (Government of India, Planning Commission 1981).

2. "It is noteworthy that fluctuations in paddy production have been higher in areas where new technology has not yet become fully entrenched. This is evident from the (analysis of) regionwise decline in output during the drought years 1972–73, 1976–77 and 1979–80. During these three years, decline in paddy production due to below normal monsoon was the lowest in Haryana and Punjab. The most seriously affected States were the traditional paddy growing areas where the new technology is yet to make a significant mark. In the case of wheat, the production in Punjab and Haryana in fact increased during these years of drought" (Government of India, Ministry of Finance 1982).

11 Growth and Equity in Indian Agriculture and a Few Paradigms from Bangladesh

RAISUDDIN AHMED

In chapter 10 of this volume, M. L. Dantwala presents an excellent overview of growth-with-equity issues in Indian agriculture. Although he does not attempt to define the problem of measuring *inequality* and *absolute poverty*, his arguments imply that absolute poverty is the most urgent concern of Indian policy makers.[1] Since my disagreements with Dantwala are few, I shall attempt primarily to amplify and supplement some of his points on institutional policies and present some paradigms from Bangladesh.

Institutional Policies

Dantwala asks whether the emphasis on the new seed-cum-fertilizer technology has resulted in the neglect of institutional changes and tilted the balance of social justice against the poor. Development of market institutions, particularly those related to new technology, has been impressive. Credit and marketing cooperatives, special programs for small and marginal farmers, intensive agricultural development in selected districts, and special employment programs for rural laborers are some of the institutional arrangements that have few parallels in other low-income market economies. Some studies indicate that in recent years about 33 percent of the institutional credit was shared by small farms holding less than 2 hectares, which had only about 25 percent of the total cultivated area (as reviewed in Sarma 1981). The interest rate was reduced 10–15 percent in the informal credit markets of the Punjab and Haryana by innovative credit institutions and new technology. Although most of these institutions did not reach their goals, their achievements are by no means inconsequential.

The new market institutions contributed only marginally to alleviating poverty because they contributed little to the income of those who had no access to land. Egalitarian distribution of land not only redistributes

124

access to productive assets but also broadens the power structure in rural areas, so that benefits from other policies are spread more evenly among rural people. Dantwala has indicated that the distribution of land may be less unequal than it appears if differences in quality of land are considered. But even if these differences and those caused by the positive correlation between farm size and family size are allowed, the inequality could still be large.[2]

The setting of land ownership ceilings in India has in practice provided little land for distribution. Even with a lower ceiling (say, 4–12 hectares, depending on the state), the supply of surplus land for redistribution to small and landless households is adequate only in the northwestern states, where other employment opportunities are available. In the eastern and most southern states, where landlessness and absolute poverty are widespread, there is not enough land to redistribute even with a low ceiling (Singh 1982).

Bangladesh Paradigms

Because of similarities in regional resource endowment, population density, and production patterns, the experience of Bangladesh has much in common with that of India, particularly eastern India.

A little more than 90 percent of the population of Bangladesh lives in rural areas. Most have few assets of any kind. A large proportion of cultivators are small and marginal. About 50 percent of the farms are less than 2.5 acres, 19 percent of the cultivated areas being under some form of tenancy. These small and marginal farms buy much of their foodgrain supply from the market (Ahmed 1981). They supplement income from their farm by earnings from petty trades, services, and labor, which themselves are closely related to agriculture. The Agricultural Census of 1977 indicates that the proportion of rural households not operating any land and depending primarily on wages from work as hired agricultural laborers ranges from 23 percent in Tangail to 34 percent in Rangpur. The country average is 29 percent. If economic progress is as slow in the future as in the past, and if the population continues to grow, even if at a slower rate, the proportion of landless households in rural areas will double by the year 2000.

The behavior of wage rates and employment of unskilled agricultural labor in the wake of agricultural growth is one of the most important links between poverty and agricultural growth. The average index of the real agricultural wage rate fell from 97 in the first half of the 1960s to 51 in the first half of the 1970s and 72 in the second half. The choice of different years would still lead to the same conclusion. Apparently, failure of the money wage rate to keep pace with the prices of commodities generally consumed by laborers resulted in this decline. But a primary cause of the decline in real wages was the failure of agricultural productivity to keep pace with the growth of the labor force. Econometric analysis shows significant and positive relationships between real wage rates of agricultural labor and agricultural production. However, the growth rate of agricultural production has to be higher than the growth rate in population to affect real wage rates perceptibly. If the aggregate demand for labor does not grow as much as family labor supply, then the demand for hired labor tends to stagnate or fall, and so does the real wage rate (Ahmed 1981). Between 1960 and 1980, agricultural production grew by about 1.8 percent annually, and the population grew by 2.6 percent. Some estimates indicate that agricultural employment grew by only 1.2 percent.[3]

High-yield varieties have covered no more than 18 percent of the area sown with rice. Although high-yield varieties are 50–60 percent more labor-intensive, the resulting increase in employment has been substantially offset by a reduction in the area sown with jute, which also is labor-intensive. Rural trade, services, and industries, which provide some employment for the rural poor, indirectly depend on agricultural production. Therefore, the growth in employment in these pursuits may not have been much different from that in agriculture. This implies that stagnation in agriculture, high population growth, and the increasing proportion of landless households in rural areas caused rural poverty to increase.

Redistribution of land has often been suggested as a prerequisite for fast agricultural growth that includes the poor. The immediate question in Bangladesh is whether enough surplus land is available for distribution. Eleven percent of rural households in Bangladesh did not own any homestead land in 1977, 22 percent owned land only to accommodate homesteads, and 38 percent cultivated less than 2.5 acres per household (Government of Bangladesh, Bureau of Statistics 1979). Assume that a six-person household owning 3.0 acres of land is a subsistence unit[4] and also the ceiling for land ownership. This ceiling would result in about 4.44 million acres of surplus land. This would only be enough to provide homestead land to landless households and to raise the size of marginal farms to 0.5 acre per capita. Even if it were politically possible, there is not enough land in Bangladesh to organize farming into viable units and provide land to all landless and small, submarginal farm households for long.

Although labor-intensive nonagricultural development is emphasized as a long-run solution to the problems of Bangladesh, agricultural development will be crucial during the coming decade. Production can be doubled with known technology. Presently, only about 12 percent of the cultivated area has a controlled supply of irrigation water; no more than

20 percent of the area under rice is sown with high-yield-variety seeds; and only about 40 percent of crop area is fertilized at two-thirds of the recommended amounts.

Until 1973/74, about 80 percent of government allocations for irrigation went to large-scale projects, which covered only about 10 percent of the area irrigated under all projects (Ahmed 1977). In recent years larger shares of public resources have gone to small-scale irrigation, but a big push to develop irrigation primarily through small-scale tube wells is yet to come. Technical studies indicate that enough ground water is available (World Bank 1972). Incentives involving a large number of farmers would be a key factor in the success of such a strategy. Formation of local institutions to organize farm groups to operate tube wells would be a second important element.

The new agricultural technology and tube-well irrigation do not discriminate against small farmers as much as has been suggested (Gauhar 1982). Independent studies by the Bangladesh Institute of Development Studies show that much of the criticism is baseless (BIDS 1980). The proportion of total irrigated land operated by the small farmers under these projects is no less than the proportion of total land operated by small farmers. No evidence was found in the project area of any unusual transfers of land. Nevertheless, with the new emphasis on private initiative in small-scale irrigation, large farmers probably would benefit more than small farmers. But increases in the demand for labor and in the expenditures of well-to-do farmers on consumer goods would offset some of these negative consequences.

Notes

1. This concern is expressed explicitly in Government of India, Planning Commission (1973).

2. The Indian National Sample Survey (26th Round) indicates that in 1970/71, 75 percent of Indian farmers were classified as small and marginal, owning only about 25 percent of the total cultivated land. On the other hand, only about 2 percent of the large-farm households owned about 23 percent of the land. The trend was a slight increase in the proportion of small and marginal farms with a decreasing share of land.

3. This includes family labor. The employment of wage labor must have increased at a slower rate because aggregate demand increased at a slower rate than did the growth in family labor. For growth in aggregate employment see Clay and Khan (1977).

4. The average farm size in Bangladesh is about 3.5 acres. Calculations based on farm income, costs, and living expenses indicate a subsistence unit of about 3.0 acres for a family of six, at the current level of technology. Technological change would change this subsistence threshold, as would population growth.

12 The Data on Indian Poverty and the Poverty of ASEAN Data

MAHAR MANGAHAS

All of the chapters in this volume suggest elements of a trickle-down mechanism in India. This mechanism is evident from the inverse relation of agricultural income per capita and other agricultural productivity variables to poverty.

The strength of the trickle-down mechanism, however, is somewhat controversial. According to Bardhan and Rao et al. (chaps. 8 and 9 in this volume), even the productivity factors do not always carry the "right" signs for different cross sections and different equation specifications, while according to Ahluwalia (chap. 7), the trickle-down mechanism is significant but there simply hasn't been enough growth to trickle down.

What is fascinating about the Indian debate, however, is more the richness of the empirical base than the substantive positions of the researchers. India has a time series of 17 annual observations for rural poverty between 1956/57 and 1977/78, courtesy of the National Sample Surveys. No other developing country has comparable data. Using the head-count measure, the incidence of Indian rural poverty steadily dropped from 54 percent in 1956/57 to 39 percent in 1960/61 (5 observations), rose to 57 percent in 1966/67 (5 observations), and then declined again to 41 percent in 1971/72 (4 observations). It moved up to 46 percent in 1973/74 but dropped to the previous low of 39 percent in 1977/78 (1 observation). It is highly significant to me that the various authors never question the general accuracy of this series.

This series includes at least one complete cycle, perhaps two. It shows that the incidence of poverty is dynamic, changing substantially even from one year to the next. The task of explaining these changes is a great challenge for Indian social scientists. Does poverty incidence move cyclically, as does growth of GNP, and if so, are these cycles related? What explains the turning points in poverty?

The move to collect Indian data at 5-year intervals, beginning with 1973/74, rather than annually is most regrettable. Frequency will then be the same as in the Association of South East Asian Nations (ASEAN) countries. One can only hope that India's potential for arriving at a scientific understanding of the most effective means of solving the poverty problem will not become as limited as has been the case for ASEAN (Mangahas 1979, 1983).

The ASEAN countries certainly have not lacked high economic growth for the trickle-down process. The region as a whole has had one of the highest average growth rates in the world over the past three decades, perhaps second only to the East Asian newly industrializing countries (NICs)—the Republic of Korea, Taiwan, and Hong Kong.

Like the Government of India, all of the ASEAN governments have expressed strong dissatisfaction with poverty and inequity. Equity is an important goal in the development plans of Indonesia, the Philippines, Malaysia, and Thailand. Malaysia has set quantitative (five-year) targets for the reduction of poverty and, according to data in its development-plan reviews, has been meeting these targets. Malaysia also has adopted an official poverty line for estimating poverty incidence. Those in use in Indonesia, the Philippines, and Thailand have been designed by academic researchers and the World Bank. The few surveys available indicate small but significant reductions in poverty incidence in Indonesia and Thailand. Overall income inequality as measured by the Gini coefficient and other indices has remained unchanged. Owing to the large public-housing program, the post-fiscal inequality in Singapore is significantly narrower than the pre-fiscal inequality.[1]

In the Philippines, the poverty incidence rose in the 1960s but remained below the level registered by the lone survey in the mid-1950s.[2] The trend for the 1970s cannot be ascertained, owing to the extremely poor quality of the data. In all the ASEAN countries, the absolute levels and the trends in per capita income from the (occasional) household surveys are not strongly consistent with those from the (annual) national income accounts. The aggregate underreporting of income from the former source could range from 20 percent to 50 percent of national accounts income. The underreporting is most serious in the Philippines.

As in most mixed free-enterprise economies, growth-oriented policies in the ASEAN countries have taken precedence over redistributive policies. The relative lack of official monitoring of distributive trends can be traced to policy priorities. In turn, the resulting weak scientific under-standing of distributive issues reinforces these priorities. Where poverty incidence is not measured frequently, there may be a tendency to assume that (a) it cannot fluctuate much from year to year and (b) any changes are for the better, since per capita income is always growing. Greater dissemination of the data on the Indian experience may help to dispel such facile assumptions.

This does not mean that ASEAN governments are unaware of or unconcerned about their substantial poverty problems or that they are relying on the trickle-down mechanism to eventually solve them. They may be too accustomed to using indirect policies to uplift the poor. One of the most important of these indirect policies is to influence basic consumer commodity prices. Thus, ASEAN policy makers would be highly sympathetic to the Narain relation. The price of rice is a highly sensitive matter in all countries, whether importers or exporters. Indonesia also controls the price of kerosene, and the Philippines controls the price of cooking oil. Invariably, the objective of low and stable prices for consumers has taken precedence over more remunerative prices for producers.

The danger is that the instrumental variables may be mistaken for the objective variables, since the former are being monitored and the latter are not. Without monitoring of the results, the search for the most effective instruments does not get very far from guesswork. As far as I know, no ASEAN study has set a poverty index on the left-hand side of a regression equation. The data are simply too limited.

Further progress will require not only technical but also political skills. The job will be much simplified when ASEAN political leaders overcome, as in India, their allergies to distributive data, as they have already done for data on inflation, foreign-exchange deficits, and the external debt. On the other hand, there is a need for technical innovations in measurement that will reduce the cost of annual monitoring of poverty and other distributive conditions. Simpler yet accurate means should be designed to *measure* (perhaps it would be sufficient to *indicate*) levels of income, expenditures, consumption, calories, assets, and so on. Perhaps some variables in money units should be replaced by physical units such as weight for age among children, incidence of certain sicknesses related to poverty, ownership or access to certain consumer durables. Simple means of classifying households into vertical socioeconomic classes could be designed.[3]

More consideration should be given to tapping survey respondents' recall of economic *changes* in their earning ability or in their living standard. Respondents are not likely to report a change unless it is significant to them. Thus, empirical data on a group of no-change respondents would become available. Direct measurement of real changes would circumvent problems of (*a*) comparability of successive surveys and (*b*) selection and construction of appropriate price deflators for socioeconomic classes.

Perhaps the accuracy of the magnitudes of change may not be as important as simple head-counts of those who experienced positive or favorable changes, those who had negative or unfavorable changes, and those who experienced no change. The traditional measure of income growth amounts to subtracting the losses from gains and dividing the remainder by the population, as though gainers shared their gains with losers. In contrast, a simple development score of "gainers" minus "losers" has a clear democratic bias.

In a market economy, there are always some losers at certain times. Experimental surveys in the Philippines show that the proportion of losers can vary widely according to socioeconomic class. Socioeconomic-class membership can be easily determined—using housing criteria, for instance—without measuring either income or expenditures if there are only three to five classes. A relatively simple way of testing whether economic growth has trickled down to the poor is to measure the relative plurality of gainers over losers in every class and to check whether the lower classes have a higher plurality than do the upper classes.

Notes

1. Post-fiscal income is income that results after taxes borne have been subtracted and government subsidies enjoyed have been added.

2. The surveys of the 1960s are not comparable to that of 1956/57. For more details on inconsistencies in the data see Mangahas (1982).

3. In the Philippines, market-research firms have for many years been using a dwelling-rating system, with five classes. These are not quintiles; a typical urban distribution could have 30 percent in the lowest class E; 35 percent in class D; 25 percent in class C; 8 percent in class B; and 2 percent in class A.

13 Directions of Agrarian Change: A View from Villages in the Philippines

YUJIRO HAYAMI and MASAO KIKUCHI

A deep-rooted popular belief is that modern market institutions and technology destroy traditional agrarian communities. This view has been asserted repeatedly since the days of the first enclosure movement in England by Russian *Narodniks*, U.S. Populists, and the followers of Mahatma Gandhi. The issue was revived a decade and half ago with the advent of the green revolution. It has been feared that the diffusion of modern rice and wheat varieties and the application of modern cash inputs would promote polarization of peasant communities and greater misery for the poor. This chapter investigates this problem by comparing two villages located in the same district in the Philippines but characterized by different patterns of agrarian change.

A theory advanced by Karl Marx and later elaborated by Karl Kautsky and Vladimir Lenin asserts that modern technology and the institutions of capitalism polarize the peasantry into large commercial farmers and wage laborers. Institutions of precapitalist village society such as communal land ownership, mutual-aid associations, and patron-client ties are thought to provide for an egalitarian distribution of assets and income that assures at least a minimum subsistence. As those traditional institutions are replaced by modern market institutions, village elites begin to accumulate land for commercial production by encroaching on commons, evicting tenants, and purchasing small peasant holdings. This process is augmented by modern agricultural technology based on large machinery, which raises the efficiency of large-scale operations relative to small-scale operations. The higher efficiency of large commercial farms drives off small peasants and converts them into landless laborers, many of whom are not able to find employment in the rural sector and are forced to migrate to the cities.

As conceived by Marx, large-scale commercial farming based on land-lords, capitalist tenants, and wage laborers, established in England after the second enclosure movement, is the ideal type of the polarization

132

process. Marx realized, however, that patterns in other countries would likely deviate from the ideal. In fact, Germany and other European countries in the late nineteenth century showed the opposite trend. Even in the United States, despite dramatic increases in mechanization, family farms continued to exist. Large-scale farms characterized by hired labor and management hierarchy did not become a dominant mode of production in agriculture, and this led to a major controversy between Marxian orthodoxy and revisionists (de Janvry 1981; Mitarny 1951).

A major reason for the failure of Marx's prediction seems to be the inherent difficulty of labor enforcement in agricultural production. In urban industries, work is highly standardized and easy to monitor. The biological process of agricultural production, however, is subject to infinite ecological variations. Different ways of handling crops or animals are often necessary because of slight differences in temperature and soil moisture. The dispersal of agricultural operations over wide areas adds to the difficulty of monitoring.

This difficulty multiplies as the farming system becomes more complex, involving more intensive crop care, crop rotations, and crop-livestock combinations: "In areas more suitable for multiple enterprise farms, family operations have the advantage. Increasing the enterprises so multiplies the number of on-the-spot supervisory management decisions per acre that the total acreage which a unit of management can oversee quickly approaches the acreage which an ordinary family can operate" (Brewster 1950, 71).

The effects of "modern technologies" are not homogeneous. Mechanization that substitutes capital for labor is usually characterized by scale economies and saves the labor-enforcement cost. For example, supervising one tractor driver is much easier than supervising many laborers and bullock teams. Therefore, mechanization tends to increase the relative efficiency of large farms and to promote polarization. On the other hand, a biological-chemical technology requiring intensive on-the-spot management decisions per unit of land area would increase the relative effficiency of small family farms and promote the unimodal farm-size distribution. Our hypothesis is consistent with historical changes in the size distribution of operational holdings in Japan (table 13.1). It appears that Marx and his followers underestimated the unique nature of the biological production process and the potential for development of biological-chemical technology.

Green Revolution Controversies

The green revolution, based mainly on modern, semidwarf varieties and fertilizers, is biological-chemical by nature. Yet, in both scientific and popular literature it has often been claimed to be a major force

Yujiro Hayami and Masao Kikuchi

Table 13.1. Percentage Distribution of Farms by Size of Cultivated Area in Japan, 1908–40

| Year | Farm Size | | | |
	Less than 0.5 ha.	0.5–2.0 ha.	Larger than 2 ha.	Total
1908	37.3%	52.1%	10.6%	100.0%
1910	37.5	52.4	10.1	100.0
1920	35.3	54.0	10.7	100.0
1930	34.3	56.4	9.3	100.0
1940	33.3	57.3	9.4	100.0

Source: Institute of Developing Economies (1969), 116.

promoting polarization. The arguments run as follows: In contrast to small subsistence farmers, large commercial farmers have better access to new information and the financial capacity to adopt modern varieties and use modern inputs such as fertilizers and chemicals. Profit resulting from adoption of the new technology would stimulate the large farmers to enlarge their operational holdings through the purchase of small farms or tenant eviction. They also would introduce large-scale machinery, which would reduce employment opportunities and wage rates for the landless population (Cleaver 1972; Frankel 1971; Griffin 1974; Warriner 1973).

Nevertheless, empirical evidence accumulated in the past decade indicates that, in general, the new, seed-cum-fertilizer technology diffused widely among farms irrespective of farm size and land tenure, at least in the areas where decent irrigation was available. Both large and small farms recorded similar efficiency gains from adoption of the new technology (Hayami 1981; Hayami and Kikuchi 1981; Ruttan 1977).

Although polarization has occurred with diffusion of modern varieties in some cases, there is considerable doubt as to whether the real cause is the new technology or other factors, such as the pressure of growing population on limited land resources and its bearing on agrarian structure. In most developing countries, the growth in the agricultural labor force has exceeded the labor-absorptive capacity of nonagriculture. As a result, land-labor ratios have been declining, often accompanied by increases in land rent at the expense of labor wage rates. In general, the higher rate of return to land provides a strong incentive to accumulate more land, especially where alternative investment opportunities such as stocks and securities are not easily available. The concentration of landholding induced by the higher rate of land rent makes income distribution more skewed, which promotes further concentration of land.

Another factor promoting polarization is inadequately designed land-reform laws and regulations. A number of cases were reported in which regulations on land rent and tenure or land confiscation and redistribution plans resulted in the large-scale eviction of tenants and the establishment of landlords' direct cultivation with the use of agricultural laborers (Dutt 1977; Joshi 1970; Narain and Joshi 1969; Raj 1976; Warriner 1969).

Agrarian Change in Two Philippine Villages

To identify the causes of polarization, it is necessary to analyze the interrelationships among agrarian structure, new technology, population pressure, and government policies such as land reform. Since the problem involves highly sensitive issues such as illegal eviction of tenants, we cannot expect deep insights from official statistics based only on such sources as national censuses and large-scale sample surveys. For this reason, we made detailed case studies of two villages (*barrios*) in the province of Laguna, south of Manila. One, on the east coast of the Laguna de Bay, the largest lake in the Philippines, we shall call the East Village. The other, located on the south coast of the lake, about 15 kilometers from the East Village, we shall call the South Village. Both are in a rice-monoculture area.

We surveyed the East Village from November 1976 through January 1977 and the South Village in September 1977. Both surveys comprised interviews with the heads of all households, and with other family members when necessary. Similar surveys conducted for the East Village in 1966 and 1974 provided benchmark information. Data on the South Village for earlier dates are based mainly on recollections of the villagers.

Almost all of the land of the two villages is in wet paddy fields, and double cropping is common. As in other rice-producing areas in the Philippines, absentee landlordism is widespread. Only 2.4 hectares of the 108 hectares of rice land in the East Village are owned by villagers, and only 3.0 hectares of the 208 hectares in the South Village.

The land-ownership pattern in the East Village, characterized by scattered holdings of small landlords, is typical of this region. A majority of the landlords live in the town (*poblacion*) or in nearby municipalities. Usually they have close personal contacts with their tenants. In the South Village in 1977 more than 70 percent of land was owned by five large landlords who lived in Manila.[1] In fact, the whole area of the village was originally owned by two landlords but was subdivided through inheritance.

The East Village is a typical peasant village consisting of small farms none of which is larger than 10 hectares. In contrast, in the South Village more than 60 percent of the total rice land is in three farms averaging 45 hectares each.

These differences are based on settlement histories reflecting different ecological conditions. The South Village is subject to frequent floods and waterlogging. It was marshy jungle until the 1930s, when two wealthy men purchased the area and installed drainage and irrigation facilities. They cultivated the major area under direct administration and let marginal areas be cultivated by sharecroppers.

Settlers in the East Village used family labor to open the land. Landlords usually allowed them to keep all of the harvests for five years; afterwards harvests were shared equally. Settlement began much earlier and took a much longer time than in the South Village. In both villages, cultivation frontiers had closed by the 1950s.

During the decade 1966–76 the two villages were under strong population pressure. In the East Village, total population increased at an annual compound rate of 4.8 percent between 1966 and 1976 (table 13.2). The high rate of natural increase was augmented by an inflow of migrants from surrounding upland areas, where agricultural technology was stagnant and there was no increase in employment opportunities. Since the land area remained virtually constant, the man-land ratio deteriorated sharply. The available evidence indicates similar changes in the South Village.

One consequence of the strong population pressure on land was an increase in the number of landless laborers (table 13.2). While the total number of households paralleled the growth in the population, the number of landless-worker households increased much faster. As a result, landless-worker households rose from 30 percent of the total to 50 percent.

Extension of the national irrigation system to the East Village in 1958 made double cropping possible in all paddy fields, thereby doubling rice yields per hectare of the net sown area. Another major change was the introduction of modern, semidwarf varieties of rice. According to the 1966 survey, no one had tried the modern varieties, but in 1976 all the farmers planted them. They also applied fertilizers and chemicals and adopted improved cultural practices such as intensive weeding and straight-row planting. Similar advances in technology were reported for the South Village. As a result, the average rice yield per hectare of crop area rose from 2.7 tons in 1966 to 3.4 tons in 1976 in the East Village and from 2.5 tons in 1967 to 3.4 tons in 1977 in the South Village.

Land-reform programs implemented mainly in the early 1970s changed land-tenure relations drastically. Sharecroppers were permitted to become leaseholders, with the land rent fixed at 25 percent of the average yield for the previous three years. The percentage of rice area under the share tenure dropped from about 70 percent to 30 percent in the East Village and from about 70 percent to 0 percent in the South Village.

In the East Village, however, about 30 percent of the rice area continued under sharecropping contract, even though share tenants could obtain

Table 13.2. Changes in Population, Rice Land Area, and Number of Households in the East Village, 1966–76

Year	Population	Land Area (ha.)	Man-Land Ratio (persons/ha.)	Number of Households		
				Total	Farmers	Landless Workers
1966	398	105	3.8	65	45	20
1974	532	111	4.8	95	54	41
1976	635	108	5.9	109	54	55
Annual growth rate	4.8%	0.3%	4.5%	5.3%	1.8%	10.6%

leasehold titles if they applied to the Agrarian Reform Office. Because of their relations with their landlords, who were relatives or friends, they did not try to change their status. In the South Village, on the other hand, there were no personal ties between tenants and the large landlords living in Manila.

In the East Village, average farm size declined from 2.3 hectares in 1966 to 2.0 in 1976, reflecting strong population pressure on the land. Farms below 2.0 hectares accounted for increased percentages of the total number of farms and the total land area, while the shares of large farmers decreased (table 13.3). However, income distribution probably became more skewed. The number of landless laborers increased sharply. Although demand for labor increased owing to the new, seed-cum-fertilizer technology, especially for weeding and other crop cares, the labor supply also rose, and real wage rates measured in rice changed little. Meanwhile, farmers' income rose. Since rent payments to landlords were fixed by land-reform regulations, the increased income resulting from higher rice yields per hectare went to farmers.[2] In other words, the land reform benefited tenant farmers by the difference between the fixed rent and the economic rent, defined as the marginal productivity of land, which should have increased cumulatively with the advance of yield-increasing technology. Since this benefit was proportional to the size of the operational holding under lease, income gaps between large and small farmers and between farmers and landless laborers probably widened.

Although subtenancy is illegal under the land-reform code, the number of subtenancy contracts increased from one in 1956 to five in 1966 to 16 in 1976. Under these contracts, a tenant subrents part or all of his operational holding to landless laborers or other farmers and extracts from the sublessee a surplus of the rent revenue over the payment to his original landlords.

Table 13.3. Farm-Size Distribution in the East Village, 1966 and 1976

	1966				1976			
	Farms		Rice Area		Farms		Rice Area	
Farm Size	No.	% of total	Ha.	% of total	No.	% of total	Ha.	% of total
Below 1.0 ha.	6	13	3	3	13	24	6	5
1.0–1.9 ha.	17	38	23	22	20	37	28	26
2.0–2.9 ha.	5	11	11	10	8	15	19	18
3.0–4.9 ha.	13	29	46	44	11	20	41	38
5.0 ha. and above	4	9	22	21	2	4	14	13
Total	45	100	105	100	54	100	108	100
Average area per farm (ha.)		2.3				2.0		
Gini coefficient		0.33				0.39		

Note: Farm size is expressed in terms of the operational holding of paddy field.

In order to test the hypothesis that the gap between the economic rent and the actual rent provided an opportunity for leasehold tenants to become intermediate landlords, the factor shares of rice output were estimated for different tenure types by imputing unpaid factor inputs by market prices. Results show that in both absolute and relative terms, the share of land was lowest, and the operators' surplus highest, for land under leasehold tenancy (table 13.4). In contrast, under subtenancy, the share of land was highest, and no surplus was left for contracting farm operators. The share of land for subtenants was very close to the sum of the land share and the operators' surplus for other tenure classes. These observations indicate that a substantial portion of economic rent was captured by leasehold tenants in the form of operators' surplus.

As supporting evidence, the production function for rice was estimated using the same set of data as that used for the calculation of factor shares. The function employed was the unrestricted Cobb-Douglas production function, relating the rice output per farm to the following independent variables: (1) land, the number of hectares harvested per farm; (2) labor, the number of man-days applied per farm; (3) capital, the sum of the irrigation fee paid and/or imputed rentals of carabaos, tractors, and other machines per farm; (4) current inputs, the sum of paid and/or imputed costs of current inputs per farm; (5) a subtenancy dummy, subtenancy equaling 1 and others equaling 0; (6) a share-tenancy dummy, share-tenancy equaling 1 and others equaling 0; and (7) a scale dummy, farms larger than 2.0 hectares equaling 1 and others equaling 0.

Table 13.4. Factor Payments and Factor Shares in Rice Production per Hectare in the East Village, 1976 Wet Season

Input/Output	Factor Payments (kg./ha.)[a]			Factor Shares (%)		
	Leasehold Tenancy	Share Tenancy	Sub-tenancy	Leasehold Tenancy	Share Tenancy	Sub-tenancy
Rice output	2,889	2,749	3,447	100.0	100.0	100.0
Factor payments						
Current inputs	657	697	801	22.7	25.3	23.2
Land	567	698	1,305	19.6	25.4	37.8
(Paid to landlord)	(567)	(698)	(504)	(19.6)	(25.4)	(14.6)
(Paid to sublessor)	(0)	(0)	(801)	(0)	(0)	(23.2)
Labor	918	850	1,008	31.8	30.9	29.3
Capital[b]	337	288	346	11.7	10.5	10.1
Operators' surplus[c]	410	216	−13	14.2	7.9	−0.4

[a] Factor payments converted to paddy equivalents by the factor-output price ratios
[b] Sum of the irrigation fee and the paid and/or imputed rentals of carabaos, tractors, and other machines
[c] Residual

Table 13.5. Estimation of the Cobb-Douglas Production Function for Rice Using Farm Survey Data for the East Village, 1976 Wet Season

	Regression Number			
	1	2	3	4
Coefficients of				
Land	0.343	0.343	0.333	0.352
	(0.203)	(0.207)	(0.206)	(0.215)
Labor	−0.299	0.299	0.300	0.292
	(0.200)	(0.204)	(0.203)	(0.210)
Capital	0.135	0.135	0.130	0.139
	(0.099)	(0.101)	(0.101)	(0.104)
Current inputs	0.240	0.241	0.248	0.242
	(0.094)	(0.096)	(0.096)	(0.096)
Subtenancy dummy		−0.005		
		(0.147)		
Share-tenancy dummy			−0.058	
			(0.099)	
Scale dummy				−0.019
				(0.129)
Total	1.018	1.017	1.011	1.024
	(0.055)	(0.061)	(0.057)	(0.072)
R^2 (adjusted)	0.931	0.928	0.929	0.928
Standard error of estimate	0.248	0.253	0.291	0.253
Intercept	1.019	1.038	0.994	1.041

Note: Standard errors of regression coefficients are enclosed in parentheses.

The results of estimation by the ordinary-least-squares method are summarized in table 13.5. All estimates of the production elasticities of inputs have positive signs, as was expected. Although these estimates are not significant at conventional levels of significance except for current inputs, they are at least larger than their standard errors. In contrast, the coefficients of dummy variables are smaller than their standard errors.

Under the assumption of market equilibrium, the production elasticities are equivalent to the functional shares of factors. On the whole, the estimates of production elasticities in table 13.5 are similar to the values of relative factor shares in table 13.4. In particular, the estimates of the production elasticity of land are surprisingly close to the relative share of land for subtenants. The results support the hypothesis that subtenants have to pay rent at a rate equal to the marginal-value product of the land.

On the other hand, leasehold tenants can capture the surplus of the marginal return to the service of land over the actual rate of rent payment to the landowners in the form of operators' surplus by using the land for their own farming operations. Alternatively, they can capture the surplus by subrenting the land. Thus, population pressure, technological change, and the land-reform regulations on the land-rent market are basic forces underlying the emergence of a multistage landlordism.

Multistage landlordism may increase even further. In 1976, two cases were reported of sublessees renting a part of their subrented land. Thus, if the economic forces that induced the emergence of subtenancy increase, the number of layers in multistage landlordism may multiply.

The economic forces that induced changes in the land-tenure system also affected labor-employment relations. The most significant change was a shift from *hunusan* to *gama*. *Hunusan* is a traditional system by which all villagers participate in harvesting and receive a certain share of output (one-sixth in the East Village). *Gama* is a new system in which participation in harvesting is limited to the workers who helped to weed the field without receiving wages. The *gama* system was introduced to the East Village shortly after the construction of an irrigation system in 1958. By 1976, more than 80 percent of the farmers had adopted the system.

The *gama* system enables employer-farmers to reduce the wage rate for harvesting to a level equal to the marginal productivity of labor. In earlier days, when the rice yield per hectare was lower and labor was scarcer, the one-sixth share of output under the *hunusan* system might have represented a wage rate equal to the marginal product of the harvesters' labor. However, as the productivity of rice farming increased and labor became more abundant, the one-sixth share of output became substantially larger than the marginal product of labor for harvesting.

In such a situation, farmers could increase their income by replacing the *hunusan* with daily wage workers (*upahan*). However, resistance to

Table 13.6. A Comparison of the Imputed Value of the Harvesters' Share and the Imputed Cost of *Gama* Labor in the East Village, 1976

Labor Input	Based on Employers' Data	Based on Employees' Data
Number of working days of gama labor (days/ha.)[a]		
Weeding	20.9	18.3
Harvesting/threshing	33.6	33.6
Imputed cost of gama labor (P/ha.)[b]		
Weeding	167.2	146.4
Harvesting/threshing	369.6	369.6
(1) Total	536.8	516.0
Actual share of harvesters		
In kind (kg./ha.)[c]	504.0	549.0
(2) Imputed value (P/ha.)[d]	504.0	549.0
(2) − (1)	−32.8	33.0

[a] Includes labor of family members who worked as *gama* laborers
[b] Imputed using market wage rates (daily wage = P8.00 for weeding, P11.00 for harvesting)
[c] One-sixth of output per hectare
[d] Imputed using market prices (1 kg. = P1)

change in a long-established custom can be costly. Two large farmers in the South Village were reported to have reduced the share of harvesters from one-sixth to one-seventh. Their crop was destroyed during the night.

The *gama* system is designed to equate the cost of the harvesters' share of output to the marginal productivity of labor under the basic institutional environment of the village community.[3] As a test, an imputation of labor inputs applied to rice production under the *gama* system was made by using market wage rates; imputed wage costs were compared with shares of *gama* harvesters. The results show a remarkable affinity between the imputed wages and the actual harvesters' share (table 13.6). Such results indicate an equality between the actual payment to *gama* workers and the marginal product of labor, assuming that the marginal products equal their market wage rates.

Changes in the agrarian structure of the East Village represent "peasant stratification" rather than polarization. Increasing class differentiation occurs in a continuous spectrum ranging from landless laborers to non-cultivating landlords. People in the village communities remain tied to one another in a variety of personal relations, and all community members

Table 13.7. Farm-Size Distribution in the South Village, 1967 and 1977

| | 1967 | | | | 1977 | | | |
| | Farms | | Rice Area | | Farms | | Rice Area | |
Farm Size	No.	% of total	Ha.	% of total	No.	% of total	Ha.	% of total
Small farms								
Below 1 ha.	7	16	4.2	2	22	39	11.2	5
1.0–2.9 ha.	27	60	46.4	24	26	47	44.8	22
3.0–9.9 ha.	7	15	26.0	14	5	9	17.5	8
Total small farms	41	91	76.6	40	53	95	73.5	53
Large farms								
A			14.0	7			80.0	38
B			27.0	14			41.0	20
C			14.0	7			14.0	7
D			60.0	31			—	—
Total large farms	4	9	115.0	60	3	5	135.0	65
Total farms	45	100	191.6	100	56	100	208.5	100
Average farm size (ha.)								
Small farms		1.9				1.4		
Large farms		28.8				45.0		
Gini coefficient		0.60				0.71		

Note: Farm size is expressed in terms of operational holding of paddy field.

have some claims to the output of land. For example, even landless workers receive a share of output after participating in the harvest. Unlike in the bimodal differentiation between kulak and proletariat, semisubsistence peasants survive, while the strata of peasant subclasses multiply.

The pattern of agrarian change in the South Village contrasts sharply with that of the East Village. Farmland is unusually concentrated, with three large farms covering 135 ha. (65 percent) of the total rice area, whereas 53 small farmers operated the rest (table 13.7).[4]

Formerly, this village had two large-scale farms (C and D in table 13.7) under the direct administration of two landlords and a number of small share tenants. Later, two tenant farmers (A and B) gradually accumulated landholdings through direct renting from landlords and purchase of tenancy titles from other tenants (table 13.8). One of the large tenant farmers (A) took over management of one of the large farms (D). Although the contract specified that farmer A was employed as manager,

Table 13.8. Accumulation of Operational Holdings by Large Tenant–Operators in the South Village, 1949–77, Selected Years

Year	Area Added (ha.)	Tenure Status[a]	Cumulative Total (ha.)	Means of Acquisition
Operator A				
1949	1	S	1	Rented from landlord
1962	6	L	7	Purchase of tenancy title
1962–67	7	L	14	Rented from landlord
1970	60	L	74	Rented from landlord
1973	3	L	77	Purchase of tenancy title
1975	3	O	80	Purchase of ownership title
1977	—	—	80	
Operator B				
1949	3	S	3	Tenancy title inherited from father
1962–65	14	L	17	Rented from landlord
1967	10	L	27	Rented from landlord
1968	2	L	29	Purchase of tenancy title
1970	6	L	35	Purchase of tenancy title
1972	6	L	41	Purchase of tenancy title
1977	—	—	41	

[a] S = Share tenancy area; L = leasehold area; O = owned area

it was actually a leasehold contract in that farmer A paid a fixed rent to the landlord.

Because of the accumulation of operational holdings by the two large tenant farmers, the skewness in the farm-size distribution worsened from 1967 to 1977 (table 13.7). The number of farms below 1 ha. tripled within the 10 years, while the number in the 1–3 ha. class decreased. The average size of operational holdings by small farms declined from 1.9 ha. in 1967 to 1.4 ha. in 1977, while the average size of large farms increased from 28.8 ha. to 45.0 ha. The transfer of land from small and medium family farms to large-scale commercial operations is typical of the polarization process.

Under the land-reform programs, the land-retention limit of landlords was reduced from 75 ha. to 7 ha. But the holdings of the two large landlords were not confiscated, because ownership transfer was limited to "tenanted land." There was no retention limit for land under the direct administration of landlords. Major areas owned by the two large landlords were officially under their direct administration. Areas under tenancy contracts were subdivided into units below the retention limit under the titles of family members and relatives. Land-reform programs have also tried to limit the tenant-farm size below 3 irrigated or 5 nonirrigated hectares. Such a regulation could easily be evaded, however, by registering tenancy titles under the names of family members.

From an economic standpoint, the large and small farms differed considerably in organization, but the new, seed-cum-fertilizer technology was applied in much the same way by both groups. The large farms were completely dependent on hired labor. A manager was in charge of coordination and supervision, and a number of overseers supervised laborers. On small farms a large portion of labor input was supplied by operators and family members.

Despite organizational differences, farming practices on large and small farms were similar. Both completely adopted modern varieties and straight-row planting. Weeding was done to more or less the same degree of intensity. The average fertilizer application per hectare for both was four bags (50 kg./bag). The same situation existed in the use of farm chemicals and weeding.

There was little difference in the degree of mechanization. One of the large farms owned five hand tractors and the other three. While less than one-third of the small farms owned a tractor, both large and small farms relied heavily on custom-tractor work, and nearly 100 percent of the area was cultivated by tractor. The only major difference in the use of machinery between the large and the small farms was that threshing on the small farms was done mostly by hand beating on wooden tables, while the large farms used mechanical threshers.

Labor inputs per hectare for rice production on large and small farms were about the same in the 1977 dry season (table 13.9). The former relied much more heavily on hired labor. Total labor input per hectare was 20 percent higher on the large farms, owing to the use of labor for management. With similar input use, there was little difference in paddy yield per hectare on large and small farms.

Overall, there is no evidence that the large farms were more efficient technically than the small. Although they required more management labor, their wage payments were lower. Large farms paid the same cash wages as did small farms, but the latter also provided snacks amounting to about 20 percent of cash wages.

The stronger bargaining position of the large farms is also reflected in the output-sharing rates for harvesting workers. The traditional rates in the South Village were one-sixth for the dry season and one-fifth for the wet season. In 1975, the two large tenant farmers reduced the sharing rates to one-eighth and one-seventh, respectively. Their action was successful despite substantial resistance from workers.

The relative economic positions of large and small farms can be evaluated by comparing farm output values with input costs (table 13.10). The data in table 13.10 show no significant difference in the levels of

Table 13.9. Labor Inputs for Rice Production per Hectare on Large and Small Farms in the South Village, 1977 Dry Season

Labor Input	Large Commercial Operations			Small Family Farms		
	Man-days/ha.		% Hired Labor	Man-days/ha.		% Hired Labor
	Total Labor (1)	Hired Labor (2)	([2]/[1])	Total Labor (3)	Hired Labor (4)	([4]/[3])
Land preparation	12.0	12.0	100	10.5	7.3	70
Transplanting	9.6	9.6	100	9.5	8.9	94
Weeding	34.0	34.0	100	35.1	18.4	52
Harvesting and threshing	30.0	30.0	100	34.4	30.8	90
Seedbed preparation and care	2.0	2.0	100	1.6	0.3	19
Fertilizer and chemical application	3.0	3.0	100	2.8	0.5	18
Clearing and repair of dikes	16.0	16.0	100	7.9	1.9	24
Management	16.0	14.0	88	3.0	0	0
Total	122.6	120.6	98	104.8	68.1	65

operators' surplus of large farms and small farms with leasehold titles. This raises the question as to why large tenant farmers have accumulated landholdings and consolidated them into larger units of operation. The reason is that it was a safer way to capture a part of the economic rent of leased land than subrenting small parcels. As the comparison of the cost-return structures between subtenants and leasehold tenants in table 13.10 shows, the large surplus for leasehold operators was really the gap between the economic rent and the actual rent paid to landlords. Thus, profits for the large leasehold tenants should be the same, irrespective of whether they cultivate land by themselves or subrent it, at least in the village studied. However, under the land-reform laws, subrenting is dangerous for the lessor because he may forfeit his leasehold title if the sublessee reports to the Agrarian Reform Office. Under these circumstances, the transaction costs involved in subtenancy arrangements beyond a limited circle of relatives and close friends are prohibitive. The cost of managing large-scale farms for large holders would have been much less than the expected transaction cost involved in subtenancy contracts. This seems to be the basic reason for consolidating their holdings into large units. Regulations based on land-reform laws designed to protect the rights of tillers have actually blocked the chances for landless laborers to become farm operators.

Table 13.10. The Cost-Return Structure of Rice Production on Large and Small Farms in the South Village, 1977 Dry Season

Input/Output	Factor Payments (kg./ha.)[a]			Factor Shares (% of output)		
	Large Farms (Leasehold)	Small Farms		Large Farms (Leasehold)	Small Farms	
		Leasehold	Subtenancy[b]		Leasehold	Subtenancy
Rice output	3,960	3,996	3,866	100	100	100
Factor payments						
Current inputs	540	477	544	14	12	14
Land	697	873	1,742	18	22	45
(Paid to landlord)	(697)	(873)	(662)	(18)	(22)	(17)
(Paid to sublessor)	(0)	(0)	(1,080)	(0)	(0)	(28)
Labor	1,143	1,085	1,215	29	27	31
Capital[c]	531	333	383	13	8	10
Operators' surplus (residual)	1,049	1,228	−18	26	31	0

[a] Measured in rice equivalents
[b] Excluding subtenanted farms in which the two contracting parties are relatives
[c] Sum of paid or imputed rentals of carabaos, tractors, and other machines

Conclusion

Our Philippine village studies do not support the popular argument that the new, seed-cum-fertilizer technology is a major factor contributing to polarization. No significant difference in levels of farming technology was observed between large and small farms. Both adopted modern varieties for 100 percent of their area. There were no major differences in the levels of fertilizer and chemical applications, seedbed preparation, transplanting, weeding, mechanization, and labor input applied directly to rice production. Rice yields per hectare were the same. Overall, there seems to be no technological advantage for large operations.

Nevertheless, inequality increased in both villages. The basic factor was strong population pressure on land, which raised the return to land relative to labor. Under the land-reform laws, the increase in economic rent accrued to tenant farmers, widening income gaps between large and small farmers and between farmers and landless laborers.

The factors that promoted polarization in the South Village did not operate in the East Village. Operational holdings became smaller but more uniform, and the peasant mode of production continued to dominate. Subtenancy and *gama* arrangements were more common than in the South Village. The reason lies in the difference in social structures of the two villages.

Development in the South Village was based on the landlords' investment in land infrastructure. Land-ownership distribution was highly skewed from the beginning. The distribution of operational holdings also was skewed because of the existence of large farms under the direct administration of landlords. In contrast, the East Village was settled by smallholders and squatters in an unorganized way. Both ownership and operational farm-size distributions were relatively equal. Therefore, people in the South Village were more used to the *modus operandi* of large farms, including the exercise of monopsonistic powers. In the East Village, there would have been stronger resistance to the exercise of such powers. Also, the landlords in the South Village were able to commission large areas to tenants.

The South Village was developed in a shorter period through an organized settlement by large landlords. Therefore, kinship relations are less common there. Only 33 percent of families shared common names, compared with 59 percent in the East Village. Migration into and out of the South Village has been more frequent. Overall, there was much less community solidarity in the South Village, which made it easier for landlords to abolish snack services to workers and reduce output shares of harvesters.

In contrast, even landless workers in the East Village were guaranteed shares of the village income through the *gama* system. The close personal relations reduce the risk of a subtenancy arrangement, since subtenants are less likely to take legal actions against sublessors who are friends or relatives.

A comparison of the response of the two villages to population pressure, technological change, and the land-reform programs shows that the same economic forces can produce different institutions, in different social environments. What is more important, it suggests that there is a threshold of inequality in wealth and power beyond which polarization will occur.

Policies designed to achieve equity and justice without due consideration of variations in community structures will be counterproductive. Effective policy design should begin with the accumulation of detailed socio-economic studies at the village level that are free from ideological preconceptions.

Notes

This paper draws heavily on Hayami and Kikuchi (1981, chaps. 5 and 6) and Kikuchi and Hayami (1980a, 1980b).

1. This type of landlordism is uncommon in this region; however, it is common in central Luzon, north of Manila (see Hayami and Kikuchi 1981, chap. 4).

2. The land-reform regulations were not the only reason for the fixity of leasehold rent. In fact, even before the land reform the rent on leasehold land had been fairly stable, partly owing to insufficient information on yield changes and partly owing to the time lag involved in contract renegotiations (ibid., 110).

3. In addition, *gama* has the merit of saving the cost of monitoring weeding labor, because an incentive scheme is incorporated in the output sharing. Also, the availability of labor at harvest time is guaranteed by contract. From the employees' side, the *gama* is more secure; it involves less risk of being left without employment. However, those merits do not explain why the diffusion of the gama system coincided with increases in the rice yields.

4. The percentage of landless laborers in the total number of households was also very high in this village: 57 percent at the time of our survey.

14 Poverty as a Generation's Problem: A Note on the Japanese Experience

S. HIRASHIMA

The Japanese experience indicates that for the majority of the poor—rural or urban—escaping the poverty trap is a task for a generation.[1] If the income status of a particular family is a function of the quality and the size of productive assets and the quality of family labor, then it is difficult to suppose that the economic position of the family could improve substantially in the short run. As long as poverty is deeply rooted in the current economic system (excluding pure socialistic states), the basic solution requires a long-run perspective.

This chapter focuses on two components of Dharm Narain's "trend" factor—irrigation and drainage, and technical education in agriculture—taking prewar Japan as an example. Three aspects of Japanese agricultural growth are particularly relevant to the development process. First, high productivity was accompanied by labor-intensive technology (high labor absorption) and relatively low demand for domestic as well as foreign capital. Second, at the beginning of industrialization the agricultural sector was not a bottleneck in terms of production, labor supply, and mobilization of rural savings. Finally, the state played an effective role in institution building and the successful implementation of land reform.

The average growth rate during the pre–World War II period (1889–1940) was 1.34 percent, and that of the postwar period (1956–76) was 2.09 percent (table 14.1). These rates do not look impressive in the face of the 2.7 percent rate of growth in Indian agriculture during the postindependence period (1949/50–1978/79) (Sarma 1981, 19). However, the per capita growth rate was accompanied by the consistently low rate of population growth (1.01 percent and 1.10 percent during the two reference periods). Levels of land productivity and labor input were high (fig. 14.1). In fact, the level of yield per hectare of rice in prewar Japan is comparable to that achieved by many Asian countries after the green revolution. Similarly, labor input per hectare in Japanese agriculture was

Table 14.1. Sectoral Growth of GDP in Real Terms in Japan, 1889–1976

Years	$A+M+S^a$	A	M	S	P
	%	%	%	%	%
1889–1900	2.92	1.37	6.25	3.16	—
1901–10	2.62	1.66	6.44	1.55	1.18[b]
1911–20	4.13	1.62	6.46	4.26	—
1921–30	2.41	0.75	5.57	0.44	1.26[c]
1931–40	4.86	1.30	7.17	3.64	—
Prewar average	3.31	1.34	6.34	2.59	1.01
1956–60	9.50	3.34	14.99	7.83	0.98
1961–70	10.45	2.11	13.48	9.23	—
1971–76	5.82	1.04	6.11	6.10	1.26[d]
Postwar average	8.90	2.09	11.73	8.05	1.10

Source: Minami (1981), 32, 80.

[a] A = Agriculture, forestry, and fishery; M = Manufacturing, mining, construction, transport and communication, and public works; S = Commerce and services; P = Rate of population growth

[b] 1901–5

[c] 1921–25

[d] 1971–75

consistently higher during the prewar period—and is still higher—than that of many other Asian countries.

Up to 1900 Japan was a net exporter of foodgrains, and the agricultural sector produced the major export items.[2] The revenue burden on agriculture was 1.83 million tons of rice in 1836 and 1.77 million tons in 1873 (Hayashi 1965, 170). In 1883–87 the tax burden borne by the agricultural sector was 20 percent of net produce, compared with 2 percent for the nonagricultural sector. The figures for 1930 were 7 percent and 4 percent, respectively (Minami 1981, 75).

The number of farm households was surprisingly stable at around 5.5 million during the prewar period (table 14.2). Gainfully employed workers per farm household decreased by only 0.2 person in 65 years owing to the primogeniture system legally instituted in 1898. Towards the end of the Tokugawa period, the land-man ratio had deteriorated to such an extent that given the level of technology and the heavy burden of feudal rent, further subdivision was prohibitive for the majority of farm households. This system laid the foundation for the supply of cheap labor to the nonagricultural sector, notably to the small- and medium-scale industries and the service sector.

Irrigation associations, farmers' associations, and other cooperatives are well-known institutions in rural Japan. Japan also is one of the few countries where drastic land reform was successfully implemented, in

Figure 14.1. National average labor input per crop per hectare and rice yield (in tons of brown rice) per hectare in Japan, 1883–1969

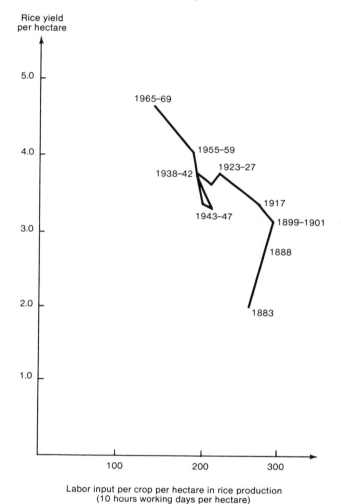

Source: Ishikawa, Yamada, and Hirashima (1982, 52).

1946. With this reform, the proportion of pure owner-cultivators jumped from 31 percent in 1940 to 62 percent in 1950, while pure tenants fell from 27 percent to 5 percent (table 14.2).

By the end of World War II, the agrarian situation had become unstable and discouraging for many renters. This resulted in the rice riot of 1918, a series of tenancy disputes in the 1920s, and a series of constraints imposed

Table 14.2. The Land-Labor Ratio and the Land-Tenure Structure in Japan, 1875–1977

Year	Gainfully Employed Agricultural Workers (thousands) (1)	Farm Households (thousands) (2)	Cultivated Land (thousands of hectares) (3)	(3)/(1) (4)	(3)/(2) (5)	(1)/(2) (6)	Percentage of Total Farmers		
							Owners (7)	Part owners (8)	Tenants (9)
1875	14,886	5,517	4,556	0.306	0.826	2.7	—	—	—
1880	14,655	5,500	4,664	0.318	0.848	2.7	37.3[a]%	41.8%	20.9%
1890	14,279	5,448	4,836	0.339	0.888	2.6	—	—	—
1900	14,211	5,502	5,112	0.360	0.929	2.6	35.4[b]	38.4	26.2
1910	14,929	5,517	5,477	0.391	0.995	2.5	33.4	39.2	27.4
1920	13,939	5,564	5,903	0.423	1.061	2.5	31.3	40.6	28.1
1930	13,944	5,613	5,863	0.420	1.045	2.5	31.1	42.3	26.5
1940	13,549	5,484	6,023	0.445	1.098	2.5	31.1	42.1	26.8
1950	15,990	6,156	—	—	—	2.6	61.9	32.4	5.1
1960	13,390	5,966	6,071	0.453	1.018	2.2	75.2	21.6	2.9
1977	12,643	4,835	5,536	0.438	1.145	2.6	79.2[c]	18.8	1.6

Source: Ishikawa, Yamada, and Hirashima (1982), 74 (table 36).

[a] 1883/84
[b] 1899
[c] 1970

by the state on prices, food production, procurement, and distribution. However, there was no significant difference in output per unit of land between owner-cultivators and tenant farmers. Also, if scale of operation is considered, there was no difference between the two in labor input per unit of land.[3] A high productivity level and a high labor intensity were achieved in the context of a high tenancy ratio in pre–land reform Japan. Consequently, the redistribution of land from landlords to the existing tenants did not affect social productivity.

How was this possible? There are three plausible factors: the strength of community relations, investment in irrigation and drainage, and the interaction among institutions concerned with agriculture, namely, technical education, research and experiment, and farmers' associations. Since I have dealt with the relationship among these factors elsewhere (Hirashima 1982), here I shall discuss only irrigation and drainage and technical education.

Investment in Irrigation and Drainage

Irrigation and drainage are leading inputs in farming by which productivity, labor absorption, and equity can be increased. Higher productivity comes mainly from the possibility of a better combination of necessary inputs. Labor absorption can definitely be increased when irrigation and drainage permit expansion of the area under cultivation in the dry season. However, the economic condition of the poor in rural areas can be improved by investment in irrigation and drainage only if it is directed properly. Let us look at some cases.

As every farmer knows, those who cultivate land with better ecological, locational, and morphological characteristics get higher returns at the same input level than those who cultivate poor land. Equity can be maintained in two ways: by taxing the extra returns that accrue to the natural differences of soil, that is, the differential rent of the first type; or by equalizing productive capacity of soil by land improvement, which can be done most effectively by investment in irrigation and drainage.

The experiences of most developed countries in providing equity in either of these ways do not look impressive, and those of the developing countries are also quite discouraging, for several reasons: First, land revenue and water revenue are negligible in amount and do not rise with productivity. Second, investment in irrigation and drainage tends to concentrate on the already better-endowed regions or regions where a higher return per unit of capital invested is possible. Third, in many cases investment is made by the public sector, which fails to recover the costs. In other words, a substantial portion of rent generated by such investment goes into the private income stream. Fourth, private investment in the form of new seeds, fertilizer, and so on, tends to concentrate on improved land. Consequently, the disparity between land with and without public investment has been widening. Finally, extra benefit has been accumulated by those exploiting underground water. As Dantwala rightly points out in chapter 10, this will be a major source of disparity in the future, since underground water is mistakenly regarded as a free good, which enables farmers in the sweet water belt to capitalize their situational advantage. Private investment in this venture also tends to concentrate on the better-endowed land.

Irrigation as a Source of Equity

Although investment in irrigation and drainage can worsen inter-regional and interpersonal disparity, it also can reduce differences in the productive capacity of land. One possibility is for the state to direct the investment towards this end. The other is for investment in land improvement to be decentralized, preferably at the community level, using communal funds and labor.

Japan was fortunate in these two respects. Taking advantage of a relatively balanced distribution of rainfall and relatively small rivers and a favorable institutional set-up, the basic investment in irrigation (not much in drainage) was made during the feudalistic period before the Meiji Restoration (1868) in a decentralized way.

During the Tokugawa period in particular, the power of a feudal clan was measured in terms of the rice production of its territory. There was, therefore, a strong incentive for each clan to enhance the productive capacity of its farmland by expanding the area under rice and increasing productivity. To achieve this objective, many clans developed technologies that were kept secret within the clan territory.[4] Only irrigation technology was diffused among the clan territories, because irrigation and flood-control works on rivers running through several clan territories were usually undertaken by the center (the shogunate).[5]

At the community level within the clan, irrigation practice has long been the field-to-field irrigation in small and fragmented fields. The individual farmer had little choice as to seeds, cropping pattern, and the timing of farm operations. Choice of technology, water management, and cultural husbandry tended to be a community matter. This is one reason for the homogeneity in technology and productivity among farmers.

After the Meiji Restoration, the new government tried to improve paddy land at the macro level in several stages. Up to 1900 the major efforts were geared towards reparceling fragmented plots[6] and improving drainage in northern Japan.[7] In 1909 the Land Consolidation Act was amended to name irrigation and drainage as the key component of land-improvement works undertaken by the state. In the 1920s, however, the state started allocating public funds to the agricultural sector by subsidy and direct investment in which the irrigation and drainage works were given high priority. This coincided with the agrarian unrest during that decade. The agricultural sector's share in the total government subsidy rose from less than 5 percent up to 1910 to 21.2 percent in 1920, 26.6 percent in 1930, and 52.1 percent in 1940 (Minami 1981, 286). The increased public expenditure was reflected in a sharp increase in the marginal capital-output ratio of agriculture from 1.36 in 1900–1920 to 5.00 in 1920–42 (table 14.3).

These efforts substantially reduced regional differences in land productivity that had existed in the early part of the Meiji period. If we take the 5-year average rice yield of the lowest five prefectures as 100, the index for the highest five prefectures dropped from 180 in 1883–86 to 128 in 1952–56 (Imamura et al. 1977, 71).

Technical Education in Agriculture

The Japanese experience indicates that an interregional or interpersonal disparity in land productivity can be reduced if the investment in irrigation and drainage is properly directed. However, such an investment would not be an adequate solution to the disparity and poverty that originated in the ownership and size distribution of productive assets in agriculture. Disparity of this kind was not reduced until after the land reforms in 1946.

Under the skewed distribution of productive assets prevalent in prewar Japan, the chief option for poor tenants and small farmers was to invest in their children's education. They hoped to get out of the poverty trap by sending their children to the nonagricultural sectors and by upgrading the quality of manpower that remained in farming.

The role of technical education in agriculture should be examined from four points of view. First, it plays an important role in training local people for leadership as well as in upgrading the technical capacity of farmers. Second, too much emphasis is being given to higher education in developing countries; more attention should be paid to technical education at the lower level. Third, the fact that normal education leaves out a substantial portion of the children of the poor should be more widely recognized. Fourth, problems associated with the unemployment of the educated are used to justify the slow development of education, without regard to the kind of education available.

Japan installed a formal education system in 1872. As in many other countries, compulsory education was introduced at the primary level, beginning with four years in 1886; it was extended to 6 years in 1907 and to 9 years in 1947. The enrollment rate was 28.1 percent in 1873, 48.9

Table 14.3. Growth Rates of Capital Stock, Employment, and GDP (in Real Terms) and the Capital-Output Ratio and Employment Coefficients for Japan, 1885–1940

Variable	1885	1885–1900	1900–20	1920–40
Capital (K)	—	0.3	1.0	1.3
Employed (N)	—	0.0	−0.5	0.1
GDP (Ya)	—	1.7	1.8	0.7
K/Ya	3.35	2.75	2.33	2.67
$\Delta K/\Delta Ya$	—	0.57	1.36	5.00
N/Ya	9.85	7.65	4.81	4.25
$\Delta N/\Delta Ya$	—	0.41	−1.65	0.41

Source: Extracted and modified from Nakamura (1980), 24.

percent in 1890, and 98.1 percent in 1910. The student-population ratio became comparable to that of England in 1910 and to that of the United States in the 1930s (Minami 1981, 12). The enrollment rate of girls lagged behind that of boys, but it was almost the same by 1920 (UNESCO 1975, 10).

Despite the rapid development of education in Japan, technical education in agriculture, industry, and commerce was not emphasized in the earlier years. As figure 14.2 indicates, the education system had a dualistic structure. Even though technical education was a part of the regular school system in 1880, it was regarded as inferior, and few students registered in the initial period. Nevertheless, it was realized that upgrading the quality of labor was essential to modernizing the country.

As in many contemporary developing countries, technical education started at the college level. The Sapporo Agricultural School (currently the Faculty of Agriculture, Hokkaido University) was opened in 1876 following the framework of the Massachusetts College of Agriculture. The Komaba Agricultural School (currently the Faculty of Agriculture, University of Tokyo), which opened in 1878, followed European models. In 1893, post-primary agricultural education was instituted by the Technical Supplementary School Ordinance. Six years later the basic structure of the agricultural middle school was completed—type A at the prefectural level and type B at the county level. The agricultural high school was the last to be developed, the more important ones being established during the two decades after 1900. By 1935 there were 5 universities with agricultural colleges, 14 agricultural high schools, 361 agricultural middle schools, and 17,300 post-primary agricultural schools in Japan (Zenkoku Nogyo Gakkocho Kyokai 1941).

Agricultural schools provided an opportunity to learn to those who could not afford the normal education. Since most of the students coming

Figure 14.2. The education system in prewar Japan

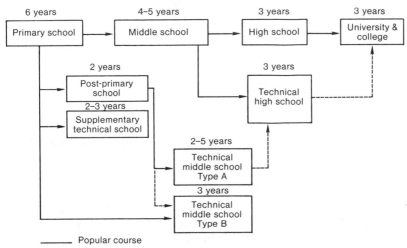

_____ Popular course

_ _ _ _ _ _ Opened but less popular course

Note: There were basically three kinds of technical schools: agricultural, commercial, and industrial. Up to 1906, compulsory education was four years, and at that time post-primary schools were four years, which was reduced to two years after 1907.

to technical schools were from the lower-income strata, they were already an important labor source to their families. Those who could not afford to go to normal middle school went to either post-primary schools or agricultural supplementary schools in villages and towns. Some went to type B agricultural middle schools, located in the county. However, as figure 14.2 shows, those who studied at supplementary agricultural schools or type B technical middle schools did not go further. Type A agricultural middle schools were popular for those who could afford them, but very few graduates went on to high school.[8] Also, a few students who could not afford a normal course of education were able to go to a university.

The agricultural supplementary schools were expected to supplement the primary education of those working or going to work and to give knowledge and skills needed in those occupations. The schools were open at night and on Sundays and were closed during peak agricultural seasons. In many cases, they shared facilities with local primary schools. Subjects taught included ethics, arithmetic, reading, introductory agriculture, plowing, manuring, pesticides, irrigation and drainage, agricultural implements, livestock, sericulture, forestry, and soil science.

The agricultural middle school was expected to educate local leaders and others who could improve agriculture. There were 30 lecture hours a week for type A schools and 27 hours for type B. Practical training was adjusted in accordance with the agricultural seasons.[9] Subjects taught at type A schools included ethics, reading, composition, mathematics, physics, chemistry, economics, and gymnastics. Geography, history, foreign language, bookkeeping, and law were optional. Practical training covered soil science, manuring, plant science, agroindustry, dairy, sericulture, climatology, forestry, veterinary science, and fishery. Sophisticated subjects such as physics, economics, and so on, were not taught in type B schools.

Agricultural high schools and colleges were intended to train those who could lead agricultural development at the national as well as the prefectural level. Almost 70 percent of the graduates of agricultural high schools went into government service and teaching institutions, and less than 10 percent remained in farming (table 14.4).

Graduates of agricultural schools found jobs in various related fields. Some remained in farming, some worked in various agencies related to agriculture, including the Ministry of Agriculture, experiment stations, and farmers' organizations. Many became local leaders and politicians. Graduates of agricultural schools formed a network that was effectively utilized by the state in the implementation of the agricultural policies. Also, the network provided a channel through which local problems could be brought to the attention of decision-making bodies. The system contributed to the high degree of homogeneity in productivity among Japanese farmers.

Conclusion

About 70 percent of the farm households in prewar Japan operated less than one hectare, and the same percentage cultivated rented land. As late as 1950, when the yield per hectare reached four tons, the majority of operators of less than one hectare of land could not meet household expenditures with agricultural income (Nakamura 1980, 333–34). Under these conditions, the overall poverty situation would have worsened rapidly if the investment in irrigation and drainage had been made according to the economic feasibility alone and if the government had not invested in agricultural education. Without these investment policies, the homogeneity of technology and productivity among those different in tenure status and scale of operation would not have been possible.

This chapter does not claim that the Japanese experience was a success story in alleviating rural poverty during the prewar period. As already mentioned, the land reform of 1946 played a major role in solving the problems of land tenure, the basic cause of low incomes for the majority of tenants and small farmers. Nevertheless, land reform would not have been as effective if the homogeneity in land productivity had not been

Table 14.4. Employment of Agricultural High School and Middle School Graduates in Japan, as of 1935 and 1938

Employment	Agricultural High School[a]	Agricultural Middle School			
		Type A		Type B	
		Male	Female	Male	Female
Total number of graduates[b]	13,419.0	206,677.0	11,891.0	116,565.0	20,741.0
Government office	50.3%	26.8%	3.7%	9.9%	2.4%
Teaching institution	18.4	10.7	3.7	2.7	1.2
Higher education and military service	2.3	7.8	2.0	5.3	0.8
Engaged in					
Farming	8.6	41.9	67.4	68.0	72.8
Nonfarming	1.9	6.8	13.6	10.4	15.0
Private company	12.5	—	—	—	—
Overseas	1.8	3.9	1.1	1.9	1.1
Other	4.1	2.1	8.6	1.8	6.6
Total	100.0	100.0	100.0	100.0	100.0

Source: Calculated and compiled from Zenkoku Nogyo Gakkocho Kyokai (1941).

[a] These figures relate only to those who graduated from 11 public agricultural high schools; there were 14 agricultural high schools in 1935.

[b] As of 1935 for high schools and 1938 for middle schools, excluding those graduates unidentified or dead

achieved during the prewar period. As has been emphasized, this was owing to the deliberate efforts of the state to direct investment in irrigation and drainage in a decentralized way and to develop education in rural areas, particularly technical education in agriculture, commerce, and industry.

Notes

The author is grateful to Dr. Wilbert Gooneratne of ILO-ARTEP for his valuable comments.

1. The current migration to the Middle Eastern oil-producing countries may be an exception. But even in this case, unskilled migrant laborers would remain so in the short run, despite their acquisition of assets.

2. Morita (1969, app.). The proportion of agricultural commodities, including raw silk, in total export was 83 percent in 1870 and 29 percent in 1930 (see Minami 1981, 50, 71).

3. For a detailed discussion see Yamada (1982, 27–58).

4. The source of growth in agricultural production from the Meiji Restoration up to 1900 was the nationwide diffusion of these clan-specific technologies (Hirashima 1982).

5. Two major schools of irrigation technology authorized by the shogunate, namely, the Kanto school and the Kishu school, spread all over the country.

6. The first land consolidation act, based on the German model, was passed in 1899.

7. Horse plowing, an advanced technology developed in the well-drained paddy land of western Japan, could not be introduced in the poorly drained land in the north.

8. For example, out of 255 resident students of Morioka Agricultural High School in 1909, 48 were graduates of type A schools, and the rest came from the normal middle schools (see Kokuritsu Kyoiku Kenkyusho 1973, 732 and table 7).

9. In the 1890s the proportion of specialized subjects taught to ordinary subjects taught was 7 to 3, but in the 1900s it was reversed (ibid., 716).

15 Terms of Trade, Agricultural Growth, and Rural Poverty in Africa

UMA LELE

Dharm Narain's formulation for India stresses the size of agricultural production and the level of nominal prices as the determinants of the percentage of the population living below the poverty line. This chapter explores the significance of this line of enquiry for Africa.[1]

The chapter first identifies the structural characteristics of the small, open African agricultural economies that distinguish them from large, densely populated Asian countries such as India or Indonesia.[2] Through a simple model, the chapter then outlines the role of international and domestic terms of trade and the size of agricultural production in influencing the incidence of poverty in Africa, arguing that the major determinants of African rural poverty are the size of overall agricultural production, the international prices of African agricultural tradeable commodities relative to prices of importables, and the domestic producer prices of food and export crops. International prices of exportables and importables, hereafter referred to as the international terms of trade, are exogenously determined, whereas domestic producer prices are affected by both the international terms of trade and the rate of revenue extraction by the government. The size and composition of agricultural production are a function of the various relative prices and investment in the agricultural sector. Investment in agriculture is largely influenced by the pattern of government expenditures in the agricultural sector. The chapter illustrates that given international and domestic prices, technological change in agriculture is fundamental to the achievement of overall agricultural growth as well as to the alleviation of poverty and that the pattern of public investments is critical in influencing the rate of technical change.

The role of prices has received a great deal of attention by economists concerned with African development in recent years,[3] and a further controversy has arisen as to the relative importance to be attached to import substitution of food versus export promotion in agricultural development.[4] However, even in this price-focused analysis, the precise links of international to domestic prices have not been adequately explored. In particular, the role of government interventions in creating multiple markets and prices, and consequently the differing nature of domestic markets for food and export crops, has not been examined adequately in terms of their effect on resource allocation between production of food and production of export crops. But what is most important, the role of public investments in influencing the size of overall agricultural production has received relatively little attention, although public goods are generally known to be critical in ensuring agricultural development in less developed countries and, in particular, technological and internal market constraints are known to be severe in holding back African agricultural growth.[5] Using a three-sector model, this chapter illustrates the implications of these considerations for the growth and composition of agricultural production and its relation to African poverty.

There are several respects in which the African agricultural production and pricing relations are different *in degree* from those in Asia. First, the problem of access to land for cultivation, popularly referred to in Asia as the "incidence of landlessness," is far less frequent in Africa than in Asia, although the growing population pressure on the land has already made landlessness a problem in some countries, and it is expected to increase in the near future.[6] And despite the great variability among groups within rural Africa, on the average the extent of market dependence for food, particularly for cereals and cereal substitutes, is routinely well below that in South Asia.[7] Crop failures, however, occur more frequently in Africa than in Asia, given African agriculture's nearly complete reliance on rain. This means that the dependence of the African rural population on the market is markedly greater in some years than in others. Later in this chapter, I discuss the relations of market dependence and market failures with the levels and composition of agricultural production and rural poverty in Africa.

Second, unlike in countries such as India, international trade represents a large portion of the African GNP, and agriculture's share in such trade is quite large. Further, for most of their exports, Africans are price takers. This is illustrated by the African shares of selected individual crops in world trade (table 15.1). With a few exceptions—crops such as cocoa, sisal, pyrethrum, or burley tobacco—the size of African agricultural production does not influence international prices. Thus, by and large, increases in African exports should not have an adverse effect on African income. Of the commodities for which African production exercises an influence on international prices, only cocoa is important from the viewpoint of the total agricultural export earnings of the African countries. In the case of sisal, burley tobacco, and some others, while African

Table 15.1. The Share of Main Export Crops of Selected African Countries in World Trade, 1980

Country and Commodity	Value (thousands of 1980 $U.S.)	Percentage of World Trade
Ethiopia		
Coffee	272,338	2.17%
Cotton	11,252	0.14
Ghana		
Cocoa	788,300	15.82
Coffee	2,900	0.02
Ivory Coast		
Cocoa	857,565	17.21
Coffee	485,645	3.88
Cotton	66,274	0.81
Kenya		
Coffee	291,384	2.33
Tea and mate	156,227	10.24
Vegetable fibers, except cotton and jute	23,889	6.07
Malawi		
Tobacco	124,420	3.61
Tea and mate	36,724	2.41
Cotton	5,607	0.07
Nigeria		
Cocoa	485,445	9.74
Cotton	34,323	0.42
Oilseeds, nuts, kernels	38,650	0.41
Senegal		
Cotton	10,300	0.13
Sudan		
Cotton	238,209	2.91
Oilseeds, nuts, kernels	85,982	0.91
Tea and mate	2,507	0.16
Tanzania		
Coffee	138,655	1.11
Cotton	52,030	0.64
Vegetable fibers, except cotton and jute	30,303	7.71
Tea and mate	22,482	1.47
Uganda		
Coffee	340,726	2.72
Cotton	4,185	0.05
Zaire		
Coffee	166,440	1.33
Cocoa	6,941	0.14
Zambia		
Cotton	8,360	0.10
Tobacco	3,423	0.10
Oilseeds, nuts, kernels	839	0.01
Zimbabwe		
Tobacco	176,136	5.11
Cotton	85,295	1.04

Source: UNCTAD (1983).

production influences world prices, the crops do not represent an important share of Africa's total exports and incomes. Exogenously determined international terms of trade can thus be assumed. These terms of trade are a significant determinant of African real incomes as well as of the size and composition of African agricultural production.

The domestic terms of trade between the agricultural and the urban sector influence the distribution of income between the two sectors (and within agriculture) and hence the extent of rural poverty. Given agriculture's importance in the GNP, it is natural that the agricultural sector should constitute the major source of government revenues and that governments should control internal agricultural trade to generate revenues. However, it is the public expenditure patterns that determine the extent to which these revenues extracted from the agricultural sector are plowed back into agriculture for influencing current and future agricultural production. In Africa, revenue generation has been used largely to support consumption of the urban population or to carry out capital-intensive investments with low rates of return and relatively few linkages with or benefits for the rural sector.[8] If expenditures were directed more towards agricultural technology development, rural transport and communications, or the education and training of the rural entrepreneurial class, the productivity and production of rural commodities and services would increase. Through a simple model, I outline below the effect of exogenously determined international and domestic terms of trade and public-expenditure patterns on rural prices and production and hence on poverty in Africa.

The Model

Nominal rural household income may be defined as

$$Y_R = P_A Q_A + S_b + S_s + R, \qquad (15.1)$$

where Y_R = rural household income, P_A = producer prices of agricultural commodities, Q_A = the quantities of agricultural commodities, S_b = subsidies received by the agricultural sector, S_s = social services provided to the rural sector, and R = remittances of rural workers working in the nonagricultural sector.

For the purposes of this chapter, I assume that the rural sector is synonymous with the agricultural sector and that the urban sector is synonymous with the public sector. I also assume that the income received in the form of subsidies on agricultural inputs (S_b), food supplies, or other factors entering into rural production or consumption is negligible. This is a realistic assumption, given that purchased inputs constitute a small portion of value added in African agricultural production, even though rates of subsidies on inputs are frequently quite large.[9] Also, except in periods of extreme emergency, such as the drought of 1973/74, most official food-supply systems do not reach rural Africa even to the extent that they reach rural Asia. Subsidies on transportation are frequently large in Africa. These are most notable in eastern and southern African countries, where the policy of uniform official agricultural (producer and consumer) pricing is rigorously implemented. However, in effect, transport subsidies do not benefit the rural sector to the extent that they would appear to on the surface, either because governments do not buy all the agricultural surpluses offered on the market, especially of food crops, or because these subsidies are largely compensated for by the high cost of government marketing monopolies, which support a large and inefficient urban public sector.

Social services received by the rural population in the form of free schooling, water supply, or health clinics can be important. But these depend on the patterns of public expenditures, which, in turn, influence the size of agricultural production and are influenced by it. Their implications for the levels of poverty are spelled out later in the chapter. Finally, remittances of wage earners to rural households constitute a significant portion of household income in some African countries, such as Botswana, Lesotho, Swaziland, Zambia, and Nigeria. In my formal presentation I abstract from this income on the ground that in overall terms such remittances are unlikely to constitute a major source of future rural income in most African countries unless rapid agricultural productivity growth allows a more sustainable pattern of overall economic development.[10] Their implications for our findings are nevertheless explored qualitatively later in this chapter.

Thus we assume that agricultural household income

$$Y_R = P_A Q_A = P_{F_i} Q_{F_i} + P_{F_f} Q_{F_f} + P_E Q_E,$$

where P_{F_i} and P_{F_f} are the nominal producer prices of food crops in the informal and formal markets, respectively, and P_E is the producer price of export crops in the formal market. A formal market is defined as an exchange either between the producer and the government or between the producer and the large processor or exporter. An informal market is the "traditional," mostly rural market, where small surpluses are exchanged among producers and consumers at market prices. Q_{F_i} and Q_{F_f} are the quantities of food crops sold in the informal and formal markets, respectively, and Q_E is the quantity of export crops. P_F and Q_F are the weighted average prices and total quantities of food crops, respectively. Export crops in this model are the traded goods, and food crops are only internally traded. Food crops may, however, be imported.[11]

Poverty in Subsistence Agriculture

Certain areas of the African rural sector are completely subsistence-oriented where export-crop production is constrained by physical-resource endowment, especially the unsuitability of land. In such situations, $Q_E = 0$, and all Q_F is used in domestic consumption. Any increase in food-crop production should lead to an increase in food available for household consumption, supporting Dharm Narain's hypothesis of the direct relation between production and poverty alleviation. Whether it would increase nominal household income would depend on what happened to informal and formal market prices, P_{F_i} and P_{F_f}. This issue will be discussed later in this chapter.

The extent to which production of subsistence crops is increased frequently depends on the difficult trade-offs between considerations of household food security and of growth in production. For instance, the new high-yield varieties of sorghum and maize introduced in Africa are frequently more susceptible to climatic fluctuations than their traditional varieties or the substitute root crops typically grown. This means greater variance in production even though the mean value of the new crop output may be higher. Interyear household storage of these new crops often is not effective, since their storability is poorer than that of traditional crops. Consumer prices in the informal markets increase sharply in periods of food shortages. Moreover, for a variety of reasons, governments and informal markets are unable to stabilize supply effectively from year to year through their own market interventions. Formal food imports, almost always made on government account, typically arrive late and are smaller than the extent of domestic excess demands. In periods of food shortages, governments do not give the rural sector the same priority in the distribution of food as they give the urban sector.[12] The low density of African rural areas and the associated great distances lead to high unit costs of public distribution in the rural sector, and the absence of a free press reduces the likelihood that governments will be responsive to the needs of rural families.[13] Thus, when producers adopt new crops that are susceptible to droughts, they increase their market dependence in times when supplies and prices are uncertain. The incentive to adopt the new high-yield varieties is consequently lower than the average yield of these varieties over the years may imply, limiting the possibilities in the short and the medium run of reducing poverty levels through production programs.[14]

The Tanzanian government's efforts to promote hybrid maize in the arid Dodoma region through a national maize program after the drought of 1973/74 encountered much resistance from farmers owing to the lower drought resistance of hybrid maize relative to that of the traditional varieties of sorghum and cassava, as well as the unwillingness of producers to depend on the National Milling Corporation for food supply.

Poverty in Export-Crop-Producing Agriculture

Rural households may produce both food crops and export crops and may generate marketed surpluses, which they exchange for other subsistence needs.[15] Their consumption may then be defined as

$$C_R = P_F Q_F + \gamma P_N Q_N,$$
(15.2)

where γ = the fraction of imported production consumed in the rural sector, P_N = the prices of nonagricultural goods,[16] and Q_N = the quantities of nonagricultural goods.

We now turn to the determination of the quantities of nonagricultural goods consumed in the rural sector. We assume that all export-crop production in the country is exported and that all nonagricultural goods consumed are imported. The foreign-trade balance is thus presented in foreign currency as follows:

$$P_E^* Q_E^* = P_N^* Q_N^*,$$
(15.3)

where P_E^* = the price of African exports in foreign currency and P_N^* = the price of African nonagricultural imports in foreign currency. International terms of trade may then be defined as

$$P = P_E^* / P_N^*.$$
(15.4)

As the prices of Africa's exports in foreign currency decline (or rise) and/or prices of its imports increase (decline), the volume of African imports will decline (rise) unless price changes are compensated for by increased production of exportables. Increased (reduced) capital transfers may also help counter the trade imbalance.

Agricultural export volumes stagnated or declined in most of Africa in the period 1970–82, with a few exceptions, such as the Ivory Coast and Malawi (see table 15.2). With the two oil-price shocks, the international terms of trade moved against many African countries, especially since 1978–79 (table 15.3). Capital transfers mainly through donor assistance did not increase sufficiently in all countries during this period to compensate for the adverse terms of trade and export-volume effects (table 15.4). The result of volume and price effects has been a general decline in the capacity to import. The extent to which reduced imports affect the rural poor depends on the initial pattern of imports and subsequent responses to various price changes. To the extent that reduced foreign-exchange availability reduces imports of agricultural inputs, spare parts, or consumer goods consumed in the rural sector, this should adversely

Table 15.2. Growth of Trade in Selected African and Asian Countries, 1960–80

| | Annual Average Growth Rate | | | | Indices of Terms of Trade (1980 = 100) | |
| | Exports | | Imports | | | |
Country	1960–70	1970–82	1960–70	1970–82	1979	1982
Africa						
Ivory Coast	8.9%	2.6%	10.0%	4.6%	119	91
Kenya	7.5	−3.3	6.5	−2.7	108	87
Malawi	11.7	5.1	7.6	1.2	111	106
Nigeria	6.6	−1.6	1.5	17.2	67	103
Senegal	1.4	−1.8	2.3	1.3	110	89
Sudan	2.1	−5.1	0.5	3.5	98	85
Tanzania	3.8	−5.8	6.0	−1.5	105	86
Zambia	2.3	−0.5	9.7	−6.8	118	72
Sub-Saharan	5.9	−0.8[a]	6.0	3.3[a]		
Asia						
Bangladesh	8.1	−0.8	7.0	5.5	96	98
India	4.7	4.7	−0.9	2.6	118	96
Indonesia	3.5	4.4	1.9	12.3	73	108
Philippines	2.3	7.9	7.2	2.1	112	83
Sri Lanka	4.6	0.1	−0.2	1.8	126	85
Thailand	5.2	9.1	11.3	4.3	121	78

Sources: World Bank (1981a), 149; (1984a), 124–25.
[a] 1970–79 only

Table 15.3. Indices of International Terms of Trade in Selected African and Asian Countries, 1960–81, Selected Years (1975 = 100)

Country	1960	1978	1979	1980	1981
Africa					
Cameroon	106	168	144	123	90
Ivory Coast	113	150	129	102	78
Kenya	133	144	110	94	99
Malawi	115	108	84	76	82
Nigeria	32	102	119	173	190
Senegal		97		63	68
Sudan	83	86	78	86	88
Tanzania	98	121	102	100	113
Zambia	115	89	100	82	67
Zimbabwe		81			94
Asia					
Bangladesh	201	99	90	84	79
India	134	108	88	71	66
Indonesia	63	95	119	135	154
Philippines	112	98	107	75	68
Sri Lanka	203	151	116	93	80
Thailand	121	87	73	63	62

Sources: World Bank (1981d, 1982, 1983c).

Table 15.4. Net Official Development Assistance, 1979–82, and the 1982 Current Account Balance for Selected African Countries (in millions of U.S. dollars)

Country	Net Official Development Assistance				1982 Current Account Balance
	1979	1980	1981	1982	
Cameroon	274	264	202	210	−525
Ghana	169	192	145	142	83
Ivory Coast	162	210	124	136	15
Kenya	351	396	449	482	−509
Malawi	142	143	138	121	−78
Nigeria	27	36	41	35	−7,324
Senegal	307	263	400	279	—
Sudan	570	620	681	702	−248
Swaziland	50	50	37	26	—
Tanzania	588	666	673	676	−268
Zaire	416	428	394	330	−375
Zambia	277	295	231	237	−252
Zimbabwe	12	162	207	214	−706
Sub-Saharan Africa	9,344	10,755	10,512	10,407	−10,876

Sources: For the net official development assistance, OECD (1983), 206; for the current account balance, World Bank (1984a), 244.

affect the rural sector. To the extent that import cuts reduce unproductive investments or urban consumption, they should have no effect on the rural sector. Capital investments, however, tend to be lumpy and subject to pressure from both domestic political and international financiers' sources against being cut. Similarly, urban consumption tends to be protected owing to the political weight of the urban constituencies. Thus, except in the case of food, imports to meet urban demand may not benefit the rural sector even indirectly by increasing supplies for rural consumption. Food imports may lead to reduced food prices, but these will have substitution effects in consumption as well as in production. (This issue is discussed more fully below.) For these various reasons, in reality foreign-exchange constraints have hurt rural consumption both directly and indirectly through their adverse effects on the domestic production of essential commodities, caused by shortages of imported agricultural inputs, raw materials, and spare parts. Commercial food imports have risen in recent years in many countries (table 15.5). It can be safely assumed that a substantial portion of these imports is used to meet urban food needs. This means even greater constraint on other imports, although this situation varies from year to year and among countries, depending on the importance of food imports in total imports.

The importance of agricultural production growth to compensate for the international terms-of-trade losses cannot be overemphasized. The

Table 15.5. Food Aid and Commercial Imports of Selected African Countries, 1975–78 (in thousands of metric tons)

Country	1975	1976	1977	1978
Cameroon				
Food aid	0	0	0	0
Commercial imports	69	74	116	122
Ethiopia				
Food aid	38	5	53	31
Commercial imports	29	87	139	87
Ghana				
Food aid	33	21	52	47
Commercial imports	52	95	220	253
Ivory Coast				
Food aid	3	0	0	0
Commercial imports	79	122	282	309
Kenya				
Food aid	5	3	7	5
Commercial imports	81	9	28	95
Nigeria				
Food aid	0	0	0	0
Commercial imports	444	852	1239	2044
Senegal				
Food aid	28	4	15	73
Commercial imports	192	414	414	355
Tanzania				
Food aid	105	51	122	65
Commercial imports	356	46	34	58
Zambia				
Food aid	1	2	20	12
Commercial imports	163	84	85	96

Source: Huddleston (1983), app. 3.

World Bank analysis in Tanzania indicated that a 2 – 4 percent rate of annual growth of export-crop production during the 1970s in place of the 4.5 percent annual decline experienced would have considerably narrowed the trade deficit. (Lele 1984; World Bank 1983b.) This was not an unrealistic growth rate of production to expect, given Tanzania's agricultural record. Export-crop production had experienced a growth rate of about 3 percent annually from 1930 to 1950, and this rate had accelerated to well over 6 percent during the 1950 – 70 period. Malawi experienced a terms-of-trade loss similar to Tanzania's. However, it realized growth of export volumes of well over 5 percent annually in the 1970s, leading to an increase in its purchasing power of close to 2 percent annually, compared with a decline of nearly 6 percent in Tanzania. How much of this export growth benefited the rural poor in Malawi is, however, questionable owing to the low proportion of the consumer or export price passed on to the peasant producer by the government's marketing agency (Kydd and Christiansen 1982; Ghai and Radwan 1983).

Government as a Surplus Extractor

Even if international terms of trade rise as they did in many African countries during the beverage boom in the second half of the 1970s, the benefits to producers will depend upon the rate of surplus extraction by the government and patterns of public expenditures. We now explore the issue of government as an intermediary in influencing the domestic terms of trade.

Let

$$P_{F_f} = P_C - M_C, \tag{15.5}$$

where P_{F_f} = the official producer price of food in the formal market, P_C = the official consumer price of food, and M_C = the marketing cost of the official agency. Many African governments attempt to exercise a monopoly power in the urban sales of food. P_C is then determined exogenously by governments to maintain prices of food attractive to the urban consumers.

Poverty levels depend on the ability of governments to effectively exert a monopsony in food-crop purchases. But for the present,

$$M_C = M_T + G, \tag{15.6}$$

where M_T is the transport cost of buying food from the rural producers and G = the amount extracted by the government. Further,

$$G = A_C + T_A,$$

where A_C = the administrative costs of the parastatals and T_A = the tax on the rural sector.

The size of G may be exogenously determined by a combination of rather large administrative costs which exceed any "legitimate" costs even of formal marketing, and the tax. This latter may be used by governments for further investment or consumption. The extent of monopsony power exercised by governments in crop purchases in Africa varies significantly by country and by crop. Thus, while Tanzania has tried to control purchases of all major food crops and export crops, in Malawi the marketing parastatal ADMARC is a residual buyer of food crops and a monopsonist in the purchases of export crops from peasant producers. Note that production of estate crops in Malawi is allowed to be sold directly by estates to private exporters; the government intervenes only in wholesale and retail pricing of sugar (World Bank 1981c). In Cameroon, there is effectively no control on domestic purchases of major cereals, although the government controls consumer prices and releases foodstocks. Whatever the variation in the domestic purchases and sales by governments of food crops, in most African countries governments are the monopsonists in the purchases of export crops either directly or through publicly sponsored cooperatives.

Internal transport costs (M_T) of parastatals in the formal market could be described as being a function of T, F, and S, where T is the amount of transportation equipment and spares, F is the fuel imported by the government through an administrative fiat, and S is the stock of transport equipment. Given that relatively few African countries follow free-trade policies and the import content of the cost of transport used by marketing parastatals is typically well over 80 percent, this is not an unrealistic assumption.

The amount of transportation equipment and spares (T) imported may be defined as

$$T = \alpha \cdot [P_E^* Q_E^* - (P_{F_1}^* \cdot F + P_{F_2}^* \cdot Q_F + \ldots + P_{FN}Q_{FN})]/P_T^*, \quad (15.7)$$

where α = the fraction of foreign exchange allocated to transport, $P_{F_1}^*$ = the international price of fuel, F = the quantity of fuel, $P_{F_2}^*$ = the international price of food, Q_F = the quantities of food imported, P_N = the price of other essential importables, and Q_N = the quantities of other essential importables.

The price elasticity of demand for fuel has been significantly lower in developing countries than in developed countries.[17] It is expected that this would be lower still in Africa, because much of the fuel consumption is by the public sector. Similarly, the quantities of food imported have been influenced by the exogenously determined weather factor and by a decline in the per capita marketed surpluses of food production available for urban consumption to formal market agencies. Therefore, as any of the international prices of fuel, food, or transport equipment rise, *ceteris paribus*, terms of trade (P) would move against Africa, and less foreign exchange would be available for importation of transport equipment.

Assume for static analysis that the total level of African exports is fixed, so that

$$(\partial M_T / \partial T) < 0,$$

$$(\partial M_T / \partial P) < 0.$$

This means that internal marketing costs in the formal sector would increase both because of the direct price effect of the increased fuel costs on domestic transport costs and because of the decline in the amount of transport equipment that can be imported. Indeed, since the second oil-price shock, owing to foreign-exchange constraints a number of African countries have reduced their importation of essential transport equipment and spare parts. While African official pricing policies do not reflect the differences in interregional costs of transportation, the effect on the producers of the rising fuel costs and foreign-exchange constraints is the decline in the effort by official agencies to purchase crops, thereby reducing the effective producer price of food and export crops in the formal market. Similarly, delays in payments to farmers by parastatals and cooperatives have been reported extensively in a number of countries, owing to the deteriorating financial situation of the parastatals as a result of their increased marketing costs. It is, therefore, necessary to examine the implications of multiple prices prevailing in African markets.

The Role of Dualistic Markets

The official producer price of food crop may be defined as

$$P_{F_f} = P_C - M_T - G_1, \tag{15.8}$$

where $G_1 =$ the government revenue extracted from food crops.

The informal market price is

$$P_{F_i} = P_{C_{F_i}} - M_{t_i},$$

where the consumer price in the informal market $(P_{C_{F_i}})$ is determined by the supply and demand for food in the informal market and M_{t_i} is the transaction cost in the informal market. Note that there is no surplus extraction by the government. The transaction costs in the informal market (M_{t_i}) would be expected to be lower than those in the formal market, since transactions in the informal market are mostly for local consumption on headloads, in contrast to transactions by the formal market, which are for consumption in the distant capital city. The import content of headloads of transport in the informal market would also be lower. Thus, when terms of trade move against African countries, while the formal food- and export-crop markets may both experience a rise in transport costs, this would not occur to the same extent in the case of the informal market. Thus the producer price of food in the informal market (P_{F_i}) is more than the producer price of food in the formal market (P_{F_f}) when terms of trade move against Africa.

The producer price of the export crop may be defined as

$$P_E = e P_E^* - M_T - G_2, \tag{15.9}$$

where $G_2 =$ the government revenue extracted from export crops and $e =$ the exchange rate.

Equation (15.9) demonstrates how a decline in the international terms of trade would lead to a decline in the producer price of export crops unless the government's rate of extraction or the exchange rate changed. We assume no domestic consumption of export crops and thus no welfare effect of reduced P_E on domestic consumers. On the other hand, food-crop production is consumed in the country, and the effect of reduced P_F should be to increase food consumption. Thus, equations (15.8) and (15.9) suggest that as the terms of trade move against Africa, the change in the relative prices of food crops and export crops will be less than zero.

The price of nonagricultural products is determined as

$$P_N = e P_N^* + M_T + G_3 \qquad\qquad (15.10)$$
$$= [e P_N^* + M(aP) + G_3],$$

where G_3 = the tax imposed on nonagricultural goods.

Equation 15.10 uses similar reasoning as previously but notes that here marketing costs *add on* to the international price that agricultural producers have to pay.

Behavior of Government Revenues

The size of revenue from the agricultural sector (G) would decline with a decline of agricultural marketing in the formal sector or if revenues were being collected as a percentage of the international price that declined. If a fixed tax per ton of crops exported is imposed, the decline in the price may be passed on entirely to the producer. Since both practices are followed by governments, the actual incidence of price decline between the producer and the government varies among crops and countries.[18] Governments would be expected to increase tariffs on importables to maintain the level of revenues arising out of price and quantity declines of exportables.

When the balance of trade tends to be persistently negative, donors who provide the large portion of the capital transfers to Africa typically demand, as part of their conditions for lending, that African governments devalue their currencies. They also ask that the terms of trade be moved in favor of agriculture in order to provide increased incentives to producers. Governments find it difficult to turn the domestic terms of trade in favor of agriculture when adverse international terms of trade have already led to an income loss for the urban sector. Typically, the operating efficiency of marketing parastatals (A_C) cannot be increased in the short run (requiring, among other things, reductions in the staff of parastatals and changes in pricing policies, so that they actually reflect transport costs to producers and urban consumers). Nor are expenditure patterns of governments changed easily in the short run, given the tussle between the urban and the rural sectors to maintain their respective shares of the smaller income pie. The urban sector should be expected to win this battle, given the balance of political power outlined earlier. This does not necessarily mean, however, that rural-urban shares of the final export-crop price would not move in favor of the producers; rather it means that in all likelihood *the extent* of adjustment taking place would be far less than that *required* to compensate for the rural income loss from the terms-of-trade effects or to stimulate a significant *overall* agricultural production response.

Determination of the Composition of Agricultural Production

We assume that

$$Q_F = Q_F(l, L, P_{F_f}, P_{F_i}, P_E, t_F, GR), \tag{15.11}$$
$$Q_E = Q_E(l, L, P_{F_f}, P_{F_i}, P_E, t_E, GR, P_N),$$

and

$$t_F = t_F(GR), \tag{15.12}$$
$$t_E = t_E(GR),$$

where L = land; l = labor; t_F and t_E are levels of technologies in the food- and export-crop sectors, respectively; and GR is the government expenditure on public goods, such as agricultural technology, rural transport, and so on.

We would expect

$$\frac{\partial Q}{\partial L} > 0, \frac{\partial Q_F}{\partial L} > 0, \frac{\partial F_F}{\partial P_{F_f}} > 0, \frac{\partial Q_F}{\partial P_{F_i}} > 0, \frac{\partial Q_F}{\partial P_E} < 0, \frac{\partial Q_F}{\partial t_F} > 0, \frac{\partial Q_F}{\partial GR} > 0, \frac{\partial t_{F,E}}{\partial GR} > 0.$$

If land is not in surplus and there is no technical change, diminishing returns to labor would prevail in the food-crop sector, with increased population implying a reduction in average food production. The demand for food (Q_D) would be a function of population, income, and relative prices between food crops and imported goods. Thus demand for food should increase with population growth and a decline in Africa's international terms of trade.

The excess demand for food in the domestic market should increase the ratio of P_F/P_E even further than outlined above as a result of transport costs alone. The inability of African countries to import adequate food owing to foreign-exchange constraints posed by international terms of trade should also reinforce increases in informal market prices. The reduced official producer prices of export crops P_E in relation to P_F (for which an informal market exists) should have the same effect. A shift in production in favor of food crops should therefore occur. The substitution effect of relative price changes between food crops and export crops should not be expected to be symmetrical, however, since an informal market exists in the case of one but not in the case of the other. While food-crop production data are much too incomplete to allow us to detect these patterns, such *relative* price shifts and supply responses in favor of food crops seem to be noticeable in a number of African countries especially since the late 1970s.

Increases in the official producer prices of food crops do not explain all of the production shift. In Zambia, for instance, the official producer prices for most crops were increased in real terms by an average of 30 percent between 1979 and 1984 (World Bank 1984b, 31). In Tanzania, on the other hand, official price adjustments have been on the order of 25 – 40 percent annually since 1980/81. In contrast, by 1980–81 the informal market prices of food crops were up to six times the official prices (World Bank 1983b, 16–17).

The extent to which informal trading of food crops would lead to a supply response in food production, however, depends on a variety of factors, including the transaction costs and risks associated with small-scale informal trading and the availability of consumer goods in the informal market. Where a strict government monopsony is enforced in food-crop purchases by the government, as in Tanzania, both the trans-actions costs and the risks associated with informal-market sales are considerable. Also, import constraints would mean that the possibilities of obtaining nonagricultural goods demanded by the rural sector through such informal-market transactions would depend on the growth of the domestic manufacturing-and-service sector or the possibility of carrying out illegal trade across national boundaries. For all these various reasons, informal trading should be expected to be less efficient in Tanzania than in Nigeria or Cameroon, where fewer controls exist on markets. Hazell's studies in Nigeria and Malaysia suggest that even when these regional variations in the growth linkages of increased agricultural production are taken into account, on the whole, economic linkages are much weaker *within* the rural sectors in Africa than in Asia (Hazell and Röell 1983). This implies that while some response of productive resources to relative price changes should be noticeable from export crops to food crops, this would not be significant enough to increase *overall* agricultural production owing to the various market failures discussed above. Indeed, the com-bination of public-expenditure patterns and price incentives in Africa that have neglected rural infrastructure and technological development in many countries seems to have led to a decline in factor productivity, resulting in an increased use of traditional (land and labor) inputs simply to maintain per capita availability of food production. Of course, the greater the resources that have to be allocated to the production of basic food-consumption needs of the rural population, the lesser the resources available for the production of marketable goods and services that can be exported in exchange for other consumables.

Falling marketed surpluses going through official channels have other ramifications. They lead to a fall in government revenues and a decline in the government's ability to maintain services. While increased capital transfers from donors may help to alleviate the situation in the short and the medium run, government policies that substantially redirect public expenditures in favor of the agricultural sector would be needed on a sustained basis to increase agricultural productivity and production.

Summary and Conclusions

It is evident from the presentation above that Dharm Narain's emphasis on the size of agricultural production and prices as determinants of poverty is as significant for Africa as for India. I have pointed out, however, that rather than the nominal prices of agricultural commodities assumed by Dharm Narain in India, it is the relative prices between exportables and importables and between food crops and export crops that influence patterns of production and consumption and thus levels of poverty in Africa. The domestic terms of trade are influenced by the international terms of trade and the extent of net surplus extraction by the public sector. The latter influences levels of poverty through its effect on both prices and public expenditures, which in turn can determine levels of agricultural productivity and avert market failures through investment in transport infrastructure, which increases factor and product mobility.

The current debate concerning the relative importance of food- and export-crop production in Africa seems facile in this context, given the need for increased volume of agricultural output. Technological change in the food-crop sector would release resources for export-crop production; technological change in the export-crop sector would increase import capacity more directly. The relative importance to be attached to technological change and other investments in the two sectors should depend on the likely marginal returns to investments in particular crops. These are areas about which too little, if anything, is known empirically in Africa to enable us to provide precise policy guidance for agricultural growth and poverty alleviation. Further analytical concerns thus need to shift from generalized debates to concrete, data-based analyses of individual circumstances that would increase our understanding of determinants of growth and poverty.

Notes

The views expressed in this paper are those of the author and should not be interpreted as reflecting those of the World Bank. The author has benefited from comments on earlier drafts of this paper by T. N. Srinivasan, John Mellor, Chandra Ranade, and Yaw Ansu. Ton T. Long and Clara Else provided research assistance.

1. *Africa*, as used here, refers to sub-Saharan Africa unless noted otherwise. Sub-Saharan Africa, according to the World Bank, includes Angola, Benin, Botswana, Burkina Faso, Burundi, Cameroon, Cape Verde, Central African Republic, Chad, Comoros, Congo, Djibouti, Equatorial Guinea, Ethiopia, Gabon, Gambia, Ghana, Guinea, Guinea-Bissau, Ivory Coast, Kenya, Lesotho, Liberia, Madagascar, Malawi, Mali, Mauritania, Mauritius, Senegal, Seychelles, Sierra Leone, Somalia, Sudan, Swaziland, Tanzania, Togo, Uganda, Zaire, Zambia, and Zimbabwe.

2. Myint (1977, 327–54) does this by identifying the conflicts and complementaries in the four roles of agriculture in overall economic development. These roles were discussed earlier in Johnston and Mellor (1961, 566–93). Johnston and Mellor focused mostly on the large and rather closed Asian economies. This chapter takes these distinctions further in a more applied way.

3. Most notable in this regard is World Bank (1981a), usually referred to as the Berg Report, after its author, Elliot Berg.

4. See, for example, Sender and Smith (1984).

5. See Schultz (1978). For technological and market constraints see Baker, Crawford, and Eicher (1982); and Lele (1984).

6. In Africa, landlessness is difficult to measure because of the prevalence of the customary land-tenure system. Traditionally, farmers have the right to cultivate land but not to own it. The measurement is further complicated by the slash-and-burn agricultural method, widely practised in Africa. Thus there exist few statistics on landlessness in Africa that are strictly comparable to those in Asia. A variety of available data, however, point to a better land access in Africa. The World Bank's agricultural-sector report for Lesotho points out that in the late 1970s up to 15 percent of rural villagers (adult males) did not have any land (World Bank 1979, 17). Collier and Lal estimated that in Kenya, in the 1970s about 7.5 percent of the rural population was landless *and* likely to be poor (see Collier and Lal 1980). Given the existing knowledge of the relative population pressure in Kenya and Lesotho, these estimates seem plausible, abstracting of course from land-quality considerations that affect those with land access in both countries. By contrast, in India, for example, 40 percent of the households in rural areas own less than 0.50 acre of land (landlessness is taken to apply to those with 0.5 acre of land or less) (see Cain 1983, 149–67). If the access to tenancy of small and marginal farmers, whose agricultural incomes do not enable them to depend totally on their own production for survival, is taken into account, the landless tend to be on the order of 15 percent of the rural households in India. Similarly, in Bangladesh, 33 percent of the 12 million rural households own no land under cultivation (see Rosenberg and Rosenberg 1978, 27). Thus, in Africa land access is currently a relatively small problem; however, in many African countries population growth

rates have accelerated, reaching well over 3 percent annually and an all-time high of 4 percent annually in countries such as Kenya. Thus the land-access problem is expected to become serious in Africa in the near future.

7. Data for Asia and Africa are not strictly comparable in this regard. But speaking conservatively, well over 50 percent of the calories consumed by the rural poor in South Asia may be derived from food bought in the market. In Sri Lanka, about 75 percent of calories consumed by the low-income group in the rural sector come from rice bought on the open market (see Gavan and Chandrasekera 1979, 39; see also Mellor 1978). By contrast, preliminary results from ongoing research by S. Kumar, at IFPRI, indicate that about 15 percent of the total value of food is bought in the market in Zambia, according to a national survey, and about 30–40 percent is generally reported in the more marginal areas in Africa.

8. This pattern of public expenditures is illustrated by the case of Nigeria, where 35 percent of the capital budget allocated to agriculture in the 1981–85 plan has been allocated to large-scale irrigation schemes [unpublished World Bank data]. In Senegal, 40 percent of the capital budget for agriculture went to irrigation during the Fifth Plan (see Government of Senegal, Ministry of Rural Development 1982). Christiansen (1984) estimated that in Malawi, about K 200 million were devoted to the development of the estate sector during the 1970s by taxing smallholders through a variety of means, such as control of which crops they could grow, what prices they received, and how much land they could cultivate. A large share of the profits made by the public-sector marketing parastatal, ADMARC, have been invested in the large-scale estate sector.

9. While up to 75 percent of the price of fertilizer was subsidized in Tanzania in the mid-1970s, and 85 percent in Nigeria in the early 1980s, consumption of fertilizer per hectare of arable land in 1981 was only about 5.6 kg. and 7 kg., respectively, compared with 33.8 kg. in India (World Bank 1983b, 1984a, and unpublished World Bank data).

10. The modern sector in Lesotho, for instance, was expected to provide only about 2,500 to 3,000 jobs per year, while the annual addition to the total labor force would be 10,000 to 12,000 (see World Bank 1979). In Kenya, for the period 1979–83 it was expected that only about 20 percent of the approximately 270,000 yearly increase in the working-age population would be able to find employment in the modern sector (see Government of Kenya 1979).

11. Food accounted for 14 percent of total merchandise imports of low-income economies in 1981 (World Bank 1984a, 238).

12. See, for example, Sen (1981b).

13. The distribution costs resulting from long distances and low population densities should not be overlooked; the cost of official domestic distribution by Tanzania's National Milling Corporation amounts to approximately U.S. $100 per ton (Lele and Candler 1981). Transport costs from north to south in Cameroon are so prohibitive that one source estimates that up to 80 percent of the northern rice crop (where the majority of Cameroonian rice is grown) was smuggled into Nigeria in 1981 (unpublished World Bank data). In Malawi, weaknesses in internal transport networks have forced the state marketing agency to drop procurement of cassava despite its role in the food-security program as a drought-resistant

staple. Further, the fact that governments are typically late to acknowledge the incidence of a drought and mobilize international food aid has been observed repeatedly in Africa, as for instance in Ethiopia in 1972/73 and most recently in Kenya (see Cowell 1984). Amartya Sen contrasts the role of the free press in India in averting famines with the role of the controlled press in China (see Sen 1982). Low population densities in the rural sector also mean less political power for overthrowing the government because of food shortages, whereas the large urban centers benefit from the power of population concentration.

14. The typical pattern of production is frequently the use of traditional varieties to produce quantities needed for domestic consumption and the adoption of new varieties if there is a guaranteed market through a public agency.

15. Indeed, many export crops tend to be more drought-resistant than food crops and are frequently cultivated as a way of reducing risks, even if relative producer prices between export crops and food crops decline, as has happened in recent years in the case of cotton in central Tanzania.

16. These "nonagricultural" goods may include such goods as sugar, salt, edible oil, cloth, and so on.

17. Different studies find a wide range of price elasticity for fuel consumption in the short and long run. For a summary of seventy-eight studies see Brodman and Hamilton (1979); and World Bank (1981b). There is a consensus that the short-run price elasticity for fuel is greater for OECD countries, i.e., -111 (see Pyndick 1979, 241), than for less-developed countries, i.e., -0.037 to -0.081 (see Wolf et al. 1980).

18. In Cameroon, for instance, producer prices for some food staples seem to be derived from an estimate of production costs, while the government's control of import duties gives it de facto power to determine relative levels of the same crops grown domestically. In Kenya, price-setting criteria include consideration of border prices, production costs, supply trends, the income effect on consumers, and the promotion of specific crops (World Bank 1983a, 75). Prices for smallholder produce in Malawi also vary by crop, with the general aim of ensuring a "reasonable return" to the farmer and providing surplus revenues to the marketing organization for national development programs. Nigeria's Technical Committee for Producer Prices set producer prices for export crops as a small proportion of international prices until the late 1970s. By 1981, however, a new incentives policy and falling international prices led to domestic prices that for the first time *exceeded* international prices. The two major exports, groundnuts and tobacco, were heavily taxed under the pricing system in the 1970s, while the price for rice (a very minor export) was subsidized.

16 Dharm Narain's Approach to Rural Poverty: Critical Issues

G. PARTHASARATHY

The insights underlying the formulation of Dharm Narain's approach to rural poverty are of much greater value than the formulation per se. These pertain to the inclusion of the consumer price index for agricultural laborers as a key variable. The largest group of people below the poverty line in India are the landless and the near-landless (Ali et al. n.d., 82). Case studies in the deltas of Andhra Pradesh show that the bulk of the poor are agricultural laborers. A study in West Godavari in 1971/72 showed that 70–80 percent of the households below the poverty level (depending upon the threshold norm) were landless (Parthasarathy, Rao, and Rao 1974). In neighboring East Godavari at about the same period, around 50 percent of the cultivator households and 80 percent of the agricultural laborers fell below the poverty line (Rao 1982, 65). These households were essentially nonproducers and depended upon the market for their living requirements. These case studies were in canal-irrigated areas. In other areas with lower population densities the bulk of the poor were marginal and small farmers who also were low producers. Many were net buyers of basic requirements and depended upon wage incomes for their needs.

Structural changes in Indian agriculture since the period of the first agricultural labor enquiry, in the 1950s, have accelerated the market dependence of the poorer groups in rural areas. A rapid shift from wage payments in kind to money wages eroded the built-in insurance against inflation provided by payments in kind. Other factors have contributed to increased market dependence. Despite variations among regions, there has been an overall decline in the system of attached laborers and an increase in the number employed on a daily basis for money wages. The trend towards increased concentration of surpluses of foodgrains since the late 1960s in areas with a high potential for increased use of high-yield varieties of seeds also has augmented market dependence.

Studies in several parts of India have highlighted the dramatic changes in agrarian structure since the introduction of new technology. Kurien's (1978) study on Tamil Nadu, Bandyopadhyaya's (1977) monograph on North Bengal, and Breman's (1974) study on South Gujarat emphasize shifts in modes of production contributing to the breakup of the traditional interdependence between the property-holding and propertyless classes. Dharm Narain was a perceptive student of the evolving Indian agrarian structure. His early work on prices and the distribution of the marketed surplus by the size of the landholding noted distress sales among small farmers (Narain 1961). He closely followed developments leading to the rapid decline in tenancy in the 1960s and the transformation of small tenants into agricultural laborers. As chairman of the Agricultural Prices Commission, he showed a deep awareness of the complexity of the agricultural-price problem in relation to the objectives of growth and equity, given the growing market dependence of the rural poor. While he recognized the incentive effects of prices on diffusion of new technology and growth of agriculture, he was deeply conscious of the need to protect the interests of the growing numbers of rural and urban poor. Because of the rising market dependence and price inelasticity of demand of the poor for foodgrains, weather-induced shortfalls in foodgrain production result in upward pressures on the consumer price index, while smaller harvests and lower employment add to the shortfall in real incomes. The extent to which bad harvests and higher prices increase rural poverty can be seen in the study of the Agro-Economic Research Centre, Waltair, in East Godavari, for the three years 1969/70–1971/72, cited earlier.[1] This study showed that variation in the incidence of poverty between a good year and bad year could be as high as 50 percent. Not all of this variation could be explained by changes in the net availability of food supplies and employment.

Amartya Sen's response captures the insights of Dharm Narain's formulation into the "recovery problem." Sen also has emphatically drawn our attention to Dharm Narain's insights on the inadequacy of Malthusian-type formulations, such as net food availability, to explain sharp variations in the incidence of rural poverty. But it would be less than just to Dharm Narain if the key variable in his formulation, "nominal prices," were considered a mere "recovery problem" in the market and his emphasis on the changing agrarian structure were ignored. It is in this context that the chapters of Yujiro Hayami and Masao Kikuchi on Philippine villages and Uma Lele on Africa become relevant to Dharm Narain's approaches.

Hayami and Kikuchi suggest that modern market institutions and technology do not necessarily polarize the peasantry into large commercial farmers and landless laborers. If technological advance is biological-chemical, without scale economies and labor-saving devices, it can promote a more unimodal distribution of farm sizes. They describe the development processes in two Philippine villages. There was polarization in the "South Village" and peasant stratification without polarization in the "East Village." In both situations, the income gaps between large and small farmers and between farmers and landless laborers widened. The interactions between technology, public policy, and demography were adverse to the interests of the poorest strata of rural society in both villages—in one through polarization, in the other through changes in customary arrangements that guaranteed means of subsistence. In both villages there were unrelieved pressures on land because of high demographic pressures, low rates of employment in agriculture, low rates of absorption in non-agriculture, and an increase in the share of rent relative to wages. There was less evidence of monetization in the labor market than in India. But the percolation of benefits of technology to the rural landless were as severely constrained as in Indian villages. In such situations Dharm Narain's "nominal price" variable becomes highly relevant.

Uma Lele recognizes the relevance of "nominal prices" to the African situation. Her survey is remarkable for its treatment of a complex and widely varying situation, but it needs to pay much more attention to the centrality of dualism *within* agriculture. This dualism is a colonial legacy that generally resulted from control of land by white farmers and/or investments by private farms. A few more facts are needed, especially from southern Africa. The most extreme situation was in Zimbabwe, where approximately 6,000 white commercial farmers and some plantations controlled almost 50 percent of the total land area, employed a great deal of wage labor, and produced most of the marketed agricultural goods. Farming in the Tribal Trust Land, governed by communal tenure, takes place on small units with little marketed surplus and with problems of overgrazing, crowding, and lack of infrastructural development. Dualism is also an issue in Zambia. Five hundred to six hundred large-scale commercial farmers produce about one-half to two-thirds of the maize marketed on leasehold land. In Swaziland there is a dramatic contrast between the 600 to 800 large modern farms and the traditional sector. A large number of modern farms are owned by private companies (USDA 1981, 104–5). The bulk of the households within the traditional sector have relatively little access to infrastructure, credit, and delivery systems. The relative abundance of land and communal land-tenure systems has so far restrained the emergence of the landless class. But these two favorable factors are rapidly disappearing.

Increasing demographic pressures in Africa have created scarcities of cropped land[2] and have reduced periods of fallow. Growing interactions between the modern and traditional sectors have been leading to the disintegration of communal land-tenure systems and the emergence of a landless class. Under the ecological conditions of African agriculture, there is no available technology by which the traditional farmer can adjust to the reduced fallow period and a more intensified agriculture. Both politics and increased private ownership of (privatization of rights in) land have disrupted the traditional symbiosis between pastoralists and the sedentary population (United Nations 1976, 22). Thus, the growing incidence of rural poverty in sub-Saharan Africa is rooted in the colonial legacy of state-sponsored dualism in agriculture and augmented by trends in demography, technology, and public policy. This has resulted in poor agricultural performance and loss of food security for the bulk of the people in the traditional sector. Strategies of rural development pursued by African governments have been inadequate to meet this situation, which is becoming critical. Many countries with strong ties to foreign financial interests pursued rural-development policies that conflicted with basic national interests and neglected areas vital to the people (Bezzabeh 1981, 9). As a consequence, the ratio of the incidence of rural poverty to that of urban poverty is far higher in many African countries than in India (FAO 1981, 80–81). The African situation warrants a much deeper probe into the factors underlying Dharm Narain's time trend and its effect on the incidence of rural poverty.

The responses also help clarify the issues pertaining to the trickle-down debate. Two points made by Montek Ahluwalia are relevant. First, he asks whether the rate of agricultural growth is high enough to permit a trickle-down. Second, he distinguishes between the trickle-down mechanism and its actual operation. At an all-India level there was simply not enough growth, as measured by per capita NDP in agriculture, to trickle down. But the question remains as to why a significant negative relation between per capita agricultural income and rural poverty is not established even in states such as the Punjab and Haryana, which had high rates of growth. Ahluwalia's conclusion, based on differences in the patterns of growth between the 1950s and the 1960s, that aggregative evidence does not support the view that the trickle-down mechanisms have weakened in the more recent period should not be considered conclusive. Other evidence on changes in employment-output and capital-labor ratios within agriculture also should be taken into account. What is more important is Ahluwalia's finding that reliance on trickle-down alone will not alleviate poverty. An effective public-distribution system in rural areas based in part on changes in the consumer price index for agricultural laborers should certainly be considered as part of the package of policies directly aimed at helping the poor. Dharm Narain's approach and his inclusion of "nominal price" as a key variable indicate his understanding of the limitations of trickle-down.

Hirashima's chapter (14) on the Japanese experience provides a useful historical perspective, and Rao et al. (chap. 9) emphasize the critical role of sources of agricultural growth, especially irrigation, in India. Long-term rates of growth in Japanese agriculture were not higher than post-independence rates in developing countries. In fact, they were lower. Several critical elements distinguish the Japanese experience from the current experience of developing countries. Even by the beginning of the Meiji Restoration, rates of growth of nonagriculture were high enough to limit growth in the agricultural population and the landless labor class. As a consequence, the per capita product in agriculture rose at a much higher rate than in India and other developing countries. Land-saving and labor-using technology in the agricultural sector conserved resources for industrial development and facilitated the absorption of labor into non-agriculture. This aspect is neglected in Mellor's discussion in chapter 4 on policies for promoting the small-industry sector as a means of absorbing displaced agricultural laborers into industries. The growth of capital intensity in land in Japan required more labor and raised the income per worker in agriculture. Also contributing were technology, agrarian structure, and rural institutions, which helped in the development and maintenance of irrigation, drainage works, and effective water management (Parthasarathy 1981).

To conclude, the responses to Dharm Narain's approach to rural poverty bring into sharp focus the limitations of the trickle-down approach even while agricultural performance is considered critical to the alleviation of rural poverty. It is a tribute to Dharm Narain's insights that he introduced one critical aspect of this limitation into the analysis of changes in the incidence of poverty.

Notes

1. The proportion of households below the poverty level was above 60 percent in 1969/70 and 1970/71. But it decreased to less than 30 percent in 1971/72, which was an extraordinarily good year for agriculture (Rao 1982, 54).

2. According to the World Agricultural Census, 1970, a majority of cultivators in several African countries had less than two hectares.

17 Poverty, Agrarian Structure, and Policy Options: A Note

V. S. VYAS

Dharm Narain was among the few Indian economists who discussed agricultural prices beyond the narrow confines of acreage-response-related issues. He had already made his outstanding contribution to the latter area in the early 1960s. His work on prices and poverty was done after he joined the Agricultural Prices Commission. He shared the judgment of his two distinguished predecessors, M. L. Dantwala and Ashok Mitra, that "high" agricultural prices in the absence of suitable technology cannot raise production to any significant extent and that in any case, such an approach will injure the poor. He could not provide a logical frame for the latter judgment until he started his work at IFPRI.[1] The basic elements of Dharm Narain's formulation are spelled out by Gunvant Desai in chapter 1. This chapter is addressed, in the main, to the relation between the agricultural production structure and linkages between the agricultural and nonagricultural sectors and to the impact of these relations on rural poverty. I have drawn heavily on the chapters in this volume and discussions with the authors.

Dharm Narain's formulation was in the context of a food-deficit economy with a heavy population pressure on the land. To extend it to other countries, such as the African countries, will require considerable adaptation, as discussed by Uma Lele in chapter 15. Rapid population growth is the key causal factor in poverty in the rural economies of Africa. The most progressive agriculture in the world could not have sustained a population growing at nearly 3.2–3.5 percent per annum for more than two decades. Even a slower growth could not have been supported by African economies that lacked institutions to capitalize on the gains and absorb the shocks resulting from fluctuations in international trade. The surpluses built up when export prices were high were used to import "modern" consumer goods rather than to widen the production base. When export prices declined, the import of consumption goods—to which the more articulate and influential sectors of the population had become addicted—had to be restricted, and the capacity to import inputs essential for augmenting agricultural and industrial productivity was impaired. The governments' capacity to finance day-to-day operations was jeopardized. When a downswing in export prices coincided with a rise in import prices, particularly for oil, the system virtually disintegrated. The aid agencies contributed to this process of decay by overemphasizing exports, capital-intensive technologies, and ill-suited organizational structures. The experience of some African countries supports the underlying theme of this note, namely, that strength and buoyancy in the rural sector are owing to interlinkages within the economy and equitable sharing in agricultural production by different strata of producers.

In his elegant presentation (chap. 2), A. K. Sen emphasizes the criticality of nominal prices for wage laborers. Owing to the lagged response of money wages to price increases, any increase in prices hurts the poor. Ahluwalia has rightly added (chap. 7) that even self-employed peasant producers will suffer from a rise in prices if (*a*) they produce goods that are different from the goods they consume or (*b*) prices start rising after they have sold their product and come to the market as buyers. It is sometimes argued that such effects may be transitory and that in the long run the higher prices will have a salutary impact on the employment and the income of the rural poor by providing incentive for greater production. This argument is based on a series of implicit relations that do not sound so convincing when they are spelled out. It assumes first that a rise in consumer prices will be reflected in a rise in wholesale and farm-gate prices; second, that a rise in farm-gate prices will induce higher investment for agricultural production; and third, that a higher commitment of resources for production will increase employment opportunities. At best, these relations are partial, lagged, and tenuous. Unfortunately, the relation between nominal prices and agricultural employment has not yet been systematically explored. Most of the contributors to this volume report an inverse relation between agricultural output (per head of rural population) and rural poverty. Differences arise as to whether positive association of price and rural poverty can offset the negative relation between output and poverty or whether income effect could take care of the adverse implications of rising prices. Probably, better specifications and further refinement of data, for example, lagging agricultural output by one year or taking relative prices (i.e., prices paid deflated by prices received), will help produce more acceptable results. Yet it is the magnitude and direction of the movements of the two key variables that would make a significant difference. The country-level data from India do not show a high and consistent rate of growth in output, nor do they reflect a long-term hyperinflationary situation. As a result, the interaction between the variables is not clearly brought out in any of the formulations, although most of the results recorded by the contributors to this volume suggest that the signs of the relations are of the expected nature. More work, especially in the extreme circumstances, such as a hyperinflationary trend and high rate of growth in output over a long period of time, will be needed before we can arrive at the exact nature of interaction between these variables and time.

This volume provides a starting point for further serious discussion of the relations. Two striking points emerge. First, in Ahluwalia's formulation, Sen's measure suggests a greater fluctuation in the ratio for the households below the poverty line than do the conventional head-count methods. On a priori grounds, one would have expected larger fluctuations for the latter. Does the fact that Sen's measure is more sensitive to *inter se* movement among the poor mean that there is greater heterogeneity among the poor than has been assumed?

Second and more important is the degree of indeterminancy of the state- and region-level results. Even after expanding the interpretation as much as he could, Ahluwalia, in as yet unpublished analysis, found that neither his nor Dharm Narain's equations explained the poverty situation in more than 4 or 5 out of 12 to 13 states observed. Variations in results are totally perplexing in the region-level exercises attempted by Hanumantha Rao and his colleagues (chap. 11). There are only two plausible explanations: either the specifications (or the data) used by the researchers are not correct or there is more diversity in the agrarian system than that captured by simple, three-variable models. This chapter assumes that the second explanation is nearer to Indian reality.

It can be taken for granted that agricultural growth will not be fast enough to provide gainful employment to all rural workers in the sector. With an employment elasticity of 0.5 and a rate of growth in the agricultural work force of nearly 2 percent, the growth rate of agricultural output would have to be 4 percent per annum to absorb the growth in the agricultural work force. Except for the Punjab and Haryana, no region has sustained such a rate of growth. The situation is relieved to the extent that the rate of growth exceeds the per capita consumption of the producers, which stimulates nonfarm activities and provides further employment. Up to this point, there is a large degree of agreement among the contributors to this volume. Mellor's chapter (4) clearly spells out the mechanism of such linkage. However, it has not been fully appreciated that the pattern of growth of agricultural output, rather than the rate of growth, is of critical importance.

This is especially true of countries and regions where agricultural output is growing at a rate of 2.5–3.5 percent per annum. If the rate of growth of agricultural output is less than the rate of growth of population, little spillover or linkage effect is expected. Conversely, if the rate of growth is very high, say, 5–6 percent per annum, as in the Punjab and Haryana, the trickle-down effect is bound to take place. However, for the country as a whole, as well as for many states, agricultural growth is not far in excess of population growth. For the past three decades, agricultural output in India has grown around 2.5–2.7 percent per annum, while the population has grown 2.1–2.2 percent per annum. These figures are typical of many developing countries. Two mechanisms that can facilitate supportive interlinkages and stimulate growth in employment are technology and agrarian structure.

Among the various intersectoral linkages—production, consumption, saving-investment, and foreign trade—those for production and consumption are particularly significant in the present discussion. The production linkages are further expressed as backward and forward. Both depend on the nature of technology. Agricultural growth in recent times has been closely associated with the use of fertilizers, pesticides, diesel engines, electric power, and so on, all of which are produced in the nonagricultural sector. These inputs are extremely important for boosting production but contribute only marginally to generating employment through backward linkages. Despite their critical importance, these inputs still do not make up a very significant share of total inputs. Even in the rapidly growing agriculture of the Punjab, the share of modern inputs is less than 25 percent of the total; for the country as a whole the share is only 12–15 percent. Land, human labor, animal draught power, home-preserved seeds, and so on, still account for most of the inputs of agricultural production. Most of the modern inputs are produced by capital-intensive technology and generate little additional employment. In addition, size-able quantities, particularly fertilizers, are imported and therefore generate little or no employment in the domestic sector.

Forward linkages play a more important role in generating additional employment. With the growth of income, demand for processed food and agricultural products is increasing. The elasticity of demand for processed agricultural products is higher than unity. In addition, technologies available for processing agricultural goods range from highly capital-intensive to highly labor-intensive. As a result, policy options are available for generating employment. Consumption- or demand-induced linkages, however, are the main factors in fostering intersectoral relationships. As incomes of producers rise, a greater part is spent on nonagricultural goods and services, which stimulates production and employment in these activities. In such circumstances, the pattern of agricultural production becomes as important as the rate of growth. For example, a given quantity of foodgrains produced by a few large farmers will have significantly different implications for intersectoral growth than will the same quantity produced by a large number of small farmers.

This can be illustrated by the Indian experience. In the Panse Memorial Lecture of 1978 (Vyas 1979) I reported on a study that showed that in 1971/72 nearly 90 percent of foodgrain production in India was accounted for by the top five deciles of agricultural holdings. Assuming that the shares in foodgrain production also reflect shares in total agricultural output and that all producers received the same price for their output, the bottom five deciles received only 10 percent of the income generated in agriculture. Addition of the wage incomes of the bottom five deciles of agricultural producers did not make a material difference. The demand pattern reflected the skewed distribution of income. It was heavily biased in favor of more processed goods and services, usually produced through capital- and skill-intensive technology. If there had been a large number of agricultural producers, the demand pattern would have been biased towards daily necessities of local origin. This would have resulted in fuller employment of rural labor, which would have made a positive impact on the poverty situation.

Increasing the number of agricultural producers can be brought about by land reform. Experience in implementing land reforms in nonrevolutionary or nonmilitary situations has been uniformly disappointing. Nevertheless, the existing agrarian structure can be realigned by at least three different types of policy interventions. The first is distribution of modern inputs and credit in favor of the poor. As agriculture develops, the role of these inputs becomes progressively more important. Unlike land, they are reproducible inputs. The governments of India and other developing countries have had more success in distributing these inputs more equitably than in redistributing land.

The second type of policy intervention is designed to enable marginal farmers to produce high-value agricultural products, such as vegetables, fruits, and milk, which have high-income elasticity and absorb more labor. They can be organized as complements or supplements to other agriculture activities.

The third type of intervention pertains to infrastructure creation. In a highly perceptive essay in this volume (chap. 14), Hirashima suggests that in pre-World War II Japan there was no difference either in output or labor input per unit of land between owner-cultivators and tenant farmers, irrespective of the size of their holding. Thus, a high productivity level and a high labor intensity were achieved with a high tenancy ratio and small holdings. In a labor-surplus, food-deficit country such as India, both objectives have equal importance. According to Hirashima, this was possible because of the strength of community relations, the direction of development in irrigation and drainage, and the interaction among institutions concerned with agriculture—technical education, research and experiments, and farmers' associations.

Clearly, infrastructure elements played a significant role in creating a more equitable agrarian pattern even before the postwar land reforms. As Hanumantha Rao and his colleagues demonstrate (chap. 9), infrastructure can play a similar role in India. For example, proper water management and land shaping will strengthen the production base and generate more employment and income both directly and indirectly. Roads can facilitate easier access to agricultural markets, especially for high-value perishable products, and also strengthen intersectoral linkages. These and similar policies will encourage high productivity on small farms with high labor intensity and will favor the poor. The more important role of prices in this strategy would be to provide correct signals for resource allocations rather than to act as a vehicle to transfer incomes.

Notes

1. I recall that during the early seventies, when I served as his colleague in the Agricultural Prices Commission, my only difference with Dharm Narain was on the policy regarding the issue prices (i.e., prices charged by the government-run or controlled fair-price shops to the consumers). I took a position that in addition to recommending an increase in the procurement prices, we should also suggest an increase in issue prices, in order to minimize the subsidy element. He disagreed with this proposition. But at that time his logic was that the government-issued prices acted as market leaders, and any rise in foodgrain prices issued from the public-distribution system would lead to an escalation of prices all round.

18 Agricultural Change and Rural Poverty: A Synthesis

JOHN W. MELLOR and GUNVANT M. DESAI

It is the large variations in rural poverty over time and across space that provide the laboratory for understanding the causes of rural poverty and hence the means of its alleviation. The temporal variations in poverty include not only the secular decline incident to decades-long processes of growth and the violent short-term changes brought about by famine but also the substantial intermediate-term undulations that can cause the number of people in absolute poverty to vary by 50 percent or more. The spatial variations in poverty encompass situations that differ widely in terms of the average income of the population, the land-tenure system, and the institutional organization as well as those that are quite similar.

The wide range of circumstances accompanying the spatial and temporal variability in poverty suggests the implausibility of radical, single-policy solutions to poverty. Thus, analytical understanding of the poverty phenomenon and its relation to various static conditions and dynamic forces has a valuable place in efforts to mitigate the incidence of poverty.

Dharm Narain's formulation directs attention to the substantial role in poverty determination of two major forces: agricultural production performance and the prices of goods consumed by the poor. The formulation also draws attention to the long-term effects of a wide range of other factors. Because agricultural production performance is measured relative to the size of the rural population, the powerful changes in the rural population owing to natural increases and migration from rural areas implicitly enter the formulation.

The intellectual validity of the Narain formulation received an initial scrutiny by Ahluwalia. Subsequent papers by Sen and Srinivasan intensified that scrutiny. Particularly on the basis of the latter evaluation, the formulation passed muster on technical grounds and can confidently be used for substantive discussion.

The strength of Dharm Narain's formulation, together with a caveat for its use, was summed up by Amartya Sen in a statement at the seminar organized to discuss the chapters in this volume: "In pursuing the Dharm Narain equation it may be a mistake to look for a grand design aimed at unearthing the whole truth behind poverty, and indeed he would have been most skeptical of such a design. Dharm Narain was not, I think, searching for a 'unified field theory' but pointing to the insight that we can get about nature and causes of poverty from a rudimentary and incomplete characterization involving these simple variables. He was, as usual, capturing some important aspects of a complex reality in a simple and elegant way."

The Incidence of Rural Poverty

To know that poverty is widespread and severe in the developing world hardly requires sophisticated statistical analysis. To know the appropriate means of reducing it and where and when each of these means will be effective does. This is so because poverty is a multifaceted variable that, like growth, is capable of many changes from time to time and from place to place. But for that very reason, analysis to identify the causes of poverty and the means to alleviate it should be built on empirical research that reveals the dynamic nature of poverty. Chapters in this volume based on the wealth of data for India offer immensely valuable lessons. The lack of data on poverty in the rest of the developing world must be remedied if lessons learned from the Indian experience are to be effectively adapted to other contexts.

The changing nature of poverty is implied by the concept of absolute poverty. Even if it is defined in terms of minimum biological needs, as opposed to Sen's all-embracing concept, there are problems in measuring poverty. Should its incidence be determined by minimum needs that are not satisfied or by income below a minimum level? The distinction is not superfluous, as the weak correlation between the two measures of poverty in the chapter by Rao et al. shows. Similarly, Ahluwalia's (1978b) income-based estimates of poverty, whether a head count or Sen Index is used, differ in a number of states from Bardhan's estimates based on calorie consumption. Even the ordinal rankings of states according to the level of poverty are substantially different in the two estimates.

There are further problems of definition and hence of poverty measurement. Income measures are insensitive to the differences in the efficiency with which people and groups of people convert income into satisfaction of their needs and wants. On the other hand, the measures of basic needs, such as calorie consumption, fail to encompass the variation in physical requirements needed to meet desired objectives and lend themselves to questionable value judgments about other people's needs. Furthermore, both measures mask the movement of people in and out of poverty in accordance with life-cycle phenomena. As Srinivasan points out, even if the estimated proportion of poor in a population does not change over time, in no way does this mean that an individual observed as poor at one time is necessarily poor at all times.

Kumar relates major measures of poverty to their appropriate policy areas, while pointing out that "problems are likely to arise when conclusions about one aspect of poverty are drawn from measurements based on another." She does not expect a high correspondence between measurements of poverty based on income and those based on basic needs. Her view that poverty estimates and geographical patterns of poverty differ depending on the concept of poverty used is consistent with the empirical findings of Bardhan and Rao et al.

The chapters in this volume generally define poverty in terms of income. The poverty line is defined as income so low that even those among the poor who are highly proficient at managing their resources will most likely fail to maintain a reasonable level of minimum basic needs. The simple head-count measure is supplemented in Ahluwalia's chapter by the Sen measure of the intensity of poverty below the defined line, and in the chapters by Bardhan and Rao et al. by calorie-consumption measures. The evidence from various sources shows clearly that poverty is a dynamic variable capable of instantaneous, cyclical, and secular changes over time.

The importance of discerning the dynamic nature of poverty cannot be overemphasized, because eradication of poverty is a task that will take decades to accomplish. Policy actions in this kind of time frame require not only a continuous strengthening of long-term poverty-reducing forces but also a constant effort to counter the short-term forces that aggravate poverty. This is obviously not possible unless the causes behind the different types of temporal changes in the incidence of poverty are correctly identified, which in turn requires a time series of poverty estimates. Data to generate such estimates, however, are not available for any developing country except India.

Thus, Ahluwalia's estimates of the incidence of rural poverty in India for 1956/57 to 1977/78 provide a rare opportunity to understand the dynamic behavior of the poverty variable. Although famine—and hence an instantaneous and dramatic aggravation of poverty—has not been typical during this period, the estimates clearly show strong repetitive movements in which rural poverty has increased or decreased by as much as 50 percent within periods of three to six years. The summary in table 18.1 is revealing (see also fig. 18.1):

Table 18.1. Changes in the Incidence of Rural Poverty in India, 1956/57 to 1977/78

Subperiod	Changes in the Percentage of Rural Population in Poverty
1956/57 to 1960/61	Down from 54% to 39%
1960/61 to 1966/67	Up from 39% to 57%
1966/67 to 1971/72	Down from 57% to 41%
1971/72 to 1974/75	Up from 41% to 50%[a]
1974/75 to 1977/78	Down from 50% to 39%

[a] Estimates of the head count and the Sen Index were made for these years, which are missing from Ahluwalia's analysis, by applying a modified Narain formula to the data for each year.

It is clear from Ahluwalia's estimates that for a period of more than two decades there was neither a rising nor a declining trend in the incidence of Indian rural poverty. But the "high" incidence was not constant, as shown by repetitive movements of considerable amplitude and breadth. Which factors were responsible for aggravating or alleviating the incidence of rural poverty? Aside from these factors, were secular forces reducing or increasing the incidence of rural poverty in India? The dynamic behavior of the poverty variable makes questions like these pertinent. It also gives strength to the statistical findings (discussed in the next sections) of a close association between temporal changes in the poverty incidence on the one hand and agricultural performance, food prices, and various secular forces on the other hand.

Notwithstanding the absence of either a rising or a declining trend in rural poverty over the period 1956/57 to 1977/78, Ahluwalia's estimates clearly show that the upper bound of the fluctuations in the incidence of poverty has decreased in more recent periods. In no year after 1967/68 did the poverty ratio rise above 50 percent or above 0.20 on the Sen Index (compared with the earlier peaks of 57 percent and 0.24). On the basis of this and the declining trend in rural poverty during the decade 1967/68 to 1977/78, one could argue that there is no empirical reason to contend that there was aggravation in rural poverty after the green revolution was launched. On the other hand, the lower bound of the fluctuations in rural poverty has remained undiminished at 39 percent using the head-count measure and at 0.14 using the Sen Index. Thus, a decline in the upper bound of poverty fluctuations, an unchanging lower bound, and the absence of a secular trend combined with persistent short-term fluctuations of considerable amplitude characterize the dynamic nature of rural poverty in India between 1956/57 and 1977/78.

The detailed analysis of cross-sectional data from India by Bardhan

Figure 18.1. Changes in the incidence of rural poverty in India, 1956/57–1977/78

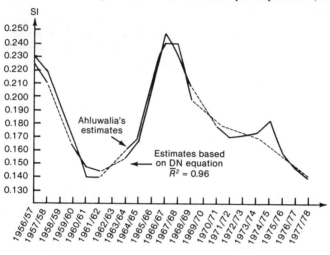

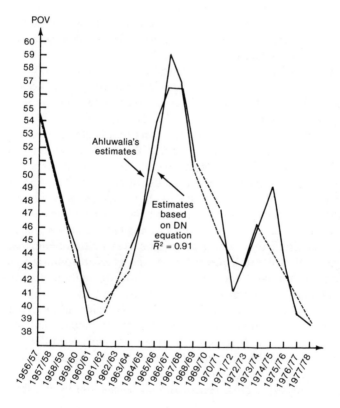

and by Rao et al. aims at identifying the causal factors of poverty. Srinivasan points out that drawing inferences about dynamic processes from contemporaneous cross-sectional data is subject to serious pitfalls, since neither the level of economic development of a region nor its achievement in the provision of infrastructure at a point in time is necessarily a good indicator of the growth process in the past that led to these levels. He also shows how Bardhan's finding of greater poverty incidence in districts with faster growth rates of agricultural production would follow if these districts happened to be the ones with above-average poverty in the initial year. This happens because the growth in agricultural production in these districts, while it reduces poverty, might not be sufficient to offset the initial conditions. Bardhan argues, however, that within West Bengal, the faster-growing districts are in general those that had below-average poverty in the early 1960s.

Mellor gives particular emphasis to the potential association, derived from the nature of the agricultural production function, between high initial levels of land productivity, a large landless class, high levels of poverty, and a high response to new technology. In these circumstances, a high growth level may be associated with high levels of poverty that derive from the initial conditions rather than from the forces of growth themselves.

In any case, cross-sectional data offer important perspectives on the varying conditions under which poverty occurs and thus suggest useful areas to explore with respect to the dynamics of poverty. Poverty levels at different locations are thus seen as an outcome of historical forces and dynamic technoeconomic processes operating under substantially different agricultural production functions. Such variation in production relations among agroclimatic regions defines a major variable in poverty determination of particular importance in predominantly rural developing countries.

Consistent with Mellor's conceptual framework, areas of high population density and high value of output per hectare are seen to be associated with high levels of poverty. The association of high population density with high road density would explain the association of the latter with high poverty levels, despite Bardhan's finding that remoteness of location is associated with high levels of poverty. The association of low agricultural production per capita of total population with high poverty would also be consistent with Mellor's conceptualization. In the analysis by Bardhan of the National Sample Survey Organisation (NSS) household data, a high growth rate of agricultural production was associated with high poverty levels for both agricultural-labor and cultivator households. Like Srinivasan's argument above, Mellor's framework also suggests that this is a plausible spatial relation but a more questionable indicator of the dynamic relations. In fact, barring some cross-sectional exceptions, high rates of agricultural growth were associated with low poverty in all empirical evidence.

It is notable that in all the analyses, high use of fertilizer was associated with low levels of poverty. In general, high levels of irrigation, specifically canal and well irrigation, were associated with low poverty. Bardhan finds a high density of oil engines and electrical pump sets associated with high poverty levels. On this latter point, and in contrast to it, Rao et al. find a high level of electrification associated with low levels of poverty. Socially, a high proportion of landless and near-landless people and of scheduled (low) castes and tribes were associated with high levels of poverty. Consistent with each other and with the Narain formulation, the analyses also associated low wages, a high price index, and low availability of nonfarm or public works employment with high poverty levels.

Of particular relevance to Kumar's discussion of income versus basic needs measures is the finding by Rao et al. that a high percentage of urban population is associated with a high level of poverty using the calorie-consumption measure, and a low level of poverty using the income measure. Surely, relative prices and differences in the nonfood-consumption options available are at work here.

Whatever conclusions may be drawn from the cross-sectional analysis about the dynamics of poverty, it is clear that a wealth of data are available in India to identify the geographic incidence of large pockets of poverty and the circumstances of that poverty. The circumstances of poverty vary so much that poverty-alleviation efforts need to be based on decentralized, area-specific approaches. Although the abundant cross-sectional data are a great help in such refined efforts, one must also note the necessity of time-series data for diagnosing the dynamic nature of poverty and lament the markedly reduced frequency of collection of the NSS data essential for such analysis. This cannot be overstressed, when the goal of poverty reduction has been quantified and the strategy to achieve it has been spelled out, as in India's Sixth Five Year Plan.

For the rest of the developing world, the most that seems possible is rough speculation based in part on the relations learned from the Indian data. For Southeast Asia, Hayami and Kikuchi demonstrate that different levels of poverty are associated with different social environments, created through different ecologies and historical processes. This is analogous to the Indian association of poverty with areas of large landlessness and high proportions of scheduled (low) castes and tribal groups. Lele observes a high incidence of poverty in Africa in areas of very high population density (for example, in the Kisii district of Kenya, in eastern Nigeria, in the Mossi Plateau of Burkina Faso, in the Western Highlands of Cameroon, and in the northern Groundnut Basin of Senegal) and in areas where the modern sector is unable to absorb the growing labor force (such as Lesotho, Kenya, and Tanzania). African poverty is also associated with poor soil; low, uncertain rainfall; increasing population pressure; skewed ownership of cattle; and rising inequalities in land ownership. Although these are generally consistent with the Indian relations, the pattern of cattle ownership; the increasing private ownership of communal land, leading to unequal distribution; and the impact of an extraordinarily high rate of population growth on poverty are variants especially notable in Africa.

Throughout the areas analyzed, rural landlessness is a basic element of poverty. This phenomenon, endemic in South Asia, is rapidly growing in importance as an immediate cause of poverty in Southeast Asia and Africa and can no longer be thought of as peculiar to South Asia. For those with land, poverty is associated with small size and low productivity of holding, a small amount of marketed surplus, a large number of dependents, low rates of participation in nonfarm work, and a low level of education. In Africa, poverty is notably associated with households headed by women or those where able-bodied men are not available for out-migration. These types of households are probably impoverished in Asia also, although they have not been especially noted owing to their lower incidence.

Beyond these broad generalizations, it is difficult to say much about the degree of poverty incidence and changes in it for the developing world outside of South Asia. Clearly, many pertinent questions remain about the relative importance of different causal factors behind poverty at different locations and changes in them over time. The Indian data make it clear that answers to these questions depend on an analytical understanding of the changing nature of the poverty problem, and data are crucial for devising location-specific policies to alleviate poverty. For Africa, the lack of relevant data leaves us with only general but nevertheless important prescriptions, especially those discussed by Lele, which are taken up in the next section.

The constraints imposed by the paucity of data on poverty for Africa also seem applicable to Southeast Asia, as pointed out by Mangahas. Hayami and Kikuchi successfully argue that the historical evidence for Japan and recent experience in the Philippines do not support the Marxian hypothesis of the polarization of the peasantry. Nevertheless, until more precise data are available on the changes in poverty over time, the kind of doubt raised by Parthasarathy—that even without the extreme polarization suggested by the Marxian hypothesis, the misery of the poor may have increased—will remain.

Finally, better data on the temporal and spatial aspects of poverty would help avoid needless and debilitating controversies that orginate from inadequate knowledge and faulty speculation.

Agricultural Performance and Rural Poverty

Most of the chapters in this volume examine the relation between poverty and agricultural production. They do so from widely different perspectives and thus reinforce each other in their central conclusions.

Raj draws attention to an earlier writing of Dharm Narain's discussing the need to raise the growth rate of India's agricultural production to 3.5 percent if poverty was to be somewhat alleviated and a recent writing of his published by IFPRI that shows the feasibility of achieving such a rate. One of the major outcomes of his final, unfinished work is a graphic substantiation of this relationship. Ahluwalia further reinforces the importance of agricultural production growth by extending Dharm Narain's data set and by adding a variable for lagged agricultural net domestic product. The positive effect of that lagged variable is consistent with Srinivasan's contention that for a trickle-down mechanism to work, accelerated growth in agriculture must be maintained for a period of several years. He points out that most of the empirical studies testing the trickle-down hypothesis have been inadequate either because they use data in which there is no indication of significant growth to trickle-down or, alternatively, because they somewhat incautiously draw inferences about dynamic processes from cross-sectional data.

The repeated and protracted ups and downs in the poverty level in India make it possible to examine the relation between temporal changes in poverty, agricultural performance, and the food-price environment. This evidence shows clearly that the accelerated growth in agricultural production (no doubt associated with rapid expansion of cultivated area and land reforms) and the stable price environment were behind the downswing in poverty during the 1950s. Poverty rose sharply in the first half of the 1960s, when the growth rate of agricultural production declined sharply because the effects of the land reforms were waning and the rate of growth of cultivated area was declining; prices rose steeply. Until then there was no green revolution to aggravate or to alleviate poverty.

Indeed, the green revolution, introduced by the dwarf wheat varieties, arrived in India at about the same time as the great 1965/67 drought. Poverty sharply declined between 1967/68 and 1971/72, although its lowest level was no lower than that attained in 1960/61. It then rose for a period of three years, after the first flush of the green revolution had run its course. It fell again between 1974/75 and 1977/78. Therefore, the problem for the poor was not the rise of the green revolution but rather its subsidence. When this evidence is combined with the need for productivity-based, accelerated growth in agricultural production, it lays to rest the question about the relevance of the green revolution in combating poverty. Still remaining, however, are the questions of how to institutionalize and maintain a green revolution; how to reduce unfavorable side effects; and what ancillary policies may help to reduce poverty in conjunction with the favorable environment provided by the green revolution. Bardhan's paper, in particular, addresses these issues.

The cross-sectional analyses, despite their severe limitations for understanding dynamic processes, are also generally consistent with the theory of giving a central role in poverty alleviation to accelerated growth in agricultural production. The analyses by Hirashima for Japan, Hayami and Kikuchi for Southeast Asia, and Lele for Africa place major emphasis on agricultural growth for alleviating poverty. Lele's treatment provides the logic for an even more dominant role of agricultural production growth in Africa than in Asia. She explains why agricultural performance has been so poor in the past decade or so in Africa and how it has aggravated rural poverty. Thus, it can be said that the relation between production and poverty holds not only for regions with heavy population pressure on land and a high degree of landlessness, as in much of India, Bangladesh, the Philippines, and some parts of Africa, but also for regions where population pressure and landlessness are not so high, as in other parts of Africa.

In stressing the importance of agricultural production growth in poverty alleviation, it must be noted that throughout the developing world the rate of growth of cultivated area has been declining. Thus, the burden for accelerating agricultural production must fall increasingly on yield per unit of land, and that requires technological change. India's experience clearly reveals this. In the first half of the 1960s the growth rate of agricultural production declined sharply because the rate of growth of cultivated area declined. The yield-increasing technology reached a critical mass in the 1970s and thereby reversed the trend towards greater poverty. Without the green revolution, the poverty situation would have been dismal.

Mellor, Srinivasan, and Ahmed all deal with the conceptual basis of the relation between agricultural production and poverty. Mellor points out that because food is the principal consumption good for low-income people and because employment is their principal source of income, alleviation of poverty depends on keeping food prices low and generating rapid growth in employment. Hence, productivity-increasing technological change in agriculture is central to achieving rapid economic growth and equity. Mellor also traces the cross-sectional variations in the incidence of poverty to extreme diversity in the technical conditions under which agriculture operates and the interactions between that diverse technological base and the dynamics of population growth, expansion in nonagricultural employment, and technical change in agriculture. Srinivasan presents a formal model to show how changes in agricultural output from land-augmenting technical change will reduce the incidence of poverty through changes in labor allocation.

Ahmed points out that agricultural performance affects the incidence of rural poverty in Bangladesh through its influence on the wage income (that is, the wage rate multiplied by the employment level) of agricultural labor. If population grows faster than agricultural production, the demand for labor will certainly grow more slowly than the supply, depressing both the wage rate and the employment per person. In Bangladesh, population has grown more rapidly than agricultural production, leading to an increase in rural poverty.

The mechanisms by which agricultural performance influences rural poverty are many and varied. The most obvious is the direct impact on the real incomes of the poor farmers and laborers, changes in which are brought about by changes in the level of agricultural production for home consumption and wage-paid employment in crop production. Wage employment may increase not only as a result of the increase in total employment but also because of the substitution of hired labor for family labor as farm incomes rise.

Another way that agriculture influences the incidence of poverty is through employment and income in the local off-farm activities tied up with crop production. The high marginal propensity of rural people to spend on locally produced nonagricultural goods and services makes these employment effects very important. Agricultural prices are dealt with separately, but the potential price-depressing effect of increased agricultural production growth should be noted. Agricultural price changes have a stronger effect on the rural poor as consumers than as producers, because they market so little of what they produce, because the wage rates are rigid, and because they are dependent on purchased food supplies.

Finally, agricultural performance influences the incidence of rural poverty through its effects on employment in the urban-based nonagricultural sector. It affects not only demand and the supply of wage goods but also the availability of capital and public-sector resources for cost-reducing, technology-based expansion. Growth in agricultural production increases the availability of public-sector resources and hence the level of expenditure on programs for uplifting the weaker segments of the economy. Even the morale of the governments in their efforts to alleviate rural poverty seems to depend on the performance of the agricultural sector, as the Indian experience after the late 1960s indicates.

Thus, there is ample logic to explain and support the strong statistical relation between improved agricultural performance and decreased poverty. To summarize, for a secular decline in the incidence of rural poverty, one needs a sustained growth rate in agricultural production that exceeds the population growth rate, is based on cost-reducing technological change, has a broad base in terms of regions and categories of farmers, and is accompanied by sustained expansion in employment in the non-agricultural sector.

Food Prices and Rural Poverty

The central role that food prices play in poverty reduction is best underlined by Dantwala's statement that the lowering of food prices is "instant socialism," transferring, as it does, income from surplus producers to poor consumers. The Narain formulation provides powerful time-series support for this role. The cross-sectional analyses of Bardhan and Rao et al. provide consistent supporting evidence. It is the role of high food prices in the exacerbation of poverty that again argues for techno-logical change rather than price adjustments as a means of expanding food production, irrespective of the elasticity of supply. That food supply tends to be inelastic with respect to price only reinforces the case.

The two periods of upswing in the incidence of rural poverty were also the periods of rapid rise in the price variable; the reverse, however, was not the case for the three periods of downswing in rural poverty. Each of these three periods began when the upward movement in prices was arrested, and prices were relatively stable during these periods.

Results of the Narain equation estimated by Ahluwalia from the expanded data set confirm a positive and statistically significant relation between the nominal price variable and the incidence of rural poverty (using both the head-count ratio and the Sen Index). That the poverty aggravation engendered by a price rise is substantially reduced when data for the 1970s are included is perhaps best explained by the expansion of the public food-distribution system and growth in the income-support programs for the poor, including public works programs. Indeed, given the roles of Dantwala and Dharm Narain in policy processes and the understanding of the role of prices shown in their work in this volume and earlier, it should not be surprising that the price effect became weaker as public policy designed to weaken it took effect.

Parthasarathy also provides micro evidence from the district of East Godavari, an intensely farmed coastal area in Andhra Pradesh, that a 50 percent rise in the incidence of poverty within three years cannot be fully explained without taking into account the relation between prices and poverty. He emphasizes that increasing landlessness strengthens the importance of food prices to the poor.

The importance of food prices in determining poverty is central to Sen's concept of change in entitlements. In his discussion at the authors' seminar, Sen emphasized the adverse impact of higher food prices on poverty and distinguishes between the indirect effects of high food prices on rural incomes and the direct effects on poverty. "Even if the indirect effects were powerful, which is far from obvious, the direct effects would remain immediate and important." He pointed in particular to "a deep conflict between the two variables, prices and income, pushing in different directions in response to a policy of high agricultural prices." The two types of effect do not necessarily—indeed do not even typically—work on the same group of people. He showed how monitoring price changes can help in anticipating rapid accentuation of poverty. His emphasis on the relation between prices and poverty was perhaps best brought out in the statement that "a major weapon in combating poverty over the long as well as the short run is to keep food prices low." The apparent conflict between this position and the need for incentives to elicit increased food production leads to the special role of cost-decreasing technological change in poverty abatement. It is notable that in India and a number of other countries as well, producer and consumer price interventions by government are determined somewhat independently, thereby relieving the dilemma pointed out by Sen, albeit at substantial cost to the public treasury.

Ahmed provides a formal argument to show how nonadoption of the high-yield varieties by India in the mid-1960s would have increased the incidence of absolute poverty, even if it would have prevented the increase in inequalities. He does so by arguing that marketed surplus would have been lower and that this would have put upward pressure on prices.

In the context of Bangladesh, the relation postulated by Dharm Narain is also considered important. Money wage rates have not kept pace with prices. This has accentuated poverty, given the importance of wage income for the poor in Bangladesh, where landlessness is high. The primary cause of falling real wage rates has been the failure of agricultural production to keep pace with the growth in the labor force. To a substantial extent, Ahmed's reasoning is similar to that of Mellor.

Mellor, Vyas, and Sen all refute the argument that lower food prices will decrease rural employment and thus aggravate poverty. For this to happen, the employment intensity of food crops must be high compared with that of nonfood crops, and the elasticity of substitution of food crops for nonfood crops with respect to price must also be high—conditions that are unlikely to be met.

Upward pressure on the nominal price of food immediately aggravates rural poverty because of the widespread dependence of the rural poor on market purchases for at least a portion of their consumption needs, the small share of the poor in the marketed surplus of agricultural production, and the increasing monetization of rural wages and rigidities in them. The higher the proportion of landless labor among the rural poor, the stronger the causal link between nominal prices and the incidence of rural poverty. Lele points out that the relation between prices and rural poverty is more complex in Africa than in Asia because there is not as much landlessness in Africa and consequently the rural poor there are less dependent on wage income. But the growing pressure of population on land, along with a persistent poor agricultural performance, makes the strength of this causal link increasingly similar to that in Asia. Sen's analysis of famines highlights the sudden impact of this effect. Even when there is no famine, the effect of prices on poverty is important, as the empirical evidence from India consistently shows. Thus, a steep increase in food prices is perhaps the most significant source of short-run aggravation in rural poverty.

The causal link between high food prices and high incidence of rural poverty is not confined to the short run. Even for secular decline in rural poverty, low food prices (in real terms) are important because of their favorable effects on the overall development process and on the growth of employment in the nonagricultural sector. Thus, the central role of food prices in poverty determination returns once again to the even more central role of improved, land-augmenting technology for agricultural production.

Now that we have made a strong argument for the effectiveness of lower agricultural prices in reducing poverty, certain caveats are in order. First, obviously agriculture should not be destroyed by unremuneratively low prices; after all, the other central factor is accelerated growth in agricultural production. Hence the centrality of improved, cost-reducing technology.

Second, it is low consumer prices that assist the poor. High marketing margins, whether they result from collusion or inefficient marketing in the public or the private sector, lead to increased poverty.

Third, in the short run a wedge between producer and consumer prices can greatly help to meet the objectives of accelerated agricultural growth and low prices for the poor while cost-reducing technology is getting under way.

Other Factors and Rural Poverty

The Narain formulation focuses attention on the causal role played by agricultural production and food prices in the dynamic behavior of rural poverty. Expressing agricultural production on a per capita basis adjusts for the important demographic forces of population growth and rural-to-urban migration. Because the swings in poverty levels run for several years at a time, there is a potential for production and prices to have an intermediate indirect influence, which greatly increases the power of this formulation. The third causal variable, trend, picks up the effects of all other factors in poverty determination over time.

It is likely that during the years 1956/57 to 1970/71, the time period used by Dharm Narain, the most powerful factor besides the causal variables of production and prices was the land reforms of the 1950s, whose influence must have gradually run out in the 1960s. This explains why Dharm Narain used the trend variable after logarithmic transformation.

It is notable that for the period that he analyzed, Dharm Narain found a downward trend in poverty after adjusting for the agricultural production growth rate and food prices. Stated in positive terms, the underlying processes in the economy were successful in reducing poverty over time. For a country of India's size, diversity, and low income, this is indeed a reassuring finding, though it does not offer any grounds for complacency. Taking a negative viewpoint, inadequate performances in agricultural production and rising agricultural prices nullified the favorable effects of these underlying forces. Again, it seems that by 1970/71 the success of the green revolution was too little, not too much.

Ahluwalia's statistical results using the Narain formulation for the period 1956/57–1977/78 do not alter the essential conclusion that other factors were influential in reducing poverty. This is true even after allowance is made for the changes in the incidence of poverty owing to the changes in agricultural production and the consumer price index. While the land reforms were important in the 1950s, the factors that were powerful in the 1970s included a range of programs to raise the incomes and employment of the rural poor through provision of inputs and credit on concessional terms, incentives to encourage livestock production, and a program to expand employment in public works. The public distribution system for foodgrains in rural areas was also expanded. All these activities, initiated to eradicate poverty in the late 1960s, gathered momentum in the 1970s. They were largely facilitated, in both the economic and the political sense, by the success of the green revolution. In a way, these public programs aimed at improving the exchange entitlements of the rural poor were more feasible than redistribution of property rights through the implementation of existing land reforms or stringent ceilings on landholdings. Again, the absence of a sharp and continuous decline in rural poverty during the 1970s was the result of too little, rather than too much, success of the green revolution. The green revolution was only partially successful because it was mainly confined to wheat and rice in areas with good water control.

The importance of technologically dynamic growth in agricultural production for a secular decline in rural poverty cannot be overemphasized. It is significant that virtually all of the chapters in this volume emphasize the deleterious effect of rapid rural population growth on rural poverty.

Dantwala, for example, maintains that even with labor-intensive small-farm technology, Indian agriculture will not be able to absorb the vast numbers of the rapidly growing labor force. Thus, reducing population growth and accelerating growth in nonagricultural employment in both rural and urban areas must be seen as vital prescriptions, especially for India, Bangladesh, the Philippines, and Africa. Returning to the problem of agricultural production and food prices, how is the shift of labor to other sectors to occur without a favorable environment on these two fronts?

Moreover, many critics of the green revolution have ignored the dynamics of the population factors not only on the side of the demand for food but also on the side of extending the land margins onto less and less productive land. This consideration is central to Dantwala's strong statement of the necessity of the green revolution for containing poverty. Lele makes note of these relations for Africa, where the population dynamics are extraordinarily strong. Mellor emphasizes the strength of the indirect influence of agricultural production growth on the growth of nonagricultural employment and argues for the expansion of infrastructure to facilitate these rural-employment multipliers. The cross-sectional data on remoteness and electrification support this view.

As stated before, Hayami and Kikuchi explicitly refute the Marxian view that a capitalist system inevitably leads to polarization of the peasantry and increased misery of the poor. The other chapters are fully consistent with their view. However, this should in no way be interpreted as denying the possibility of gradual immiserization of the rural poor or the importance of institutional structures, particularly land tenure. In fact, Hayami and Kikuchi pay special attention to the contrasting effects of technology in villages characterized by different institutional structures. Parthasarathy is particularly clear on that point, but it is a thread either implicit or explicit throughout the collection: Dharm Narain emphasizes the land reforms of the 1950s; frequent mention is made of increasing landlessness; and Lele notes the special process of privatization of land in Africa as acting to increase rural poverty.

Although Bardhan states the need for agricultural production to grow more rapidly than rural population, he also expresses concern that the very process of technological change essential to this growth may bring other forces to bear that will serve to further immiserize the poor. Bardhan particularly emphasizes a problem of tenant eviction as new technology increases the returns to, and perhaps the capacity for, self-cultivation by landowners. Such potentials must be kept in mind even though the empirical evidence for a poverty-increasing effect may seem weak.

Finally, Hirashima's presentation makes three important points. First, poverty alleviation is a process of generations, not of a few months or years. It follows that impatience with effective approaches because they do not yield quick results is counterproductive. In this context, the importance of the next two factors to the effectiveness of land reform is to be noted, even though they both take time. Second, the pattern of development of irrigation and drainage, which made agricultural production functions more homogeneous across regions, is significant in view of Mellor's technical point about the great importance of differences in the underlying production function to the effect of technology on poverty alleviation. The Japanese measures served to reduce the development of regional pockets of poverty. Third, technical education in agriculture is important in that it makes technical change proceed faster and facilitates the shift of labor out of agriculture.

Policy Conclusions

Seven broad policy conclusions can be stated based on this synthesis. First, in largely rural low-income countries, accelerated growth in agricultural production is central to alleviating poverty, and technological change is, in turn, central to that process. This leads not only to strengthening of agricultural research and rapid promulgation of research results but also to enhanced investment in infrastructure, including roads, rural electrification, irrigation, and drainage. It also leads to institutional changes and other policies to help spread the technology, especially to small farmers.

Second, all pervasive technological change in agriculture takes time. In the short run new technology may be confined to a few areas, which may exacerbate regional income disparities. If yield-based growth in agricultural production remains confined to a small geographical base, excess demand may soon push up the unit cost of agricultural output because of diminishing returns and hurt the poor as consumers. Thus, on several grounds, efforts in research and institutional change need to be expanded to broad national coverage.

Third, rapid growth in the agricultural population is a dominating factor in creating rural poverty. Population growth has this deleterious effect through added pressure on employment opportunities which reduce the income flow to labor and through the upward pressure on food prices derived from the additional demand arising from the larger population. Thus, population growth can easily nullify the favorable effects from agricultural growth rates of historically large proportions. Thus, effective policies to reduce rates of population growth and to increase nonagricultural employment opportunities as well as to absorb population in agriculture itself are vital to reduce rural poverty.

Fourth, there is a huge potential for agricultural production growth to stimulate growth of employment in the secondary and tertiary sectors of the rural economy. But this also requires policies that facilitate the growth of such employment by developing activities such as dairying, poultry raising, fisheries, and sericulture; establishing agroprocessing industries in the rural areas; and facilitating growth of consumer-goods industries and services. The role of infrastructural and institutional development, as well as technical education, in these activities is crucial. Such diversification of the rural economy counters the inequalities that may result in the initial stages of technological change in agriculture, because the diversification benefits the landless poor. It also minimizes the need for price-support programs to promote technological change, because it expands effective demand for agricultural output. In the long run, diversification of the rural economy is important because it siphons some of the rapidly growing labor force from agricultural to nonagricultural activities.

Fifth, low consumer food prices are highly favorable to the poor. Therefore, changes in food prices may be an extremely important diagnostic tool for spotting increases in poverty and taking counteractions. Food prices have an especially strong effect on changes in poverty in the short run. This leads to a concern for policies that counter high food prices by subsidizing food prices for the poor or by increasing their employment. The divergence of the calorie and income measures of the incidence of poverty leads to a further emphasis on food subsidies if nutrition considerations are to receive special weight in a market-oriented pricing system. If the fiscal and administrative burden of such antipoverty programs is not to increase so much that public resources for other development tasks are depleted, it is especially important to contain the rising cost of producing additional agricultural output. This brings us back to the need for cost-reducing technology and the need to extend agricultural growth to areas and farms with factor endowments reflecting lower costs.

Sixth, disparities in the distribution of assets and power, which are often based on the social as well as the economic structure, must be recognized, and continuous monitoring must be provided to ensure prompt initiation of special programs to ensure access to inputs, to markets, and to employment of the most disadvantaged people. The need for radical insitutional changes may have been overstated in recent years vis-à-vis technological change in agriculture, but the necessity for such change must always be examined. In this context, state-sponsored dualism, which is so frequent now in Africa, must be guarded against. Although it is beyond the scope of this volume to examine dualism in detail, a full attack must be made on all discriminatory practices that restrain the poor.

Seventh, socioeconomic reasearch is important for defining effective policies for the poor. First, it is needed to accelerate technological change and to ensure broad participation in those processes. Second, efficient price policies that are fiscally acceptable, encourage production, and protect the poor need to be generated. Third, policies must be found to reinforce indirect favorable effects on employment. Fourth, widespread studies of poor families are needed so that both long-term and short-term policies can be structured to the actual profiles of poverty as they vary from place to place and time to time.

To close on a note of humility and discretion, we quote from K. N. Raj's remarks at the seminar to discuss the papers in this volume. Raj notes that the Narain formulation

> was clearly an effort to understand whether the trends in rural poverty . . . could be explained with reference to not only the rates of growth recorded in agriculture but also the pressure on foodgrain availability as reflected in the direction and extent of foodgrain prices. This was obviously a very fruitful line of enquiry and would have in his hands led to conclusions illuminated by his many deep insights . . . .
>
> It might be risky, of course, to extrapolate any of the inferences he drew from the limited exercises he initiated, since he had his own way of examining them further and often chose to emphasize what inferences should not be drawn. It is only natural that friends, saddened by the loss of such a man, should wish to draw attention to what he was trying to do when he passed away, but we must be careful not to indulge in speculations that would violate the high standards he observed in intellectual matters.

References and Bibliography

Adelman, Irma, and Robinson, Sherman. 1978. *Income distribution policy in developing countries: A case study of Korea.* Stanford: Stanford Univ. Press.

Ahluwalia, Montek S. 1978a. Rural poverty and agricultural performance in India. *Journal of Development Studies* 14 (April): 298–323.

———. 1978b. Rural poverty in India, 1956/57 to 1973/74. In *India: Occasional Papers.* World Bank Staff Working Paper no. 279. Washington, D.C.

Ahmed, Raisuddin. 1977. *Foodgrain production in Bangladesh: An analysis of growth, its sources and related policies.* Dacca: Bangladesh Agricultural Research Council.

———. 1979. *Foodgrain supply, distribution, and consumption policies within a dual pricing mechanism: A case study of Bangladesh.* Research Report 8. Washington, D.C.: International Food Policy Research Institute.

———. 1981. *Agricultural price policies under complex socioeconomic and natural constraints: The case of Bangladesh.* Research Report 27. Washington, D.C.: International Food Policy Research Institute.

Ali, I.; Desai, B.; Radhakrishna, R.; and Vyas, V. S. N.d. India 2000: Agricultural production strategies and rural income distribution. Mimeo. Cited in Food and Agriculture Organization of the United Nations 1981.

Baker, D. C.; Crawford, E. W.; and Eicher, C. K. 1982. Agricultural technology in sub-Saharan Africa: A critical assessment. Paper presented at the 25th Annual Meeting of the African Studies Association, 4–7 November, Washington, D.C.

Bandyopadhyaya, N. I. 1977. *An enquiry into the causes of the sharp increases in agricultural labourers in North Bengal.* Centre for Studies in the Social Sciences Occasional Paper no. 12. Calcutta.

Bangladesh, Government of, Bureau of Statistics. 1979. *1977 land occupancy survey of rural Bangladesh.* Dacca.

Bangladesh Institute of Development Studies (BIDS). 1980. *An evaluation study of deep tubewells under IDA Credit in Northwest Bangladesh.* Dacca.

Bardhan, P. 1970a. The green revolution and agricultural laborers. *Economic and Political Weekly*, July, special number. Reprinted in *Some problems of Indian economic policy*, edited by Charan D. Wadhva. 2d ed. New Delhi: Tata-McGraw Hill, 1977.

———. 1970b. On the minimum level of living and the rural poor. *Indian Economic Review* 5 (April): 129–36.

———. 1973. On the incidence of poverty in rural India in the sixties. *Economic and Political Weekly*, February, annual number. Reprinted in Srinivasan and Bardhan 1974.

———. 1982. Poverty and "trickle down" in rural India: A quantitative analysis. Berkeley: Univ. of California. Mimeo.

Bardhan, P., and Rudra, A. 1978. Interlinkage of land, labor and credit relations: An analysis of village survey data in East India. *Economic and Political Weekly*, February, annual number.

Barker, Randolph; Meyers, William H.; Crisostomo, Cristina M.; and Duff, Bart. 1972. Employment and technological change in Philippine agriculture. *International Labor Review* 106 (August–September): 3–31.

Berg, Elliot J. 1961. Backward-sloping labor supply functions in dual economies: The Africa case. *Quarterly Journal of Economics* 75 (August): 468–92.

———. 1962. Reply. *Quarterly Journal of Economics* 76 (November): 662–63.

Bezzabeh, M. 1981. A review of the recent trends in agrarian reform and rural development in tropical Africa. In *Land settlement and cooperatives*. Rome: Food and Agriculture Organization of the United Nations.

Bhalla, G. S., and Alagh, Y. K. 1979. *Performance of Indian agriculture: A districtwise study*. New Delhi: Sterling Publishers.

Bhalla, G. S., and Chadha, G. K. 1981. Structural changes in income distribution: A study of the impact of the green revolution. New Delhi: Jawaharlal Nehru Univ. Mimeo.

Bhalla, Sheila. 1981. The new structure of field crop labour in Haryana and its impact on the poverty of landless agricultural households. *Anvesak* 2 (June–December).

Birla Institute of Scientific Research (BISR). 1981. *Agricultural growth and employment shifts in Punjab*. New Delhi.

Breman, Jan. 1974. *Patronage and exploitation: Changing agrarian relations in South Gujarat, India*. Berkeley: Univ. of California Press.

Brewster, J. M. 1950. The machine process in agriculture and industry. *Journal of Farm Economics* 32 (February): 69–81.

Brodman, J. R., and Hamilton, R. E. 1979. *A comparison of energy projection to 1985*. Paris: International Energy Agency and the Organisation for Economic Cooperation and Development.

Brown, G. 1979. Agricultural pricing policies in developing countries. In *Distortions of agricultural incentives*, edited by T. W. Schultz. Bloomington: Indiana Univ. Press.

Cain, M. 1983. Landlessness in India and Bangladesh: A critical review of national data sources. *Economic Development and Cultural Change* 32 (October): 149–67.

Chambers, Robert, and Farmer, B. H. 1977. Perceptions, technology and the future. In *Green revolution: Technology and change in rice growing areas of Tamil Nadu and Sri Lanka*. London: Macmillan.

Chambers, Robert, and Singer, Hans. 1980. Poverty, malnutrition, and food insecurity in Zambia. Washington, D.C.: World Bank. Typescript.

Christiansen, R. E. 1984. Financing Malawi's development strategy. Paper presented at the Conference on Malawi: An Alternative Pattern of Development, 24–25 May, Centre for Africa Studies, Univ. of Edinburgh.

Clay, Edward J., and Khan, M. S. 1977. *Agricultural employment and underemployment in Bangladesh: The next decade.* Dacca: Bangladesh Agricultural Research Council.

Cleaver, H. M. 1972. The contradictions of the green revolution. *American Economic Review* 62 (May): 177–88.

Collier, Paul, and Lal, Deepak. 1980. *Poverty and growth in Kenya.* World Bank Staff Working Paper no. 389. Washington, D.C.

Cowell, Alan. 1984. Drought spreads to Kenya, stirring fear of a food crisis. *New York Times*, 16 July.

Dandekar, V. M. 1982. On measurement of undernutrition. *Economic and Political Weekly*, 6 February, 203–12.

Dandekar, V. M., and Rath, N. 1971. *Poverty in India.* Bombay: Indian School of Political Economy.

Dantwala, M. L. 1979. The challenge of turning needs into effective demand. Paper presented at a workshop organized by the Ford Foundation, New Delhi, December, at Trivandrum.

de Janvry, A. 1981. *The agrarian question and reformism in Latin America.* Baltimore and London: Johns Hopkins Univ. Press.

Delgado, Christopher L., and McIntire, John. 1982. Constraints on oxen cultivation in the Sahel. *American Journal of Agricultural Economics* 64 (May): 188–96.

Desai, B. M. 1978. Land reforms: Concealing the surplus. *Economic and Political Weekly*, 1 July, 1051–52.

Desai, Gunvant M. 1981. Retrieving Dharm's poverty research. Ahmedabad, India. Mimeo.

Dutt, K. 1977. Changes in land relations in West Bengal. *Economic and Political Weekly*, December, A106–10.

Fergusson, C. E. 1969. *The neoclassical theory of production and distribution.* Cambridge: Cambridge Univ. Press.

Food and Agriculture Organization of the United Nations (FAO). 1981. *The state of food and agriculture.* Rome.

Frankel, F. R. 1971. *India's green revolution: Economic gains and political costs.* Princeton: Princeton Univ. Press.

Gauhar, Altaf. 1982. View from the hill. *South: The Third World Magazine*, December, 9–14.

Gavan, James D., and Chandrasekera, Indrani Sri. 1979. *The impact of public foodgrain distribution on food consumption and welfare in Sri Lanka.* Research Report 13. Washington, D.C.: International Food Policy Research Institute.

Geertz, Clifford. 1963. *Agricultural involution: The processes of ecological change in Indonesia.* Berkeley: Univ. of California Press.

Ghai, D., and Radwan, S. 1983. Growth and inequality: Rural development in Malawi: 64–78. In *Agrarian policies and rural poverty in Africa*, edited by D. Ghai and S. Radwan, 71–98. Geneva: International Labour Organisation.

Gittinger, Mattiebelle. 1982. *Master dyers to the world: Techniques and trade in the early Indian dyed cotton textiles.* Washington, D.C.: Textile Museum.

Griffin, Keith. 1974. *The political economy of agrarian change: An essay on the green revolution.* Cambridge, Mass.: Harvard Univ. Press.

Griffin, Keith, and Ghose, A. K. 1979. Growth and impoverishment in the rural areas of Asia. *World Development* 7 (April/May): 361–83.

Guino, Ricardo A., and Barker, Randolph. 1978. Time allocation among rice farm households in Central Luzon, Philippines. Paper presented at International Rice Research Institute Saturday Seminar, 7 October, Los Baños.

Hayami, Y. 1981. Induced innovation, green revolution, and income distribution: Comment. *Economic Development and Cultural Change* 30 (October): 169–76.

Hayami, Y.; with Akino, M.; Shintani, M.; and Yamada, S. 1975. *A century of agricultural growth in Japan.* Tokyo: Univ. of Tokyo Press; Minneapolis: Univ. of Minnesota Press.

Hayami, Y., and Kikuchi, M. 1981. *Asian village economy at the crossroads.* Tokyo: Univ. of Tokyo Press; Baltimore: Johns Hopkins Univ. Press.

Hayashi, T. 1965. *Nihon niokeru Sozei Kokka no Seiritsu* (Formation of the revenue state in Japan). Tokyo: Univ. of Tokyo Press.

Hazell, Peter B. R. 1982. *Instability in Indian foodgrain production.* Research Report 30. Washington. D.C.: International Food Policy Research Institute.

Hazell, Peter B. R.; Bell, C. L. G.; and Slade, Roger. 1982. The prospects for growth and change in the Muda Project region, Malaysia. In *Village-level modernization in Southeast Asia,* edited by G. B. Hainsworth. Vancouver and London: Univ. of British Columbia Press.

Hazell, Peter B. R., and Röell, Ailsa. 1983. *Rural growth linkages: Household expenditure patterns in Malaysia and Nigeria.* Research Report 41. Washington, D.C.: International Food Policy Research Institute.

Hirashima, S. 1982. Growth, equity and labour absorption in Japanese Agriculture. In Ishikawa, Yamada, and Hirashima 1982.

Huddleston, Barbara. 1983. Closing the cereals gap with trade and food aid. Research Report 43. Washington, D.C.: International Food Policy Research Institute. Draft.

Imamura, Narami, et al. 1977. *Tochi Kairyo Hyakunenshi* (A century of land improvements in Japan). Heibonsha.

India, Government of, Department of Statistics, National Sample Survey Organisation. N.d. *Report on consumer expenditure of the weaker sections of the rural population.* 25th Round, no. 232, New Delhi: Controller of Publications.

———. N.d. National sample survey: Tables on land holdings, all India. 26th Round (1971–72). Draft report.

———. 1976. *The national sample survey: Tables on land holdings, all India.* 26th Round, No. 215. New Delhi: Controller of Publications.

———. 1981a. National sample survey report on household consumption. Draft Report No. 297. January. Mimeo.

———. 1981b. Report on the second quinquennial survey on employment and unemployment. 32d Round. Draft Report No. 298. May. Mimeo.

India, Government of, Labour Bureau. 1975. *Rural labour enquiry, 1963–65.* Final Report. Chandigarh.

———. 1979. *Rural labour enquiry, 1974–75.* Final Report. Chandigarh.

————. 1980. *Rural labour enquiry, 1974–75.* Summary Report. Chandigarh.

India, Government of, Ministry of Agriculture and Rural Reconstruction. 1981. *All India agricultural census, 1976–77.* New Delhi: Manager of Publications.

India, Government of, Ministry of Finance. 1982. *The Economic Survey, 1981–82.* New Delhi: Manager of Publications.

India, Government of, Ministry of Food and Agriculture. 1971. *1971 livestock census report.* New Delhi: Manager of Publications.

India, Government of, Planning Commission. 1973. Approach to the fifth five-year plan: Draft paper. In *Some problems of India's economic policy. See* Bardhan 1970a.

————. 1981. *Sixth five year plan, 1980–85.* New Delhi: Manager of Publications.

India, Government of, Registrar General of India. 1971. *1971 census village directory.* New Delhi.

India, Government of, All States. 1970/71. *Season and crop reports.*

Indian Council of Social Science Research (ICSSR). 1980. *Alternatives in agricultural development.* New Delhi: Allied Publishers.

Institute of Developing Economies. 1969. *One hundred years of agricultural statistics in Japan.* Tokyo.

Ishikawa, S. 1981. *Essays on technology, employment and institutions in economic development: Comparative Asian experience.* Tokyo: Kinokuniya Co.

Ishikawa, S.; Yamada, S.; and Hirashima, S., eds. 1982. *Labour absorption and growth in agriculture—China and Japan,* Bangkok: Asian Regional Team for Employment Promotion and the International Labour Organisation.

Johnston, Bruce, and Mellor, John W. 1961. The role of agriculture in economic development. *American Economic Review* 51 (September): 566–93.

Joshi, P. C. 1970. Land reform in India and Pakistan. *Economic and Political Weekly,* December, A145–52.

————. 1982a. The dilemma of growth and inequality. In *A survey of agriculture,* supp. to *New Delhi Patriot,* 19 May.

————. 1982b. Poverty, land-hunger and emerging class conflicts in rural India. In *Rural poverty and agrarian reform,* edited by S. Jones, P. C. Joshi, and M. Murmis, 72–76. New Delhi: Allied Publishers.

Kautsky, K. 1899. *Die Agrarfrage.* Stuttgart: Diez.

Kenya, Government of. 1979. *Development plan for the period 1979–1983.* Vol. 1. Nairobi: Government Printer.

Khan, A. R. 1977. Poverty and inequality in rural Bangladesh. In *Poverty and landlessness in rural Asia,* edited by Keith Griffin and A. R. Khan. Geneva: International Labour Organisation.

————. 1983. Institutional-organizational framework for egalitarian agricultural growth. In *Growth and equity in agricultural development,* edited by Allen Maunder and Kazushi Ohakawa. Aldershot, England: Gower.

Kikuchi, M., and Hayami, Y. 1980a. Inducements to institutional innovations in an agrarian community. *Economic Development and Cultural Change* 29 (October): 21–36.

————. 1980b. Polarization of an agrarian community. *Land Economics* 56 (August): 350–65.

Kohli, A. 1980. Does rural wealth trickle down in India? Department of Political Science, Univ. of California, Berkeley. Typescript.

Kokuritsu Kyoiku Kenkyusho (National Institute of Educational Research), ed. 1973. *Nihon Kindai Kyoiku Hyakunenshi* (A century of Japanese modern education). Tokyo.

Krishna, Raj. 1979. Small farmer development. *Economic and Political Weekly*, 26 May, 913–18.

Kurien, C. T. 1978. *Poverty, planning and social transformation*. New Delhi: Allied Publishers.

Kydd, J., and Christiansen, R. E. 1982. Structural change in Malawi since independence: Consequences of a development strategy based on large scale agriculture. *World Development* 10 (May): 355–76.

Lakdawala, D. T. 1978. Growth, unemployment and poverty. Presidential address to the All India Labour Economic Conference, 31 December–2 January, Tirupati.

Lele, Uma. 1984. Tanzania: Phoenix or Icarus? In *World Economic Growth*, edited by A. Harberger. San Francisco: Institute of Contemporary Studies.

Lele, Uma, and Candler, Wilfred. 1981. Food security: Some East African considerations. In Valdés 1981.

Lele, Uma, and Mellor, John W. 1981. Technological change, distributive bias and labor transfer in a two-sector economy. *Oxford Economic Papers* 33 (November): 426–41.

Lewis, W. Arthur. 1954. Economic development with unlimited supply of labor. *The Manchester School* 22 (May): 139–91.

Mangahas, Mahar. 1979. Planning for improved equity in ASEAN, Hong Kong and the Republic of Korea. *Economic Bulletin for Asia and the Pacific* 30 (December): 1–19.

———. 1982. What happened to the poor on the way to the next development plan? *Philippine Economic Journal* 21(3–4).

———. 1983. Measurement of poverty and equity: Some ASEAN social indicators' experience. *Social Indicators Research* 13: 253–79.

Mansergh, N., ed. 1971. *The transfer of power, 1942–7*. Vol. 3. London: Her Majesty's Stationery Office.

Marx, Karl. 1967. *Capital*. Vol. 3. New York: International Publishers.

———. 1968. *Theories of Surplus Value*. Moscow: Progress Publishers.

Mehra, Shakuntala. 1976. Some aspects of labour-use in Indian agriculture. *Indian Journal of Agricultural Economics* 31(4).

———. 1981. *Instability in Indian agriculture in the context of the new technology*. Research Report 25. Washington D.C.: International Food Policy Research Institute.

Mellor, John W. 1963. The use and productivity of farm family labor in early stages of agricultural development. *Journal of Farm Economics* 45 (August): 517–34.

———. 1968. The functions of agricultural prices in economic development. *Indian Journal of Agricultural Economics* 23 (January–March): 23–27.

———. 1976. *The new economics of growth: A strategy for India and the developing world*. Ithaca: Cornell Univ. Press.

————. 1978. Food price policy and income distribution in low-income countries. *Economic Development and Cultural Change* 27 (October): 1–26.

Mellor, John W., and Johnston, Bruce. 1984. The world food equation: Inter-relations among development, employment, and food consumption. *Journal of Economic Literature* 22 (June): 531–74.

Mellor, John W., and Lele, Uma. 1973. Growth linkages of the new foodgrains technologies. *Indian Journal of Agricultural Economics* 28 (January–March): 35–55.

Mellor, John W., and Stevens, Robert D. 1956. The average and marginal product of farm labor in underdeveloped countries. *Journal of Farm Economics* 28 (August): 780–91.

Minami, R. 1981. *Nihon no Keizai Hatten* (Economic development in Japan). Tokyo: Toyokeizai Shinpasha.

Minhas, B. S. 1970. Rural poverty, land redistribution and development strategy. *Indian Economic Review* 5(1).

————. 1971. Rural poverty and the minimum level of living: A reply. *Indian Economic Review* 6(1).

Mitarny, D. 1951. *Marx against peasants.* Chapel Hill: Univ. of North Carolina Press.

Mohan, Rakesh. 1982. The strategy for housing and urban development. New Delhi: Government of India, Planning Commission. Mimeo.

Morita, S. 1969. *Kome no Hyakunen* (A century of rice in Japan). Tokyo: Ochanomizu Shobo.

Myint, H. 1977, Agriculture and economic development in the open economy. In *Agriculture in development theory*, edited by L. G. Reynolds, 327–54. New Haven: Yale Univ. Press.

Naidu, I. J. 1975. *All India report on agricultural census, 1970–71.* Ministry of Agriculture and Irrigation publication. New Delhi: Manager of Publications.

Nair, Kusum. 1979. *In defense of the irrational peasant: Indian agriculture after the green revolution.* Chicago and London: Univ. of Chicago Press.

Nakamura, T. 1980. *Nihon Keizai–Sono Seicho to Kozo* (The Japanese economy—its growth and structure). Tokyo: Univ. of Tokyo Press.

Narain, Dharm. 1957. Ratio of interchange between agricultural and manufactured goods in relation to capital formation in underdeveloped economies. *Indian Economic Review* 3 (August): 46–55.

————. 1961. *Distribution of the marketed surplus of agricultural produce by size-level of holding in India, 1950–51.* New Delhi: Asia Publishing House.

————. 1965. *The impact of price movements on areas under selected crops in India, 1900–39.* Cambridge: Cambridge Univ. Press.

————. 1972. Growth and imbalances in Indian agriculture. Technical address at the Silver Jubilee and Annual Conference of the Indian Society of Agricultural Statistics, 24 March. Reprinted in *Economic and Political Weekly*, 25 March.

————. 1976. Growth of productivity in Indian agriculture. Cornell Univ. Department of Agricultural Economics Occasional Paper no. 93. Published in *Indian Journal of Agricultural Economics* 32 (January–March 1977).

————. 1979. Unpublished notes.

Narain, Dharm, and Joshi, P. C. 1969. Magnitude of agricultural tenancy, 1969. *Economic and Political Weekly*, 27 September, A139–42.

Narain, Dharm, and Roy, Shyamal. 1980. *Impact of irrigation and labor availability on multiple cropping: A case study of India*. Research Report 20. Washington, D.C.: International Food Policy Research Institute.

Oberai, A. S., and Singh, H. K. Manmohan. 1980. Migration flows in Punjab's green revolution belt. *Economic and Political Weekly*, 29 March, A2–12.

Organisation of Economic Cooperation and Development (OECD). 1983. *Development cooperation: 1983 review*. Paris.

Paddock, William, and Paddock, Paul. 1968. *Famine 1975!* London: Weidenfeld & Nicolson.

Papanek, Gustav F., and Dey, Harendra K. 1982. Income distribution, labour income and political unrest in Southern Asia in 1982. Department of Economics, Boston Univ. Mimeo.

Parthasarathy, G. 1981. Technology, employment, and institutions: A review of *Essays on technology, employment and institutions in economic development: Comparative Asian experience*, by Shigeru Ishikawa. *Economic and Political Weekly*, 19 December, 2088–91.

Parthasarathy, G.; Rao, S. V.; and Rao, G. D. R. 1974. Character of poverty among rural poor. *Economic and Political Weekly*, 30 March. Reprinted in *Poverty: An interdisciplinary approach*, edited by B. S. Rao and V. N. Deshpande. Madras: Madras Institute of Development Studies, 1982.

Pearse, Andrew. 1975. *The social and economic implications of large-scale introduction of new varieties of foodgrain: An overview report*. Pts. 1 and 2. New York: United Nations Research Institute for Social Development.

Pyndick, R. S. 1979. *The structure of world energy demand*. Cambridge, Mass.: MIT Press.

Raj, K. N. 1976. Trends in rural unemployment in India: An analysis with reference to conceptual and measurement problems. *Economic and Political Weekly*, August, 1281–92.

Ranade, C. G., and Herdt, R. W. 1978. Shares of farm earnings from rice production. In *Economic consequences of the new rice technology*, edited by Randolph Barker and Yujiro Hayami, 87–104. Los Baños, Philippines: International Rice Research Institute.

Rao, B. S. 1982. Productivity, employment and poverty in rural areas: A study of an agriculturally advanced area in Andhra Pradesh. In *Poverty: An interdisciplinary approach. See* Parthasarathy, Rao, and Rao 1974.

Rao, C. H. Hanumantha. 1975. *Technological change and distribution of gains in Indian agriculture*, New Delhi: Macmillan.

Rao, M. Ramakrishna. 1979. Nutrition situation in India during 1971–72. *Sarvekshana* 2 (January).

Reserve Bank of India. 1972. *All-India Debt and Investment Survey, 1971–72*. Bombay.

Reutlinger, S., and Selowsky, M. 1976. *Malnutrition and poverty: Magnitude and policy options*. World Bank Staff Occasional Paper no. 23. Baltimore: Johns Hopkins Univ. Press.

Rosenberg, D. A., and Rosenberg, J. G. 1978. *Landless peasants and rural poverty in selected Asian countries*. Cornell Univ. Department of Agricultural Economics. Ithaca.

Ruttan, V. W. 1977. The green revolution: Seven generalizations. *International Development Review* 19 (August): 16–23.

Saith, A. 1981. Production, prices and poverty in rural India. *Journal of Development Studies* 17 (January): 196–214.

Sanderson, Fred H., and Roy, Shyamal. 1979. *Food trends and prospects in India*. Washington, D.C.: Brookings Institution.

Sarma, J. S. 1981. *Growth and equity: Policies and implementation in Indian agriculture*. Research Report 28. Washington, D.C.: International Food Policy Research Institute.

Sarma, J. S.; Roy, Shyamal; and George, P. S. 1979. *Two analyses of Indian foodgrain production and consumption data*. Research Report 12. Washington, D.C.: International Food Policy Research Institute.

Schluter, Michael. 1971. Differential rates of adoption of the new seed varieties in India: The problems of the small farm. Cornell Univ. Department of Agricultural Economics Occasional Paper no. 47. Ithaca.

————. 1974. The interaction of credit and uncertainty in determining resource allocation and incomes on small farms, Surat District, India. Cornell Univ. Department of Agricultural Economics Occasional Paper no. 68. Ithaca.

Schultz, T. W. 1978. Politics vs. economics in food and agriculture throughout the world. In *Portfolio: International Economic Perspective*, edited by A. O. Krueger. Washington, D. C.: International Communications Agency.

Sen, Amartya K. 1966. Peasants and dualism with or without surplus labor. *Journal of Political Economy* 74 (October): 425–50.

————. 1968. *Choice of techniques*. New York: Augustus Kelley.

————. 1973. Poverty, inequality and unemployment: Some conceptual issues in measurement. *Economic and Political Weekly*, August, special number. Reprinted in Srinivasan and Bardhan 1974.

————. 1980. *Levels of poverty: Policy and change*. World Bank Staff Working Paper no. 401. Washington, D.C.

————. 1981a. Ingredients of famine analysis: Availability and entitlements. *Quarterly Journal of Economics* 96 (August): 433–64.

————. 1981b. *Poverty and famines: An essay on entitlement and deprivation*. Oxford: Clarendon Press.

————. 1982. How is India doing? *New York Review of Books*, 16 December.

————. 1983. Poor, relatively speaking. *Oxford Economic Papers* 35 (July): 153–69.

Sender, J., and Smith, S. 1984. What's right with the Berg report and what's left of its critics? Institute of Development Studies (Sussex) Discussion Paper 192. Mimeo.

Senegal, Government of, Ministry of Rural Development. 1982. *Bilan global des realisations du gouvernement en faveur du monde rural depuis l'independence*. Dakar.

Shanin, Teodor. 1972. *The awkward class*. London: Oxford Univ. Press.

Singh, Inderjit. 1982. Land reform: The unlikely panacea in South Asia. Paper

presented at the Annual Conference of the International Association of Agricultural Economists, 24 August–2 September 1982, Djakarta, Indonesia.

Srinivasan, T. N., and Bardhan, P. K. 1974. *Poverty and income distribution in
India.* Calcutta: Statistical Publishing Society.

Sukhatme, P. V. 1978. Assessment of adequacy of diets of different income levels.
Economic and Political Weekly, August, special number.

————. 1982. Poverty and malnutrition. In *Newer concepts in nutrition and their
implications for policy*, edited by P. V. Sukhatme. Pune, India: Maharashtra
Association for the Cultivation of Science.

Sundaram, K., and Tendulkar, S. D. 1982. Towards an explanation of inter-regional
variations in poverty and unemployment in rural India. Delhi School of
Economics Working Paper no. 237. New Delhi.

Swindale, L. D. 1981. A time for rainfed agriculture. Coromandel Lecture, 10
December, New Delhi.

Tyagi, D. S. 1982. How valid are the estimates of trends in rural poverty?
Economic and Political Weekly, 26 June, A54–62.

United Nations. 1976. *Progress in land reform.* Report 6. New York.

United Nations Conference on Trade and Development (UNCTAD). 1983.
Handbook of international trade and development statistics, 1983. New York:
United Nations.

United Nations Educational, Scientific and Cultural Organization (UNESCO).
1975. *Elements of the structure and terminology of agricultural education in
Japan.* Bangkok: UNESCO Press.

United States Department of Agriculture (USDA). 1981. *Food problems and
prospects in sub-Saharan Africa: The decade of the 1980s.* Foreign Agricultural
Economic Report 166. Washington, D.C.

Valdés, Alberto, ed. 1981. *Food security for developing countries.* Boulder,
Colo.: Westview Press.

Visaria, P. 1980. *Poverty and living standards in Asia: An overview of the main
results and lesson of selected household surveys.* Living Standard Measurement
Study Working Paper no. 2. Washington, D.C.: World Bank.

————. 1984. The growth of population and labour force in India: 1961–2000.
Paper presented at the Workshop on Population Growth and Labour Absorption in the Developing World, 1960–2000, 1–6 July, Bellagio, Italy.

Vyas, V. S. 1979. Mainsprings of agricultural growth in India. Panse Memorial
Lecture of 1978. *Journal of Indian Society of Agricultural Statistics*, 1979.

————. 1982. Division of gains: Organizational challenge. In *A survey of agriculture. See* Joshi 1982a.

Warriner, D. 1969. *Land reform in principle and practice.* Oxford: Clarendon
Press.

————. 1973. Results of land reform in Asian and Latin American countries.
Food Research Institute Studies 12(2): 115–38.

West Bengal, State Statistical Bureau. 1960/61–1977/78. *Statistical abstract.*
Calcutta.

Wolf, C., et al. 1980. *The demand for oil and energy in developing countries.* Santa
Monica, Cal.: Rand Corporation.

World Bank. 1972. *Land and water resources sector study of Bangladesh.* Vol. 5. Washington, D.C.

―――. 1979. *Economic memorandum on Lesotho.* Washington, D.C. 22 February.

―――. 1981a. *Accelerated development in sub-Saharan Africa: An agenda for action.* Washington, D.C.

―――. 1981b. *Energy pricing in developing countries: A review of literature.* Energy Department Paper 1. Washington, D.C.

―――. 1981c. *Malawi: The development of the agricultural sector.* Washington, D.C.: 8 May.

―――. 1981d. *World development report.* New York: Oxford Univ. Press for the World Bank.

―――. 1982. *World development report.* New York: Oxford Univ. Press for the World Bank.

―――. 1983a. *Kenya: Growth and structural change—basic economic report.* Washington, D.C.: August.

―――. 1983b. *Tanzania agricultural sector report.* Washington, D.C.: August.

―――. 1983c. *World development report.* New York: Oxford Univ. Press for the World Bank.

―――. 1984a. *World development report.* New York: Oxford Univ. Press for the World Bank.

―――. 1984b. *Zambia: Country economic memorandum.* Washington, D.C.: April.

Yamada, S. 1982. Labour absorption in Japanese agriculture—A statistical examination. In Ishikawa, Yamada, and Hirashima 1982.

Zenkoku Nogyo Gakkocho Kyokai (Association for Principals of Agricultural Schools in Japan), ed. 1941. *Nihon Nogyo Kyoikushi* (History of agricultural education in Japan). Tokyo: Nogyo Tosho Kanko.

Contributors

MONTEK SINGH AHLUWALIA is economic adviser at the Ministry of Finance, Government of India. Earlier, he was chief of the Income Distribution Division of the World Bank's Development Policy Staff. He coauthored the book *Redistribution with Growth* and is the author of several articles published in professional journals.

RAISUDDIN AHMED is director of the Food Production Policy Program and a research fellow at the International Food Policy Research Institute (IFPRI). Before joining IFPRI, he served the Government of Bangladesh as deputy chief of the Agriculture and Water Resources Division of the Planning Commission and as chief agricultural economist of the Ministry of Agriculture. He is currently doing research on agricultural marketing and price policies, rural infrastructure, and agricultural productivity and employment. His most recent published work is *Agricultural Price Policies under Complex Socioeconomic and Natural Constraints*, IFPRI Research Report 27.

PRANAB K. BARDHAN is a professor of economics at the University of California, Berkeley. He previously taught at the Massachusetts Institute of Technology, the Delhi School of Economics, the Indian Statistical Institute, and Calcutta University. He has had several articles published in technical journals on economic growth, international trade, and agrarian development. His books include *Economic Growth, Development, and Foreign Trade* (edited with T. N. Srinivasan), *Agrarian Relations in West Bengal* (with A. Rudra), and *Land, Labor and Rural Poverty*.

CHRISTOPHER BLISS has been a Nuffield reader in international economics and a fellow of Nuffield College, Oxford, since 1977. Before that he was a professor of economics at the University of Essex.

M. L. DANTWALA is professor emeritus in the Department of Economics of the University of Bombay. He is also president of the Indian Society of Agricultural Economics and a member of the central board of directors of the Reserve Bank of India. He was the first chairman of the Agricultural Prices Commission in the Indian Ministry of Agriculture.

GUNVANT M. DESAI is currently a professor at the Indian Institute of Management, Ahmedabad, India. He was a research fellow at the International Food Policy Research Institute, from 1979 to 1982. He has served as a consultant to the World Bank, the Ford Foundation, and many private and public organizations in India. He is the author of several research monographs and articles including *Sustaining Rapid Growth in India's Fertilizer Consumption*, IFPRI Research Report 31.

DEVENDRA B. GUPTA is a professor at the Institute of Economic Growth, University of Delhi. He has also taught at the universities of Birmingham and Hull in England and was recently a visiting fellow at the Economic Growth Center, Yale University. He has published several papers and books on poverty and income distribution, including *Levels of Living in India*. His current research interests include rural industrialization, urban housing, and technological choice.

YUJIRO HAYAMI is a professor of economics at Tokyo Metropolitan University. He has also been a visiting professor of agricultural economics at Minnesota University and an agricultural economist at the International Rice Research Institute. Of his three major books the most recent is *Asian Village Economy at the Crossroads*, coauthored with Masao Kikuchi.

S. HIRASHIMA is director of the International Exchanges Department of the Institute of Developing Economies, Tokyo. He is author of *The Structure of Disparity in Developing Agriculture* and *Hired Labour in Rural Asia*.

MASAO KIKUCHI is an agricultural economist at the National Research Institute of Agricultural Economics, Tokyo. He was formerly an associate agricultural economist at the International Rice Research Institute. He coauthored *Asian Village Economy at the Crossroads* with Yujiro Hayami.

SHUBH K. KUMAR is a research fellow at the International Food Policy Research Institute. She also serves as a consultant to the Food and Agriculture Organization of the United Nations. Before joining IFPRI, she was a postdoctoral fellow at the Center for International Studies at Cornell University and a lecturer in nutrition at Punjab Agricultural University, in Ludhiana, India. Her work focuses on the economic and social dimensions of nutrition problems.

UMA LELE is chief of the Development Strategy Division of the World Bank's Economic Research Service. She served as a visiting professor and senior research fellow at the Center for International Studies at Cornell University. She is the author or coauthor of a number of books and other publications on rural development in Africa and India, including *Design of Rural Development: Lessons for Africa*.

MAHAR MANGAHAS has been vice president of the Research for Development Department at the Development Academy of the Philippines since 1981 and editor of the *Philippine Ecnomic Journal* since 1974. He is also a member of the Interdisciplinary Committee of the Bishop and Businessmen's Conference on Human Development.

JOHN W. MELLOR is director of the International Food Policy Research Institute. He was formerly chief economist for the United States Agency for International Development. Before that he was a professor of agricultural economics, economics, and Asian studies at Cornell University. He is the author of several books, including *The Economics of Agricultural Development, Developing Rural India*, and *The New Economics of Growth: A Strategy for India and the Developing World*.

GOGULA PARTHASARATHY is a professor in the Department of Cooperation and Applied Economics and director of the School of Economics of Andhra University, in Waltair, India. He is also honorary director of the Agroeconomics Research Centre of Andhra University. He served as a consultant to the Food and Agriculture Organization of the United Nations from 1978 to 1981 and as a visiting professor at Cornell University from 1974 to 1975.

K. N. RAJ was a professor at the Delhi School of Economics from 1953 to 1973 and has been a fellow of the Centre for Development Studies, Trivandrum, India, since then. He previously served in the Research Department of the Reserve Bank of India and the Economic Division of the Planning Commission of India.

C. H. HANUMANTHA RAO is a member of the Planning Commission of India. He is on leave from the Institute of Economic Growth at the University of Delhi, where he has been a fellow since 1961. He has published a number of papers and books on agricultural economics, including *Technological Change and Distribution of Gains in Indian Agriculture*. He has also been interested in the analysis of problems of regional development, resource mobilization and center-state financial relations, and poverty alleviation.

AMARTYA SEN is Drummond Professor of Political Economy at Oxford University and a fellow of All Souls College. He previously taught at Calcutta, Cambridge, Delhi, and London universities and was a visiting professor at Berkeley, Cornell, Harvard, the Massachusetts Institute of Technology, and Stanford. He has written on welfare economics, social choice theory, economic development, planning and project evaluation, economic history and methodology, philosophy, decision theory, and political science. He has authored eight books, including *Choice of Techniques, Collective Choice and Social Welfare, On Economic Inequality,* and *Choice, Welfare, and Measurement*.

P. S. SHARMA is a director of the Economic Administration Reforms Commission of India. Earlier he was a director in the Perspective Planning Division of the Planning Commission. He has specialized in agricultural planning and development and has written a number of research articles and a book, *Agricultural Regionalisation of India*.

T. N. SRINIVASAN is Samuel C. Park, Jr., Professor of Economics at Yale University. He was previously a special adviser to the Development Research Centre of the World Bank and a research professor at the Indian Statistical Institute, New Delhi, India. He has written extensively on problems of Indian economic development, the theory of international trade, and economic theory in general. He coedited *Poverty and Income Distribution in India* with P. K. Bardhan and coauthored *Lectures in the Theory of International Trade* with J. N. Bhagwati.

VIJAY SHANKAR VYAS is senior adviser, economics and policy, the World Bank. He has been a director of the Indian Institute of Management, Ahmedabad,

India, a member of the Agricultural Prices Commission of India, vice chairman of the Gujarat State Planning Board, a member of the board of trustees of the International Food Policy Research Institute, and a consultant to many national and international agencies. He was team leader of the Second Asian Agricultural Survey, sponsored by the Asian Development Bank. He is the author or coauthor of six books, the latest of which is *Decentralized Planning in India*.

Index

THE JOHNS HOPKINS UNIVERSITY PRESS

Agricultural Change and Rural Poverty

This book was composed in Times Roman by South End
Typographics, India, from a design by Martha Farlow. It
was printed on S. D. Warren's 50-lb. Sebago Eggshell
Cream Offset paper and bound in Holliston Roxite cloth
by The Maple Press Company, Inc., York, Pennsylvania.